Allegories of Empire

Jenny Sharpe

Allegories of Empire

The Figure of Woman in the Colonial Text

University of Minnesota Press

Minneapolis

London

An early abridged version of chapters 2 and 4 was first published in *Genders* 10 (Spring 1992), used by permission of the University of Texas Press. A portion of chapter 4 appeared in a different form in *Modern Fiction Studies* 35 (Spring 1989). © 1989 Purdue Research Foundation, all rights reserved.

Published by the University of Minnesota Press
2037 University Avenue Southeast, Minneapolis, MN 55455-3092
Printed in the United States of America on acid-free paper

Library of Congress Cataloging-in-Publication Data

Sharpe, Jenny.
    Allegories of empire : the figure of woman in the colonial text / Jenny Sharpe.
        p.   cm.
    Includes bibliographical references and index.
    ISBN 0-8166-2059-8 (acid-free). — ISBN 0-8166-2060-1 (pbk. : acid -free)
    1. English fiction — History and criticism.   2. Women and literature — Great Britain — Colonies.   3. Imperialism in literature. 4. Colonies in literature   I. Title.
    PR830.W6S5   1993
    823.009'352042 — dc20   92-45112
                                                                                         CIP

The University of Minnesota is an
equal-opportunity educator and employer.

In return for their stories of an India past,
this book is for my parents

Contents

Contents

Acknowledgments

I began working on this book in 1987–88 with the help of a generous fellowship from the Pembroke Center for Teaching and Research on Women at Brown University. I want to thank the director of the Pembroke Center, Elizabeth Weed, for her unconditional support of feminist theory; and to acknowledge the intellectual contribution of participants in the weekly seminars on that year's topic, "Cultural Constructions of Gender, Race, and Ethnicity." The writing of the book was completed with the help of a faculty fellowship that relieved me of my teaching duties in the fall semester of 1991. I am grateful to Boston College for the fellowship that afforded me a semester's leave as well as the travel grant I received to visit the India Office and British Museum libraries at London in the summer of 1990. My discussion of the antislavery movement in chapter 1 would have been far more speculative if not for the abolitionist literature at the Burns Library on the Boston College campus; and my historical research would not have gone very far without the help of Marguerite McDonough and her staff at the Interlibrary Loan Service of the O'Neill Library. Marguerite's perseverance and sheer detective skills in tracking down obscure nineteenth-century references made the limited library resources appear limitless.

I also want to thank the people who gave their time to reading various sections of the manuscript and who offered constructive criticism at different stages of its writing: my friends and colleagues, Jeff Decker, Sandra Joshel, Robin Lydenberg, and Lata Mani; and the University of Minnesota Press readers, Nancy Armstrong, Inderpal Grewal, and Susan Jeffords. I am especially grateful to Nancy for her careful reading of the introduction as it went through its many metamorphoses. The expert knowledge, good humor, and political commitment of my editor, Janaki Bakhle, made the production process far more pleasurable than might be expected. A portion of chapter 4 appeared in a different form in a special issue of *Modern Fiction Studies* 35 (Spring 1989) entitled "Narratives of Colonial Resistance"; and an early abridged version of chapters 2 and 4 was first published in the issue of *Genders* 10 (Spring 1991) entitled "Theorizing Nationality, Sexuality, and Race." I want to express my appreciation for the enthusiasm that the guest editor of *Modern Fiction Studies*, Timothy Brennan, and the editor of *Genders*, Ann Kibbey, showed toward my work.

My writing is indebted to the fellow feminists who so generously shared their research with me: Lata Mani, Mrinalini Sinha, and Vron Ware. My work is also indebted to the program in comparative literature at the University of Texas at Austin, where I spent my graduate years, and to Barbara Harlow, Jane Marcus, and Ramón Saldívas for their encouragement. I continue to learn from Gayatri Chakravorty Spivak long after she ceased to be my teacher and always find in her writings a pleasant element of surprise. I have also learned from the essays and example of Stuart Hall, whom I was fortunate to have as a teacher back in 1983. It goes without saying that the book bears the imprint of my family: my mother, whose encouragement fueled my adolescent desires for the college education that was not yet in the picture; my father, whose amazing recounting of his memories instilled in me a love for storytelling; and Max, who proved that a sister can also be a best friend. Finally, I thank Jeff for sharing in the suspension of our lives during the writing of the book. Since I am more of a talker than a writer, the long and heated arguments we had until the early hours of the morning were invaluable to my sifting through the theoretical murkiness of race, class, and gender. Considering that the inception of this book coincided with our meeting, the shadow of his friendship and emotional support falls across its every page.

When we discover that there are several cultures instead of just one and consequently at the time when we acknowledge the end of a sort of cultural monopoly, be it illusory or real, we are threatened with destruction by our own discovery. Suddenly it becomes possible that there are just *others*, that we ourselves are an "other" among others. All meaning and every goal having disappeared, it becomes possible to wander through civilizations as if through vestiges and ruins. The whole of mankind becomes a kind of imaginary museum.

—Paul Ricoeur, *History and Truth*

The reason I can do English stuff or even sometimes French stuff is not my personal acumen. It's the history of postcolonial peoples. Our access into universality was to learn Western discourse. I call us the wild anthropologists.

—Gayatri Chakravorty Spivak

1

Introduction: Neocolonial Conditions of Reading

"This is the story of a rape." These words from *The Jewel in the Crown*, the first book of Paul Scott's *Raj Quartet*, were used in the promotion of the television series of the same name. The story is by now well known. A well-intentioned English woman, Daphne Manners, is brutally raped by five or six villagers at Mayapore in 1942, the beginning of the end of British rule in India. Five Western-educated Indians—Daphne's lover, Hari Kumar, and four of his acquaintances—are charged with the crime. But more than that, they are accused of violating English womanhood. The arrest of innocent men exposes the workings of a racist judicial procedure and corrupt imperial system.[1] Scott's story is thus also intended as an anti-imperialist allegory in which the literal rape signifies the colonizer's violation of the colonized. My question is this: How does the rape of an English woman by a gang of Indian peasants come to represent—that is, stand in the place of—the rapaciousness of the British Empire? The answer is perhaps all too simple. We are presented with the evidence of the police interrogation of their prisoner. Hari is stripped naked, bound to an iron trestle, and flogged on his bare buttocks. By suggesting that an innocent brown man accused of raping a white woman is himself metaphorically "raped," Scott produces an anti-imperialist allegory through a chain of substitutions from English woman to Indian man to India. The strategic absence of the Indian woman in this allegory of sexual and racial violence is symptomatic of the colonial discourse to which its story belongs.

Despite the starkness of the declaration, "This is the story of a rape," it carries the weight of a racial memory that has its beginnings in the "Indian Mutiny" or "Sepoy Rebellion."[2] During the 1857 revolt, the idea of rebellion was so closely imbricated with the violation of English womanhood that the Mutiny was remembered as a barbaric attack on innocent white women. Yet Magistrates commissioned to investigate the so-called eyewitness reports could find no evidence to substantiate the rumors of rebels raping, torturing, and mutilating English women. During the course of the nineteenth century, Anglo-Indian fiction gave coherence to the Mutiny narratives by lending a literary imagination to what was "unspeakable" in the first-hand reports. I locate these literary works within their historical frames in order to demonstrate that *rape* is not a consistent and stable signifier but one that surfaces at strategic moments. I examine two moments of political instability during which the racial memory of the Mutiny was revived: the Ilbert bill controversy of 1883 and the 1919 Punjab disturbances. The Ilbert bill, which permitted Indian judges to try Europeans in rural areas, faced enormous opposition from tea and indigo planters, who feared their workers bringing charges of torture and mistreatment before a native judge.[3] During the 1919 Punjab disturbances Indian demonstrations against a bill that allowed the trial of political prisoners without jury or appeal culminated in the army's massacre of unarmed protesters at Amritsar. Both in 1883 and 1919, a British implication in torture and massacre produced a crisis in colonial authority. And, in both instances, the Anglo-Indian community organized itself around the racial memory of the Mutiny and the sexual threat Indian men posed to white women.[4] I read Flora Annie Steel's Mutiny novel, *On the Face of the Waters* (1896), as a work that is critical of the restrictions imposed on colonial women following the revival of the fear of interracial rape during the Ilbert bill controversy. Another Anglo-Indian novel that intervenes in a colonial discourse of rape is E. M. Forster's *A Passage to India* (1924), which holds up for scrutiny the racism generated around the "attack of English women" during the Punjab disturbances.

It is important that we consider rape as a highly charged trope that is implicated in the management of rebellion. But, even as I say this, I urge readers to remember that the threatening aspect of the rebellious native is *not* always figured as a sexual threat to white women. In his study of historical and literary representations of the 1952–56 Mau Mau rebellion, David Maughan-Brown notices that settlers talked of "Mau Mau" (Kikuyu militants who advocated violent resistance) killing but not raping English women and that "there is no single instance of a white woman being raped by a black man" in any of the colonial novels.[5] Even one example of a rebellion that is not sexually coded should remind us that the fearful image of the dark-skinned rapist is not an essential condition of the colonial psyche but contingent upon its discursive production.

What I am suggesting is that the European fear of interracial rape does not exist so long as there is a belief that colonial structures of power are firmly in place. This might explain why one is hard-pressed to find references to the Indian male as a raper of white women in Anglo-Indian fiction and colonial records prior to the 1857 revolt. Is it not possible that the British fear of interracial rape is a more recent event that *we* project backward across time? I have presented this possibility on several occasions, and each time encountered a resistance from my audience. Yet, upon presuming the perception of the dark-skinned rapist to be the source rather than the effect of its discursive production, we essentialize the racial and sexual meaning the stereotype articulates.

The threat of the dark rapist appears with such frequency in colonial situations that it is commonly explained as the projection of white fantasies onto a racial Other. Patrick Brantlinger, for example, writes that "the rape and castration fantasies offered by Grant and other Mutiny writers, in common with those spawned in the American South and South Africa, express the incestuous wishes that lie at the root of what Dominique Mannoni calls 'the Prospero complex.' "[6] Brantlinger's understanding draws on the well-known psychological study that explains Caliban's attempted rape of Miranda in Shakespeare's *The Tempest* as an expression of the European's own "savage sexuality."[7] The difficulty I have with a psychological explanation of this sort has to do with the historical erasure it performs. Mannoni's formulation of the "Prospero complex" represents a colonialist effort to rationalize the Madagascar revolt of 1947, which was one of the bloodiest episodes in modern French history. As was the case in India almost ninety years earlier, fictitious stories of natives raping white women also circulated among European settlers in Madagascar. Upon characterizing these stories as "pure projections of the unconscious," Mannoni records them as the expression of sexual guilt.[8] But, more than that, his explanation screens a different type of savagery—namely, the army's brutal suppression of the revolt. Just as Prospero's hand is invisible in the torture he inflicts upon Caliban, Mannoni's theory of "the Prospero complex" makes the French punishment of Malagasies magically vanish into thin air. His psychological model does no less than provide an alibi for the organized violence that enabled a European minority to rule millions of natives in their own country.[9] Once we dispense with thinking of the invented stories as the expression of a repressed racism or sexuality, we see that they in fact produce value for colonialism. What is significant (for my purposes) in the historical example of India is that rumors of rape did not surface during the year Scott stages his historical fiction. By giving greater continuity to a colonial discourse of rape, *The Jewel in the Crown* makes the racial fear it represents appear natural.

I want to account for the period when sexual violence against white women begins to be talked about in India, to show how "rape" is an event that emerges in and is constituted by its enunciation. This involves addressing the moment not only when a particular representation does appear but also when it does not. It is my contention that the idea of native men raping white women was not part of the colonial landscape in India prior to the 1857 uprisings. Although this was not the first instance of an anticolonial rebellion, it was the first time that European families were massacred. Yet I do not consider the rape stories simply as the embellishment of a massacre. I argue that a crisis in British authority is managed through the circulation of the violated bodies of English women as a sign for the violation of colonialism. In doing so, I see English womanhood emerge as an important cultural signifier for articulating a colonial hierarchy of race.

Although the assumption of European superiority and native inferiority was present from the start of modern colonialism, it was so taken for granted that it did not require representation.[10] In the post-Mutiny era, the British began to represent their sovereignty in a set of discursive practices that they reenacted for themselves as much as for their Indian subjects. With the naming of India as Empire in 1858, a new imperial order was articulated through Mogul emblems of power and the fixing signs of a feudal hierarchy recoded as race. British racism comes into its own during the high era of the British Empire. There is a tendency to read the racialization of colonial relations in the late Victorian era as an application of the scientific theories originating in the metropolitan center. Since such ideas had been around at least since the late eighteenth century, we need to ask why they suddenly command respect in the mid-nineteenth century. "The question," writes Stuart Hall, "is not whether men-in-general make perceptual distinctions between groups with different racial or ethnic characteristics, but rather, what are the specific conditions which make this form of distinction socially pertinent, historically active."[11] I want to suggest that the Indian Mutiny, along with other rebellions in the colonies, activated scientific theories of race. Racial explanations occur when historical conditions make it difficult to presume the transparency of race—which is to say, "race" is all the more necessary for sanctioning relations of domination and subordination that are no longer regarded as "natural." When we deploy race as a transhistorical category of difference, we tend to read racial constructions according to their own truth effect—that is, to locate inequalities in the immutability of human nature.

The shift in European thought that I am describing was not so sudden as the naming of a historical event such as the Indian Mutiny might suggest. The beginnings of a *discourse* of race—that is, a regularity in dispersed statements that hierarchically arranges the families of man—can be traced to the New World slave rebellions and the British antislavery movement of the late eighteenth century.[12] The development of a racial argument in response to the attack on slavery shows that the fixing signification of race is intimately bound up with a humanist discourse of emancipation.[13] Biological explanations for racial degeneration articulate the impossibility of social transformation by binding human types to racially marked bodies. Racism as we know it thus belongs to an age of revolution and social progress. This is why Nancy Stepan opens her history of the racial sciences with an apparent paradox: "A fundamental question about the history of racism in the first half of the nineteenth century is why it was that, just as the battle against slavery was being won by abolitionists, the war against racism in European thought was being lost."[14] Racial explanations were particularly forceful during the second half of the nineteenth century because they sanctioned *both* the management of free slaves *and* the expansion of Empire. In making a case for the significance of India to the development of British racism, I do not mean to diminish in importance the centrality of slavery in consolidating the racial sciences. However, the latter argument requires a different set of questions belonging to a problematic that overlaps with, but is not reducible to, the one I am presenting.

My interest in the Indian Mutiny has to do with its timing, the economic and symbolic value of India to the British Empire, and the crisis in colonial authority that it represents. In the eight years between the 1857 uprisings in India and the 1865 Morant Bay Rebellion in Jamaica, revolts broke out across the Empire, many inspired by Indian predictions that the end of British rule was at hand. These revolts, as so many historians inform us, reinforced a European belief in the racial inferiority of the colonized. But I want to argue that the racialization of colonial relations is also a defensive strategy that emerged in response to attacks on the moral and ethical grounds of colonialism. To read racism as a defensive strategy is to see that it not only codes the native as a degenerate type but also carries the signs of Eurosavagery.

Rather than being a closed system of representation, colonial constructions of native inferiority bear the inscriptions of the campaign of terror conducted against Indians during the 1857 revolt. Stories describing what rebels did to English women mirror the highly ritualized form of punishment and retribution that the British army executed. Captured sepoys were force-fed pork or beef and then blown from cannons; the heads of rebel leaders were displayed on spears; the roads down which an avenging army marched were lined with the dead bodies of villagers dangling from the trees as a warning of the consequences of insurrection; entire cities were looted and then reduced to rubble. The binarism of Western civilization and Eastern barbarism is difficult to maintain when the colonizer is an agent of torture and massacre. A discourse of rape—that is, the violent reproduction of gender roles that positions English women as innocent victims and English men as their avengers—permits strategies of counterinsurgency to be recorded as the restoration of moral order. I am not suggesting that this representation was a "willed" operation but rather that it was a "reasonable" explanation within the logic of the civilizing mission. Governed by benevolence, moral fortitude, and rationality, the civilizing mission cannot accommodate signs of violence except where they exhibit the native's barbaric practices.

The image of native men sexually assaulting white women is in keeping with the idea of the colonial encounter as a Manichaean battle between civilization and barbarism. Unlike earlier forms of territorial conquest, modern colonialism is guided by the moral imperative to bring the colonized into civil society. The deferral of self-rule built into it, however, simultaneously extends Western civilization to the native and encodes its failure. The stereotype of the dark rapist speaks more strongly to the failure of the civilizing mission, which is why the rape stories tend to emerge at moments of political instability. When articulated through images of violence against women, a resistance to British rule does not look like the struggle for emancipation but rather an uncivilized eruption that must be contained. In turn, the brutalized bodies of defenseless English women serve as a metonym for a government that sees itself as the violated object of rebellion.

This book makes a case for the figure of woman being instrumental in shifting a colonial system of meaning from self-interest and moral superiority to self-sacrifice and racial superiority.[15] What often passes unnoticed in the use of the "white man's burden" as a proper name for imperialism is that the concept of self-sacrifice it embodies would have been unthinkable during the early nineteenth century. The civilizing mission did not operate as a set of ideals that concealed base economic motives because profit making was inseparable from a post-Enlightenment vision of progress. In a passionate defense of the East India Company the same year Parliament voted to end slavery in the British West Indies, Thomas Babington Macaulay envisioned the enormous possibility of new Asian markets:

> It is scarcely possible to calculate the benefits which we might derive from the diffusion of European civilisation among the vast population of the East. It would be, on the most selfish view of the case, far better for us that the people of India were well governed and independent of us, than ill governed and subject to us; that they were ruled by their kings, but wearing our broad cloth, and working with our cutlery, than that they were performing their salams to English collectors and English magistrates, but were too ignorant to value, or too poor to buy, English manufactures. To trade with civilised men is infinitely more profitable than to govern savages.[16]

Macaulay does not distinguish humanitarian from economic motives because, from its earliest inception, the human-making project of inculcating Western tastes and values was inseparable from the profit-making enterprise of creating new markets for English manufactures. The appeal that modern colonialism had for Europeans was that they could benefit both monetarily in producing a need for Western goods and spiritually in generating a desire for good government, wealth, and knowledge. "For the first time in history," remarks one historian about this period, "the more enlightened nations were beginning to understand that morality, self-interest, and human progress were mutually interdependent and were to be achieved by the same means."[17]

The domestic virtues of self-sacrifice, moral duty, and devotion to others gained currency only after the violent upheavals that encouraged the colonizers to see themselves as the innocent victims of native hostility. The crisis produced by anticolonial rebellion is managed through a recoding of European self-interest as self-sacrifice and native insurgency as ingratitude. This coding is present in Rudyard Kipling's famous poem from which the concept-metaphor of the *white man's burden* is derived: "Take up the White Man's burden— / And reap his old reward / The blame of those ye better, / The hate of those ye guard."[18] My readings of the topos of rape in Anglo-Indian fiction show how the moral superiority of the British is restored through the suturing of rebellion into the civilizing mission as a grand narrative (*grand récit*) of social progress. The purpose of my own narration is not to reconstruct the civilizing mission by acceding to its narrative demands. Rather, it is to interrupt its long history by drawing attention to the lack of coherence in colonial explanations. Since the English woman in India not only stabilizes the contradictions of colonialism but also threatens to expose them, an attention to gender can reveal the weak links in narratives of colonial legitimation.

This book, then, is *not* the story of a rape but the study of English women as an absent center around which a colonial discourse of rape, race, and gender turns. I address both English womanhood as a sign for mediating gender relations and women's negotiations for domestic power within a discourse that reproduces their subordination. Hence, my study crosses the fields of colonial discourse analysis and feminist theory by demonstrating (1) the strategic deployment of sexual difference in British narratives of an East-West encounter and (2) the place of a colonial text in a feminist recovery of European women's history.

Although my analysis of the discursive production of rape is indebted to the innovative writings of Michel Foucault, I also consider a theory of ideology to be crucial for addressing cultural constructions of race, class, and gender. What discourse analysis cannot account for (and a theory of ideology can) is the different positionings of social groups within a discursive formation. The notion of a discourse that is traversed by an omnifunctional, free-floating power breaks down any distinction between relations of domination and subordination. Power may circulate through all members of a society, but there is a difference between those who are relatively empowered and those who are relatively disempowered. In this regard, I must agree with Edward Said that Foucault's elimination of opposed social forces is "the most dangerous consequence of his disagreement with Marxism."[19] Foucault rejects a Marxist theory of ideology because, he says, it adheres to a juridical model of sovereignty and reproduces the idealism of classical philosophy.[20] In the place of power-as-exploitation and ideology-as-illusion, he proposes the truth-effects of discourse. Power is not the right or privilege of a few but a strategy that everyone undergoes and exercises; discourse is not the false representation of a truth or reality but a material practice that produces it. Foucault opens up the possibility for reading the body as a site of power (both in terms of pleasure and normalization) in a way that a Marxist privileging of consciousness cannot. This aspect of his work is useful for identifying the effaced sites of social groups that have left no records of a "consciousness." Yet he also reduces recent revisions of ideology, particularly the work of Louis Althusser, to a classical or orthodox position. In this regard, the materiality of discourse is posited at the expense of ideology as false consciousness. I consider Foucault's dismissal of Marxism to be on the order of a disavowal—that is, the recognition of a relationship that accompanies a denial.

Working from the notebooks of Antonio Gramsci, Althusser shifts the emphasis of ideology away from consciousness to that which is so obvious and taken for granted that it is unconscious.[21] This means that one does not "think" ideology but "lives" it. His description of ideology as a "relation between relations, a second degree relation" moves away from the historicism of different ideologies for different classes without losing the specificity of distinct social relations.[22] As a second-degree relation, ideology is not "the imaginary" but the articulation of an ideal (Womanhood, Nation, Democracy) with the *relations* that make that ideal active (gender and sexuality, race and ethnicity, class and status). Since a particular group interprets an imaginary relation according to its social positioning, meaning is not fixed or singular.

Instead of each social group having its own ideology in the form of a worldview or sets of ideas, the same belief system "interpellates" or hails different social groups according to their different conditions of existence. The concept of interpellation is best understood in terms of Hall's description of ideology as a process that involves not simply the encoding of events but their decoding as well.[23] Encoding provides a range of preferred meanings that are "read" according to one of three kinds of codes: dominant, negotiated, and oppositional. A dominant decoding accedes to the preexisting order, while an oppositional one wrenches a sign out of its precoded frame of reference and places it in an alternative one. "Decoding within the *negotiated version* contains a mixture of adaptive and oppositional elements: it acknowledges the legitimacy of the hegemonic definitions to make the grand significations (abstract), while, at a more restricted, situational (situated) level, it makes its own ground rules—it operates with exceptions to the rule."[24] The line between preferred and excluded meanings, normalcy and deviancy, incorporated and oppositional practices is thus continuously drawn and redrawn. To read a discourse for its ideological interpellations involves examining how meaning is decoded by men and women in a way that permits them to assume appropriate (or inappropriate) roles in society. This means that ideology not only imposes restrictions but also enables one to act. Once we cease to think of ideology as a belief system that masks or conceals real relations, we can begin to theorize it as an active and transformative principle.

A theory of ideology allows me to account for the particular inflection Victorian women give to the doctrine of woman's mission, and to show how they negotiate for power within a finite range of gender roles that constitute the cultural norm. Despite the extension of domestic virtues to the civilizing mission, English women are excluded from participating in its noble work. I am concerned with how they appropriate the moral *value* of womanhood and transform it into a female form of moral *agency*. It is an agency, however, that is contingent upon establishing their racial superiority over Indian women. English women ground their own emancipation in the moral superiority of the British as an enlightened race engaged in raising natives into humanity. Hence, it is not simply the case that domestic virtues are extended to the civilizing mission; the British feminist argument for equality appeals to the idea of social progress on which modern colonialism is founded.

Feminism and a Colonial Scene of Writing

Inasmuch as feminism calls attention to gender as a category that cuts across the discursive field of colonialism, it can be a force in displacing the binarisms of colonizer/colonized, Self/Other, oppressor/oppressed, and East/West. Yet, unless we see that gender is itself overdetermined by other relations, we risk reducing colonialism to a narrative of sexual difference. To read social contradictions as overdetermined involves seeing how the axes of race, class, and gender are "linked through their *differences*, through the dislocations between them, rather than through their similarity, correspondence or identity."[25] An analysis that begins with difference and dislocation rather than identity and correspondence is crucial if we are to perform the race, class, and gender analysis that continues to elide feminist studies. Presuming a shared identity between European women and the colonized, Euro-American feminism reduces the overdetermined contradictions of colonialism to its patriarchal structures alone. In this manner, the Western sexed subject serves as a privileged signifier of Otherness.

My literary readings make a case against treating race and gender as interchangeable functions—which means that race cannot be theorized from the functioning of gender hierarchies. The task is not to resolve the problems of white femininity by mapping race onto gender but to maintain those problems as sites of textual and theoretical production. A place to begin addressing this concern is with a dismantling of the victim/villain opposition. We need a critical model that can accommodate, on the one hand, female power and desire and, on the other, gender restrictions and sexual subordination. I begin my study by demonstrating that the sexed subject of Victorian England is also a racial identity.[26] I suggest a splitting in the domestic individual, a nonidentity that constitutes itself as a totalizing image through colonial tropes of bondage and emancipation. The domestic woman is not the source of female agency nor the passive repository of the domestic ideal but exists at the intersection of the two as a precarious and unstable subjectivity. The contradictions to white femininity are more evident in a colonial context where the middle-class English woman, oscillating between a dominant position of race and a subordinate one of gender, has a restricted access to colonial authority.

I understand the English woman in India to be positioned by, but not reducible to, the racial hierarchy of colonialism. Rather than treat "race" as a unified field of otherness, I use it as a category of difference for designating the relation between colonizer and colonized. The Indian women that appear only as an absence or negation in English women's writings are central to resolving the contradictions of Western women's sexual subordination. English women's bid for gender power passes through a colonial hierarchy of race. By showing how contemporary theories of female agency contain the sediments of this colonial past, I argue that such models are inappropriate, not only for discussions of colonized women, but for European women as well.

The challenge that a colonial scene of writing poses to academic feminism is one of transforming the way we tend to view women's history. To accept this challenge means that we should not substitute a female subject for a male one; instead we should demonstrate the contradictions, discontinuities, indeed, the accidents, of history. The exploitation of colonized peoples cannot be derived from the sexual oppression of European women. At the same time, the story of European woman cannot be told in the absence of reading for the signs of colonial exploitation. This is why the *woman* in my title refers both to the English woman as the sexed subject of colonial discourse and the Indian woman as her subaltern shadow. My characterization of "woman" as a figure is intended to emphasize the rhetorical strategies of the dominant discourses from which we derive our counternarratives. Relying on a complex of signs for its meaning, *figure* is a term that belongs to allegory. As such, it draws attention to the codified interpretative systems on which our readings depend. This complicity in narration points to the need for defining our project as something other than the recuperation of lost testimonies.

The idea of a past waiting to be recovered belongs to a historicist understanding of the passage of time as progress and discrete events as parts of a totality. The grand narrative of Europeans carrying the torch of civilization to undeveloped regions in the world is but one version of this historicist vision. The

Christian allegory of human salvation provided a powerful iconography for the social mission of the British in India. Images of
natives being freed from despotic rule, raised from their ignorance, and saved from superstitious practices accompanied a display of the pseudoaristocratic world the Anglo-Indians created
with their sprawling bungalows, country clubs, and polite parties
or "frolics." Following Walter Benjamin's famous injunction to
"brush history against the grain," I emphasize discontinuity and
disintegration in this grand narrative of social progress.[27]
Benjamin derives his understanding of the catastrophic aspect
of progress from a baroque form of allegory, the *Trauerspiel*,
which he distinguishes from the medieval Passion plays and
Christian chronicles that tell a sacred story of human redemp-
tion.[28] The props, emblems, and personifications he culls from
the *Trauerspiel* (or German tragic drama) show the signs of ruin
and destruction, rune and fragment. Ruins display the passage of
time as disintegration and work against the impulse to see the
past as a totality. "Allegories are, in the realm of thoughts, what
ruins are in the realm of things."[29] The subject matter of the plays
might explain why they do not stage the redemptive side of
human history. The themes for the *Trauerspiel* are all derived
from Orientalist histories that describe the decadent and tyranni-
cal rule of the Eastern empires.[30] If, as Said suggests, Orientalism
"has less to do with the Orient than it does with 'our' world,"[31]
then the destructive element of German tragic drama speaks to
an Occidental rather than an Oriental history. In carrying the
tone and temporality of baroque allegory over to historical materialism, Benjamin brings to the center of the writing of history
what Robert Young in *White Mythologies* calls "the West's own
internal dislocation [that is] misrepresented as an external dual-
ism between East and West."[32]

Benjamin's concept of temporality disrupts an epistemology of
progress that reconstructs the past as an unbroken chain of
events leading up to the present. In the place of the historicist
conception of "homogeneous empty time" as a uniform and universal body through which history moves, he proposes a past
that is unstable and contingent upon the present:

> The historical materialist must sacrifice the epic dimension of history.
> The past for him becomes the subject of a construction whose locus is
> not empty time, but the particular epoch, the particular life, the
> particular work.... Historicism presents an eternal image of the past,
> historical materialism a specific and unique engagement with it....

The task of historical materialism is to set to work an engagement with history original to every new present. It has recourse to a consciousness that shatters the continuum of history.[33]

Time here is represented as a series of shutter images, each consisting of the specific engagement of a particular present with a particular past. In other words, our ability to read the past is contingent upon a present that transforms it into an image we can recognize. Since the past itself changes with each new present, the writing of history is never total or complete. *Allegories of Empire* is less a writing of women's history than a reading of the narratives that go into contemporary remakings of the past. Rather than restore a buried text, my study shows that the past is not available as a hidden presence for us to recover.

What one loses in refusing to make the English woman the subject of her own story is a single and identifiable plot. In every novel that I read and every plotting that I follow, I also look for the stories that are being withheld. Viewing the past in this way means cultivating a vision that does not offer the clearly focused narrative of a single, uninterrupted plot. Instead, it requires focusing on the overlapping and blurred edges of intersecting yet related lines of narration. One of the intersecting lines of narration I trace in colonial writings is the Victorian doctrine of female self-immolation, which demanded from the domestic woman an absolute devotion to her family, and the Indian practice of *sati*, which was the religious obligation of a Hindu widow to burn herself on her husband's funeral pyre. The resemblance between the two forms of female self-immolation suggests to both nineteenth-century and contemporary Western feminists the shared oppression of Victorian and Indian women. However, unlike the Victorian woman, the Hindu widow is positioned as an object in colonial discourse and a victim to be saved. An attention to this difference requires finding alternative ways to read the signs of subaltern women's agency. There is no moment when these edges of a domestic and colonial history come together into a sharply defined narrative. The stories of European and Indian women must be maintained as discontinuous.

As we attempt to fragment the singularity of women's history, we need to be especially attentive to the historical sediments of a colonial past in the categories that enable us to posit counter-hegemonic forms of knowledge. I want to show that what may appear as an appropriate form for representing the agency of women of preliterate societies—that is, voice—is a historical trope bound up with a Western epistemology of the subject. "Women's voice" in the colonial context is often invoked as a way of addressing the inability of poststructuralism to account for human intervention.[34] However, the risk one takes in making such a move is to return to an unexamined humanism that is inseparable from the human-making project of colonialism. What do we mean when we say that there is a need to account for women's voice and female agency? Mieke Bal explains agency in its simplest narratological terms as who does what: which character speaks, sees, or acts.[35] Yet, as she proceeds to demonstrate in biblical representations of Delilah's power over Samson, the animation of a woman's speech, vision, and action can just as easily operate as discursive screens that further displace agency. Might not the invocation of Third World women's voices be screens that displace their agency, in a manner resembling the representation of Delilah's speech Bal describes? It is my own feeling that, even as "woman" is becoming deessentialized in the West, she is being reconstituted elsewhere in the voice of non-Western women. Because it implies the self-presence of living speech over writing, "voice" can all too easily efface our roles as mediators, translators, indeed, as writers. This erasure permits a slippage between the women who "speak" and academic feminists who speak on their behalf. Since poststructuralism draws attention to our construction of objects of knowledge in academic discourse, it counters the tendency to naturalize woman's voice. For this reason, its lessons should not be forgotten in any effort to address the problem of agency.

One way to avoid turning the "Third World woman" into an authenticating signature for academic feminism is to transform the way we conceptualize what intellectual work is all about. Gayatri Chakravorty Spivak addresses this concern in her call for feminists in the First World to unlearn the privilege of an elite education: "The academic feminist must learn to learn from them, to speak to them, to suspect that their access to the political and sexual scene is not merely to be *corrected* by our superior theory and enlightened compassion" (*IOW*, 135). To attend to Third World women does not involve inviting them into our arena but the much more circumscribed task of recognizing that we have something to learn from them. It means reversing the direction in which knowledge traditionally flows—a move Gramsci articulates in the concept of *subaltern*.

Subaltern Forms of Knowledge

Gramsci's extension of the military term subaltern to subordinate classes is intended to counter the elitism of the modernist concept of intellectual avant-gardism.[36] Whereas the vanguard consists of the troops that march at the head of an army, a subaltern is the inferior-ranking foot soldier. Gramsci begins with the idea that everyone is a philosopher, except that popular philosophies do not always have a language or coherent system of thought. In place of the intelligentsia as an elite vanguard that leads the masses, he posits the "organic intellectual" as one who makes "coherent the principles and the problems raised by the masses in their practical activity."[37] The term subaltern thus designates both subordinate classes and subordinated forms of knowledge. Subaltern or subordinate knowledges are composed not only of philosophies that have been assigned a nondisruptive place but also of ones that are unrecognizable according to institutionalized systems of meaning. Hence, even though subaltern groups "think" according to the terms of hegemonic discourse, their philosophy manifests itself in the *contradiction* between thought and action. Rather than being at the forefront of social change, academic knowledge lags behind—which is why Gramsci insists that theory not be separated from politics.

A group of intellectuals in India, Britain, and Australia has turned to Gramsci's notion of the subaltern to define their project of writing South Asian history "from below."[38] Finding the Marxist category of the proletariat inadequate for describing India's heterogeneous and rural-based population, the Subaltern Studies collective employs the term subaltern to designate class, caste, ethnicity, age, gender, or any other form of subordination. Ranajit Guha, a founding member of the collective, explains that the term does not identify a unified and homogeneous entity but those who stand in opposition to elite groups. This means that the same social group can either be "elite" or "subaltern" depending on how it aligns itself in any one historical situation, "an ambiguity which it is up to the historian to sort out on the basis of a close and judicious reading of his evidence."[39] The Subaltern Studies collective opposes its writings to an elite Indian historiography that presents either a colonialist or nationalist perspective. British colonial historians efface subaltern resistance by coding peasant rebellions as religious fanaticism or irrational acts of violence. Indian nationalist historians also withhold from peasants an autonomous historical agency by bringing popular struggles under the hegemony of an elite leadership.

The absence of an intellectual understanding of peasants acting on their own has prompted the Subaltern Studies collective to define its project in the humanist terms of representing a subaltern consciousness. Members read colonialist and nationalist discourses against the grain in order to find a place for the unrepresented subjects of history. In what constitutes one of her most famous formulations, Spivak calls the collective's performance of subject restoration a "*strategic* use of positive essentialism" (*IOW*, 205). The Subaltern Studies group may have an essentialist understanding of its project, she explains, but the fragmented text of the official records can only yield a subaltern consciousness in its absence and subaltern identity as a relationship of difference. Hence, the essentialism of a subaltern "will" or "consciousness" is always in tension with the antiessentialism of "the subaltern" as an unstable category of difference. Spivak describes the Subaltern Studies project as a strategic use of essentialism because essentialist claims are being made for social groups that appear only as a blank in historical records. Her point is to situate the critique of humanism within a European tradition in which the universal subject of history intersects with imperialism. In this regard, the positive term that goes into the writing of subaltern history also dismantles Western humanism, but in a way that cannot be reduced to the antiessentialist position of European poststructural theories. At the same time, it is important to remember that Spivak is addressing essentialism as a strategy of writing and *not* a strategy of political action.

Spivak emphasizes the strategic aspect of the collective's intervention over essentialism as such as a warning against conflating "subaltern studies" and "subaltern groups." Hence, she not only establishes the positive value to the collective's use of essentialism but also deessentializes its project of writing a history from below. The second part of her formulation of strategic essentialism tends to be ignored by those academics who invoke the term as an equivalent for the agency of subaltern groups.[40] In "Can the Subaltern Speak?" Spivak makes a distinction between tropological representation and political representation in order to demonstrate that the absence of a match between consciousness and its representation-as-trope means that any political articulation of subaltern subjectivity is always an act of reading.[41] She shows that upon deriving a subaltern "will" from the text of open revolt, the Subaltern Studies group produces a model of agency that cannot accommodate the sexed subaltern. It is not simply a case of demonstrating that peasant women participated in rebellions; the collective is careful about recording how both men and women are joined in struggle. Rather, when the subject of insurgency is *figured as male*, the question of sexual difference is foreclosed.[42] This is why Spivak insists on maintaining a distinction between "the subaltern" as a politically interested trope in academic discourse and subaltern groups. "The subaltern is necessarily the absolute limit," she writes, "of the place where history is narrativized into logic" (*IOW*, 207).

Spivak goes on to demonstrate that an academic writing of the subaltern as insurgent is a tropological move that displaces the sexed subaltern. The symbolic exchange of women appears at crucial moments in the historiography of the Subaltern Studies group for explaining the mobilization of peasants across villages. Yet, the collective does not raise questions about the absent text of subaltern women's consciousness as it does about peasant insurgency in elite historiography. Spivak notes that the project of writing a history from below repeats the subaltern male's indifference to sexual difference. In her own work she identifies the subaltern woman as one who cannot be simply reduced to her class or caste position. She interrupts the project of making subaltern classes the subject of history with "a text about the (im)possibility of 'making' the subaltern gender the subject of its own story" (*IOW*, 246). The "im" in parentheses suggests a story that cannot be told yet which must be told. The story that cannot be told is the one of a subaltern woman who knows and speaks her exploitation. The story that must be told is the text of her exploitation. Spivak reads this text in Mahasweta Devi's short story about an exceptional wet nurse, Jashoda, who becomes deified as Mother and eventually dies of breast cancer. Jashoda's deification shows the limits to a religious discourse that interpellates the male peasant as a militant insurgent; her employment as a professional mother shows that "mothers are divided, women can exploit" (*IOW*, 252). Although Jashoda understands her life according to a patriarchal discourse of mothering, the textual enunciation of that life offers a political critique. As an organic intellectual, Mahasweta does not speak on behalf of subaltern women, but neither does she revoke a political responsibility by claiming their stories to be self-evident.

The critical transformation of an impossibility into a condition of possibility means maintaining "subaltern consciousness" as both irreducible and irretrievable to a discourse that can only be inadequate to its object. This is the "philosophy of vigilance" that Spivak proposes for negotiating the double bind of either producing subaltern groups as the objects of academic knowledge or else disavowing an intellectual responsibility by granting them self-representation.[43] The double bind suggests to her a domestic model of intellectual work. The idea is not to get out of the double bind but to engage in a persistent critique: "But what I'm more interested in is the fact that the endless labor of work that gets regularly undone, or, in other words, work within the double bind, work that does not produce necessary progress, is defined out as women's work, domestic work.... The real question is not how to get out of the double bind, but to see how, in fact, getting out of the double bind is simply an inscribed value within the social value-coding of labor."[44] Spivak insists that we attend to our own techniques of knowledge because even a radical criticism is not "free" but bound; it too is a knowledge that subjugates. She rejects the tendency of radical intellectuals to confuse epistemology with ontology in their disavowal of elite theories when writing about nonelite groups—a confusion that leads them to simple methods of information retrieval. Her assertion that "the subaltern cannot speak" requires that we speak to the sexed subaltern by way of scrupulous readings.

Wild Anthropology

Spivak's notion of a persistent critique raises important questions about the critical models we bring to any reading of a colonial or postcolonial text. In the absence of an awareness of the hegemonic structures of our theoretical models, our writings can all too easily serve an institutional function of securing neocolonial relations. None of us escapes the legacy of a colonial past and its traces in our academic practice.

As an Anglo-Indian/Eurasian who was born in London and raised in Bombay, I am implicated in the history I am about to recount. Eurasians or half-castes (as they were initially known to note their low birth) were a racially mixed group that formed a separate community of their own. They were mocked for being inherently inferior versions of the British they painstakingly imitated, and it was the common opinion that they had inherited the vices of both races. It was not until the early twentieth century that Eurasians (who were also called Indo-Britons) were officially licensed to use the name that had historically been reserved for those of pure European descent: Anglo-Indian. Embracing the culture, religion, and language of the colonizers, Anglo-Indians dreamed of the "homeland" they had never seen but to which they imagined they might one day return. I grew up listening to stories of an ancestor who dyed her skin to escape from the Agra fort during the Mutiny. But there were also other stories, like the one of her granddaughter (my paternal grandmother), who was refused entry into "whites-only" restaurants because her skin was too dark. The Anglo-Indian is represented in the cultural revival of the raj as a tragic figure of British colonialism—she is the "unknown child" of Daphne Manners in *The Jewel in the Crown* and "quite the saddest result of British imperialism" according to Geoffrey Moorhouse in his apologia for Empire, *India Britannica*.[45] By contrast, the Anglo-Indian narrator of Salman Rushdie's epic novel, *Midnight's Children*, is a figure for the Indian nation. And, in Mahasweta Devi's short story "The Hunt," a half-caste tribal woman, whose mother was impregnated by the son of the Australian planter for whom she worked, is a reminder of the pervasiveness of colonial relations long after decolonization. While the perception of Eurasians as a tragic remnant of Empire is symptomatic of a racism that positions them as the "preferred" Asian immigrant, the writings of Rushdie and Mahasweta speak to the impossibility of cultural purity on both sides of the colonial divide. The history of the half-caste I have just recounted has something to do with the perspective on the materials I am about to articulate—one that is neither Indian nor British and yet both. My arrival at the writing of this book by way of a critical thinking formed largely in the United States, however, makes my own Anglo-Indian origins almost accidental.

The point, then, is to attend to the institutional authority of the intellectual who recovers subjugated forms of knowledge. Those of us who are literary critics might well heed what anthropologists have learned from literary theory—that ethnography exists between and not within cultures, that beside every native voice is an ethnographic ear.[46] An attention to the ethnographic ear is all the more necessary in view of the disciplinary demand for intellectuals from decolonized space to serve as "native informants." Unlike the critic who specializes in a single period or genre of English literature, the "Third World expert" is expected to know the heterogeneous cultures of the entire non-Western world—an assumption that ignores the relative autonomy of regional histories and cultural traditions. In such moments I cannot help but be reminded of Macaulay's well-known statement that "a single shelf of a good European library was worth the whole native literature of India and Arabia."[47] It is at the very least with these words in mind that we should approach the teaching of postcolonial literatures. The addition of courses on "Third World Literature" or "Global English" risks being but a modern-day configuration of the social mission of English, for it allows one to point to the good work being done in the margins in order to reinforce a cultural superiority at the center. I have worked on rather traditional British literature as a caution against the uncritical expansion of English, a discipline that historically was used to rule, manage, and control the Indian Empire.[48] Instead, I have made certain interdisciplinary moves in order to rethink the boundaries of literary studies. Given the persistence of colonial explanations in "commonsense" forms of knowledge, there is a need to enter the fraught field of postcolonial literatures with an attention to history.[49]

One of the objectives of this book is to interrupt a historicist vision of the past without abandoning history as such. The difficulty in disentangling the writing of history from history-as-past is compounded by their presumed identity (as is manifested in the single name for the discipline of history and its object). In order to understand the past as "past" rather than yet another version of the present, I make a case for reading literary and historical documents according to the systems of knowledge at the time of their writing. These chapters thus combine historical research with textual analyses of novels and colonial historiography.

Rather than treating "fact" and "fiction" as repetitions of each other, I follow Pierre Macherey in seeing the absent text of history in the margins of literature, as its unconscious or "unsaid."[50] The task of the critic is to read textual silences symptomatically, not as deficiencies to be filled in, but as necessities to be explained. History, forming the conditions of existence to the literary imagination, places limits and restrictions on what can be represented at any one moment. Fiction is granted the license to imagine events as they might have happened or in a way that history has failed to record. Since the literary work represents possible worlds rather than probable ones, I employ novels to show how they stage social contradictions and strive to resolve them. The question of what a literary work *cannot* deliver directed me to other kinds of documents. I supplement literary works with materials as diverse as official records, pamphlets, treatises, essays, public speeches, eyewitness reports, diaries, private letters, memoirs, and journals. I read these documents for what they say about the dislocations between overlapping systems of representation. My purpose is to demonstrate that it is not enough to add postcolonial literatures to English curriculum in the absence of developing new models of understanding and alternative strategies of reading.

Beginnings, as Said reminds us, are strategically posited to enable a critical enterprise.[51] Chapter 2, "The Rise of Women in an Age of Progress," begins with a powerful text of female subjectivity, Charlotte Brontë's *Jane Eyre*, as a frame for reading a colonial discourse of rape. The discursive moves the text makes for expressing the heroine's quest for self-determination allow me to find a place for female agency within the Mutiny narratives that so violently appropriate the bodies of English women. Yet, there is another reason to begin with a domestic novel like *Jane Eyre*—it permits me to displace the subject-constitution of the domestic woman into the far-flung territories of Empire. I examine the discourse of female emancipation in the self-education of Jane Eyre for the way it intersects with the civilizing mission. In doing so, I show that the agency of the feminist individual is contingent upon a racial splitting of femininity, one in which the sati serves as an icon for domestic subjugation.

Chapter 3, "The Civilizing Mission Disfigured," takes the story of the middle-class English woman overseas to India, where she gains access to the grand narrative of colonialism only in the capacity of victim. I read journalistic reports and popular histories on the Indian Mutiny to discern how they define limits, establish origins, and trace stories that go into a colonial understanding of anticolonial insurgency. A representation of rebellion as the violation of English womanhood contributes to the confinement of Anglo-Indian women to the home. Chapter 4, "The Rise of Memsahibs in an Age of Empire," examines women's writings that are critical of the restrictions racial segregation places on white women. In *On the Face of the Waters*, Steel reassigns the Mutiny role of English women by emphasizing their strategies in self-survival. Yet, this reassignment is contingent upon a transformation of sati into a space of death that the English woman, unlike her Hindu counterpart, can enter and leave at will. We see that the question of English women's agency increasingly forecloses the possibility of raising similar questions about the sexed subaltern.

Chapter 5, "The Unspeakable Limits of Civility," thus addresses the problematic status of Indian women in contemporary feminist readings of Forster's *A Passage to India*. The defense of Indian women, which involves a condemnation of Indian men, inevitably aligns the feminist position with a colonial discourse of rape. I show how an alternative plotting to a colonial one is made available through a reading guided by the novel's homosexual desire. The disruptive presence in the courtroom of an untouchable man who is the object of a homoerotic gaze breaks the either/or opposition between the English female and Indian male. Chapter 6, "The Ruins of Time," argues that the signification of rape is so implicated in a colonial production of knowledge that it cannot be used to theorize the place of Indian women or any other members of the colonized. The absence of Indian women in Scott's anti-imperialist allegory, *The Jewel in the Crown*, reveals the limitations of *rape* as a concept-metaphor for imperialism. Hence, I end by suggesting a counterallegory that shifts the terms of sexual violence from rape to exploitation.

My chapters move both in a chronological sequence and from the problematic of English women's subjectivity to that of Indian women's agency. I derive from each novel an allegory of reading that stages the problems of defining Indian women's agency according to the terms of a rational discourse of subject constitution. Since allegories of reading are allegories of the *failure* to read, the critic looks for the places where a colonial system of meaning breaks down.[52] As such, she recognizes that there are no resolutions to textual contradictions or a reconciliation of the constative and performative levels. By showing that the Indian woman exists in colonial texts as an absence, negation, or screen, I argue that her agency cannot be simply "read off" the condition of the English woman in India. My readings thus inhabit British-Indian fiction in order to demonstrate that the story of the subaltern—sexed or otherwise—is not to be found there. Inasmuch as my own narration does not recount the story of Indian women, it is complicit with the documents with which I work. This elision marks the limits to where this study ends and another one begins. Our critical models can only be partial, provisional, and subject to change. Having said this, I make my writings public so that they too can be debated, challenged, and revised.

A female Negro slave with a weight chained to her ankle. From John Gabriel
Stedman's *Narrative of a Five Years' Expedition against the Revolted Negroes
of Surinam* (1796).

2

The Rise of Women in an Age of Progress:

Jane Eyre

Britain's moral stand against slavery underwrote its self-designated mission to free enslaved peoples across the globe. As the first European nation to abolish slavery, it saw itself as a more humanitarian master. The presumed racial superiority that sanctioned an aggressive territorial expansion into the Eastern hemisphere was thus above all else a moral superiority. In the years between the end of the African slave trade in 1807 and the Emancipation Act of 1834, abolitionists were the self-appointed conscience of Europe.[1] Initiated by Protestant Dissenters, the antislavery position was delivered in a rhetoric of Christianity that described slavery not only as an inferior labor system but as an immoral one as well. By drawing attention to slavery as a coercive system that prevented black slaves from exercising their free will, abolitionists ensured that the bitter taste of human suffering lingered on the English palate. "As he sweetens his tea," a pamphleteer warned English men, "let him reflect on the bitterness at the bottom of the cup."[2] Urging his readers to boycott West Indian sugar, he reminded them of "another, and more innocent, source."[3] That new source was India. East Indian sugar production was perceived as "more innocent" than West Indian because it was based on a system of debt bondage that predated British involvement. Since abolitionists distinguished the indigenous and "natural" coercive labor system in India from the unnatural relationship of the European master to his African slave, the purchase of Indian sugar ensured the good citizen the "comfort" of a clear conscience as well as the sweetness of his cup of tea. With the restructuring of Britain's overseas colonies following the independence of the United States and the destruction of the West Indian plantation economy, India replaced the Americas as "the brightest jewel in the British crown."[4] India was a source of pride not only because of its wealth and resources but also because the British saw themselves as freeing natives from the bondage of ignorance and cruel religious practices.

The progress of the heroine of Charlotte Brontë's educational novel, *Jane Eyre* (1847), follows the itinerary of colonialism from the abolition of slavery in the West Indies to the civilizing mission in India.[5] Jane's struggle to overcome the class and gender restrictions placed on her is articulated through colonial tropes of bondage and liberation. Yet, the remoteness of the colonies to the domestic scene of action prompts one critic to offer their existence "on the edges of the novel's world" as evidence of Brontë's mastery over the mythical Angria.[6] The magical resolutions that Spanish Town, Madeira, and Calcutta provide for the novel's romantic plot suggest a mastery of a different sort. *Jane Eyre* clears a space for a new female subjectivity, the domestic individual, but it does so by grounding "woman's mission" in the moral and racial superiority of the colonialist as civilizer. Such a reading cannot be derived from the novel's own frame of reference. As narrator of her life story, Jane demonstrates a self-consciousness about class and gender hierarchies; however, race operates as a transparent category of self-representation. To refuse this transparency is to see that the moral agency of the domestic individual is contingent upon a national and racial splitting of femininity—one that binds ambitions and passions to the West Indian plantation woman and female self-renunciation to the Hindu widow.

If reversals were possible and causes could be made to follow effects, I might say that Brontë wrote *Jane Eyre* to enable my reading of race, gender, and colonialism. Yet, considering that until recently such references passed largely undetected, we know that a rethinking of the past involves more than a simple reversal. The past is not a static text waiting to be recovered but one that is touched by a critical present. This is what Benjamin means when he describes history as a fragment of the past, available only through a present that sees itself prefigured there. The task of the historian is "to become aware of the critical constellation in which precisely this fragment of the past is found with precisely this present" and in doing so to write the past anew.[7] In view of our own complicity with the texts from which we derive an understanding of the past, I want to state at the outset that my reading does not extend to charging Brontë with racism. By contemporary standards, all Victorians would stand accused. Besides, I do not find it useful to demand from authors what was often historically impossible for them to represent. Rather, my reason for going over the well-trodden ground of *Jane Eyre* is to wrench contemporary theories of female subjectivity out of the continuum of a Euro-American literary tradition and locate it elsewhere, between the shifting scenes of the aggressive territorial expansion of modern colonialism.

Gayatri Chakravorty Spivak was one of the first critics to read colonialism as the discursive field in which Jane's struggle for self-determination takes place.[8] Other revisions have followed, transforming Brontë's novel into a contested site for establishing the relationship between feminism and imperialism.[9] The problem that remains insufficiently addressed, however, is the articulation of race, class, and gender in the English sexed subject. Spivak strategically downplays the issue in her effort "to wrench oneself away from the mesmerizing focus of the 'subject-constitution' of the female individualist,"[10] and critical responses to her essay tend to be reductive in their analyses. The defense of *Jane Eyre* against Spivak's criticism often expresses the desire to establish an identity between European and subaltern women. The argument that "metaphorically Jane is on the side of Heathen women"[11] or, again, "the trope of 'race' ... evokes Jane's subjection in, yet resistance to, patriarchy"[12] reads racial difference according to gender hierarchies alone. When deployed as a metaphor for sexual difference, race ceases to designate the racial hierarchies of colonialism. Thus permitting an equivalence between race and gender, metaphoricity produces the "white mythology"[13] of a universal sisterhood. Despite Brontë's references to harem women and satis, sultans and pashas, as metaphors for sexual relations in England, one cannot presume an identity between Asian and English women. To do so would be to read subaltern women's lives according to a story of women's emancipation in Europe. Rather than pointing to the adequacy of a shared meaning, the demand for metaphoricity should reveal that something is missing—namely, the lives, histories, and subjectivities of subaltern women. My own project is not to recover those missing stories but to establish them as the shadow text to the constitution of the English sexed subject.

By emphasizing the textual displacements enacted through figures of resemblance, I argue that Jane's subjectivity is constituted through a complex system of tropes. This system, which cannot be reduced to the simple binarism of colonizer and colonized, is composed of a two-part constellation in which (1) the "rebel slave" and "harem woman" are used to articulate the forms of appropriate and inappropriate rebellion, and (2) the creole woman and sati rework the doctrine of woman's mission.[14] Whereas the first set of figures serves to negate the preexisting gender role of female submissiveness in England, the second set serves as a condition of possibility for an emergent female subjectivity. Thus, I do not begin from the premise that these figures are derived from or marginal to Jane's subject-constitution. Rather, I consider the individuated self to be the effect of what Paul de Man characterizes as "coercive tropological displacements."[15] These displacements are operative even when Jane expresses sympathy for Asian women. Upon locating the novel within the configuration of colonialism at the time of its publication, I demonstrate that such sympathy belongs to a colonial discourse of social reform that establishes the racial superiority of the European by constructing the native woman as an object to be saved. One can understand why Brontë, writing her novel in the 1840s, would be uncritical of England's noble work in India. The question that needs to be asked is why we continue to read the colonial trope of sympathy according to the tenets of the civilizing mission. What is at stake in producing a version of the past that is unfaithful to Brontë's novel is the reader positioned by the address of its autobiographical voice.

It is no accident that *Jane Eyre* is a founding text for feminist criticism, as the literary canon through which women academics gained an institutional voice retrospectively reconstructs a determinant for the biography of Euro-American feminism. Just as *autos-bios-graphein*, the "self-writing of a life," is guided by a desire to authorize the life that has been lived, academic feminism authors itself through lives that can be identified as not simply female but feminist. A poetics of women's writing that centers on selfhood and self-consciousness is undeniably informed by the consciousness raising so crucial to the women's movement of the 1970s. Writing "as a woman,"[16] to invoke Patricia Meyer Spacks's well-known formula, means demonstrating an awareness about gender hierarchies and showing a commitment to women's emancipation. As a *Bildungsroman* and fictional autobiography, *Jane Eyre* both charts the development of female consciousness and presents an authoritative narrating "I" that exercises control over the life being read. Elaine Showalter calls it a classic novel in the early feminine phase of "the female tradition"; other lineages include the work for the rebellious feminism it expresses.[17]

Critics are quick to point out the opening scene in which the ten-year-old Jane voices her oppression. The imperative she gives herself—"Speak I must" (*JE*, 30)—has been seized upon as a refusal to remain silent that transforms the passive victim into an agent. These two aspects of Jane's subjectivity—the writing of a female self and voicing of women's oppression—underpin contemporary discussions of agency. *Jane Eyre* serves as a paradigmatic text not only because its action centers on a woman writing her life, but, more important, because that "life" constitutes the record of her struggle to articulate the social injustices *all* women suffer. In this chapter I argue that, as a self-conscious practice in which women constitute themselves as individuals, female self-determination represents but one kind of action rather than female agency as such. My purpose is to establish the grounds for an academic work that can break with a nineteenth-century feminist individualism that established a Western model of emancipation as the norm.

Although it is now generally acknowledged that the early canon of British women's literature reproduced the race and class exclusiveness of the women's movement, the assumptions of that canon that persist in contemporary feminist discourse continue to pass unnoticed. Consider the following statement from Sidonie Smith's *A Poetics of Women's Autobiography*, which treats the white, middle-class woman as the norm against which other women are to be measured: "And if the autobiographer is a woman of color or a working-class woman, she faces even more complex imbroglios of male-female figures: Here ideologies of race and class, sometimes even of nationality, intersect and confound those of gender."[18] Smith's formulation presumes that the self-representation of the white, middle-class woman is not also complicated by race, class, and nationality. Her writing shows that it is not enough simply to identify the author of *Jane Eyre* as a white, middle-class English woman. What I question is not so much the exclusiveness of the "female tradition" as the transparency of "race" in tropological constructs that we take to be the norm. For this reason, I want to situate the current fascination with women's autobiography within what I have been describing as the autobiographical form of feminist criticism.

31

Studies of women's autobiographies show that the fictions of self-identity that structure all autobiography are more visible in women's texts. Following the lessons of poststructuralism, critics no longer address the gendered subject as a unified consciousness but as the locus of intersecting discourses. By understanding women's lives in terms of the difficulty they have in conforming to a feminine ideal, these critics consider autobiography to be the effect of gender hierarchies as well as the site of new subjectivities.[19] To invoke the editors of one collection of essays, "Autobiography localizes the very program of much feminist theory—the reclaiming of the female subject—even as it foregrounds the central issue of contemporary critical thought—the problematic status of the self."[20] The study of women's autobiography thus forms a double-edged criticism that, upon revealing the fictions of male authority, authorizes a female self.

I share the concern of those critics whose interest in autobiography is to transform the feminist subject who reads. And I am sympathetic to the more radical moves of the essayists who expand the genre to include memoirs, slave narratives, ethnographies, and *testimonios*. Upon encountering the latter work, I am reminded of Paul de Man's observation that "any book with a readable title page is, to some extent, autobiographical."[21] By this he means that autobiography is a figure of reading that structures all forms of knowledge, including self-knowledge. What his statement does not acknowledge, however, is that the title page is readable only to the degree to which the critic relies upon an epistemology of the individuated self. A definition of autobiography as an essential structure of self-representation thus also risks ignoring the historical specificity of the genre.

Felicity Nussbaum locates the beginnings of autobiography in the ideological construction of the gendered bourgeois subject as an individuated self.[22] As a means of avoiding "the ideology of genre" in the study of autobiography, she suggests a materialist approach to "reconsider the way that the 'individual' is implicated within power relations."[23] One way to consider the power relations in *Jane Eyre* is to read the writing of a female self and voicing of women's oppression as a privileged mode of address for the feminist individualist. It is a mode of address that is unavailable to the subaltern women who are represented in the novel.

Historically, the native woman who "speaks" does so at the prompting of colonial officials, missionaries, and anthropologists. In the Western ethnographic text, subaltern women are positioned as the speaking subject of what Foucault calls a ritual of discourse. Here, "the agency of domination does not reside in the one who speaks (for it is he who is constrained), but in the one who listens and says nothing; not in the one who knows and answers, but in the one who questions and is not supposed to know."[24] Since subaltern women do not have the same relationship to "voice-agency" as the feminist individual, their subjectivities are unreadable according to the narrative demands of autobiography. Yet, it is not simply the case that the category of the individuated self has been historically withheld from them. Rather, as I hope to demonstrate, the autobiographical voice encodes their silence. This structured silence charges us with the responsibility of prying academic feminism away from its autobiographical form.

Introducing the significance of reading to the meaning of a life, Jacques Derrida suggests that we think of autobiography not as a self-writing but as a self written anew with each reading.[25] "Otobiography," he explains, is an autobiographical text signed by the receiving ear that listens. Since the ear of the other is the reception that guarantees the meaning of a life, the signature of autobiography is a contract honored by the recipient. On the one hand, to hear an autobiographical voice is to honor it. This is what critics do when they read women's autobiography according to "the ideology of genre." On the other hand, the time lag between the signing of a proper name and its reception means that the reader is responsible for the subjectivity being produced. I want to show that the speaking subject of the fictional autobiography, *Jane Eyre*, relies on the figuration of various colonial "others." My purpose is to locate women's writing and voice-agency within history and, upon doing so, to break the bond between speech-writing and agency. My reading of *Jane Eyre* as the source of Brontë's literary authority rather than the other way around is not intended to deauthorize the woman as writer. Rather, it is directed at the receiving ear so that the "self" of a feminist biography might look different.

Fictions of Female Authority

> It was *my* time to assume ascendancy. *My* powers were in play, and in force.
>
> —Charlotte Brontë, *Jane Eyre*

Gynocritics locates agency in a female pen only by collapsing the different sites of text, signature, and author.[26] To keep these different sites distinct is to acknowledge that women's writing is also a bid for power. I argue that the literary power we attribute to Brontë as a woman writer lies in a place other than the author or signature. This other space is the fictional world in which the novel's heroine emerges as a self-determining individual. Critics who read Brontë as the real-life model for the women's lives she wrote into her fiction fix the meaning of fiction in the author's life. Yet, is it not also the case that Brontë's novels have engendered her life? The autobiography of Jane Eyre gave Elizabeth Gaskell a convenient plot for casting "the novelist as tragic heroine" in her biography, *The Life of Charlotte Brontë*.[27] But more than that, Brontë's rebellious heroines are responsible for her canonization as a woman writer; it is their lives, and not the author's life, that define the parameters of "the female imagination."

In "Writing Like a Woman," Peggy Kamuf calls on feminists to shift the emphasis of the female signature from origin to effect, from its attachment to a woman's body to its deconstruction of male authorship.[28] She attacks the feminist canon for subscribing to "the cult of the individual," which she identifies as a founding principle for literary paternity. And, she considers an author-centered criticism only capable of producing tautologies, as exemplified in Spacks's claim that women writers "must write as women." By drawing attention to the nonidentity in the simile of "women writing as women," Kamuf alerts us to the signature as something that exceeds the author.[29] In *Signature Pieces*, she locates the signature between the work and its writer, as that which both divides and joins, is inside and outside the text: "At the edge of the work, the dividing trait of the signature pulls in both directions at once: appropriating the text under the sign of the name, expropriating the name into the play of the text."[30]

Nancy K. Miller responds to Kamuf by insisting that the historical erasure of women's proper names necessitates an attachment of the "feminine" play of language to a female body.[31] Since male literary authority depends on the anonymity of women writers, she argues, only a female signature can reveal the fictionality of literary paternity. Miller is correct in pointing out that women writers do not have the same relationship to authorship as do men. However, her response to Brontë's use of the pen name *Currer Bell*—that she would "like to know that the Brontëan writing of female anger, desire, and selfhood issues from a female pen"[32]—ignores the historical conditions of the signature. The rebellious feminism of *Jane Eyre* does not issue from a female pen, but, rather, a masculine pen name is one of the conditions that permits Brontë to write a new female subjectivity. The equation of "woman" with "author" presumes the problem of female agency to be a question of literary authority alone. Miller's assertion that a displacement of the author and dispersion of the subject "foreclose the question of agency"[33] does itself foreclose yet another question. What are the *grounds* of the agency she describes—in other words, how is women's literary authority produced? One place to begin responding to this question is with the historical condition of women writers in the nineteenth century.

In *Desire and Domestic Fiction*, Nancy Armstrong argues that the literary authority of the English novel is feminine because it centers on a private space derived from the separation of a "woman's sphere."[34] Domestic fiction in particular (which includes novels primarily although not exclusively by women) is underwritten by a "sexual contract," according to which "the female relinquishes political control to the male in order to acquire exclusive authority over domestic life, emotions, taste, and morality."[35] Indicating places in *Jane Eyre* where language is empowered by the force of emotions alone, Armstrong argues that women's writing is authorized by the sexual contract.[36] Since Jane's rebellious anger is considered to be inappropriate for a woman, I would say that this particular emotion is not authorized by the sexual contract. Yet, it is precisely Jane's anger that gives the novel its distinctive signature as women's writing. In other words, the "feminine" language of *Jane Eyre* exceeds the femininity belonging to a woman's sphere. This is why, when Brontë first published her novel in 1847, reviewers censured the author for creating such an unfeminine heroine. Armstrong's study of domestic fiction does not address the contradictions of a female literary authority derived from restricting women to the home. As Mary Poovey points out, since publishing meant participating in the public domain of the literary marketplace, women writers threatened the separation of spheres that authorized their fiction.[37] A withholding of the author's name from the title page provided one means of circumventing the threat the woman writer posed.

The signature of Currer Bell is the product not only of social conventions demanding the erasure of a woman writer's name but also of Brontë's own desire for a literary authority that can only be figured as male. In a private letter to G.H. Lewes, one of the few reviewers to identify the author of *Jane Eyre* as a woman, Brontë explains why she prefers to be judged by the standards used for male writers:

> I wish you did not think me a woman. I wish all reviewers believed "Currer Bell" to be a man; they would be more just to him. You will, I know, keep measuring me by some standard of what you deem becoming to my sex; where I am not what you consider graceful you will condemn me.... Come what will, I cannot, when I write, think always of myself and of what is elegant and charming in femininity; it is not on those terms, or with such ideas, I ever took pen in hand.[38]

One should not take this protest at face value, for the performance of *Jane Eyre* undermines the meaning of these words. In her letter, Brontë defines femininity in terms of its social construction alone. In her fiction, however, she assumes a genderless signature presumed as male in order to express a woman's rage and rebellion that would otherwise be deemed unfeminine. By making a woman's voice issue from the pen of a man, Brontë wrests "feminine" writing away from the Victorian norm of grace, elegance, and charm and, upon doing so, transforms the standards of judging women's writing. To return to Kamuf's reading of the signature at the limits of work and writer, this is an instance of the signature "appropriating the text under the sign of the name."

Aware that Currer Bell was not the author's real name, reviewers searched the pages of *Jane Eyre* for evidence of "his" sexual identity. "It is no woman's writing," declares the *Era* review; "no woman could have penned the 'Autobiography of Jane Eyre.' "[39] "The writer is evidently a woman," writes G.H. Lewes for *Fraser's Magazine;* "a woman, not a pattern: that is the Jane Eyre here represented."[40] Other reviewers reveal what the reading public found so disturbing about Brontë's novel. One claims that "the work bears the marks of more than one mind and one sex" and another, that "if they are the productions of a woman, she must be a woman pretty nearly unsexed."[41] Expressing both more and less than the female sex, *Jane Eyre* crosses and recrosses the gender differentiation that the doctrine of separate spheres safeguards. Yet, the power of the domestic ideal keeps gender roles in place, and it is the author who ends up losing her "sex." The difficulty in defining a female (as opposed to feminine) writing should lead us from author to text to see how an authority that is not yet available to women writers is present in Brontë's fiction. Here is the second direction in which the signature is pulled — "into the play of the text."

The restrictions imposed in life can be lifted in fiction, where a woman's self-determination is represented as female rather than the negation of a negation that the unsexing of a woman suggests. In this regard, because there is no need for faithfulness to reality, fiction has the license to imagine new subjectivities. The unfamiliarity of the female character that is Jane Eyre is evident in the controversy her rebelliousness provoked. Yet, Brontë's first novel was also immensely popular and very quickly went into a second printing. The popularity of *Jane Eyre* is a testament to the success of the fictional autobiography in authorizing the kind of women's writing that was not yet available to its author.

Brontë relies on a common literary convention to create a fiction that transforms the narrator of *Jane Eyre* into the author of her own life. The signature appearing on the title page of the first edition — "Jane Eyre: An Autobiography, edited by Currer Bell" — inscribes a fictional character in the place of the author.[42] As a writing in which a narrating "I" exercises control over the life being narrated, autobiography is an exemplary text for establishing female literary authority. One can read Brontë's publishing of *Jane Eyre* under a genderless pen name as an act that demotes the author to the lesser role of editor so that a fictional character can speak as a woman. This means that the self-presence of the female voice in the text is predicated on a displacement of the woman writer *of* the text.

Yet, the domestic plot that structures the story of an English woman's life cannot, in and of itself, give value to a female form of writing. Rather than ending with the narrative closure of her own story, Jane concludes with the image of St. John Rivers sacrificing his life for the Christian missions in India. Autobiography suddenly gives way to allegory, as she describes the missionary cast in the role of Greatheart, that Christian warrior from an exemplary allegorical novel, Bunyan's *Pilgrim's Progress*. Unlike Jane's domestic labor of resocializing Rochester and bearing him a son with which her own story ends, St. John's labor involves no lesser work than converting an entire nation to a Western system of values: "Firm, faithful, and devoted; full of energy, and zeal and truth, he labours for his race: he clears their painful way to improvement: he hews down like a giant the prejudices of creed and caste that encumber it" (*JE*, 398). The colonial allegory that is appended to the story of Jane's life serves as the signature of her autobiography. As a grand narrative that extends beyond the narrow limits of the domestic household, the Christian missions authorize the life of a woman whose own mission is restricted to working for her family. But the novel also invokes the civilizing mission at the end in order to give greater value to domestic virtues.

Jane's personal victory occurs when she reinvents domestic labor in terms of the human-making enterprise of colonialism. Rochester, who "grew savage" (*JE*, 376) when she left him, is blind and crippled when she returns. "It is time some one undertook to rehumanise you" (*JE*, 384), she says to him. Women's work may lack the grand vision of St. John's noble enterprise, but women do not forget, as he does, "the feelings and claims of little people" (*JE*, 366). In this regard, women's work, in its own quiet and modest way, is established as having a social value.

It is possible to argue that *Jane Eyre* clears the space for a female voice, but it does so only by reworking a colonial space. Armstrong mentions the domestic violence with which female authority comes into being; Rochester is maimed and blinded before Jane can achieve self-determination in marriage.[43] Yet, there are two other scenes of violence with which the novel ends, ones that are not reducible to its domestic plot. On the one hand, we have Bertha Mason, Rochester's creole wife, dancing madly on the roof of the burning mansion before plunging to her death; on the other hand, there is St. John Rivers hewing down ignorance and superstition in India. Together, they are emblematic of a new age of colonial benevolence that emerged from the ruins of the West Indian plantations.

In the remainder of the chapter, I argue that the voice-agency of Jane Eyre is predicated on a national and racial splitting of femininity. Early readings of the novel explain this splitting in terms of a self that Jane consolidates through the negation of her doubles—Helen Burns, Blanche Ingram, and Bertha Mason.[44] I pursue a slightly different line of argument, by suggesting that the impossibility of self-identity reveals voice-agency to be a politically interested trope. To this effect, I do not read Jane's doubles in the characters that are confined to the literary text but in figures that are moored loose from their histories. At the same time, I hope to convince my readers that such a history is available between the pages of the novel.

Slave as Emancipator

A slavish bondage to parents cramps every faculty of the
mind.... This strict hand may in some degree account for the
weakness of women ... and thus taught slavishly to submit to
their parents, they are prepared for the slavery of marriage.
—Mary Wollstonecraft,
A Vindication of the Rights of Woman (1792)

Brontë deploys the feminist metaphor of domestic slavery for
staging one woman's rebellion against sexual and economic bondage. As an orphan and poor relation at Gateshead, the young
Jane has a social rank even lower than that of the servants.
When her cousin, John Reed, violently attacks her for reading
books that do not belong to her, she compares him to a Roman
slave driver: "You are like a murderer—you are like a slave-
driver—you are like the Roman emperors!" (*JE*, 8). Her triple
denouncement makes public an analogy she had previously kept
to herself. Language assumes a force of its own, transforming her
former passive resistance into active and open rebellion. The
ten-year-old Jane, "like any other rebel slave ... resisted all the
way" (*JE*, 9). Subsequently punished for her unacceptable behavior, she is locked in the haunted red room where "the mood of
the revolted slave" (*JE*, 11) keeps alive her sense of injustice.
Unable to handle the unruly child any longer, Mrs. Reed decides
to send her to the Lowood Institution for orphaned girls. Jane,
increasingly compelled to voice her oppression, responds to her
aunt's actions by accusing her of being a cruel and deceitful
woman—an outburst that gives her "the strangest sense of freedom" (*JE*, 31). This opening scene, with its movement from
bondage to freedom and from an imposed silence to speech, has
been triumphantly claimed by feminist critics. Yet, if one reads
the scene in terms of its slave references as I have, one notices
that assertions of a rebellious feminism are enacted through the
figure of a rebel slave.

Although Jane identifies the master/slave relation as Roman,
the idea of a *revolted* slave had to have come from a more recent
past. There were the slave uprisings of Jamaica in 1808 and 1831,
Barbados in 1816, and Demerara in 1823. Brontë's novel clearly
draws on the moral language of the abolitionists. And it is important to recognize the degree to which the active resistance and
open rebellion of black slaves shaped the language of the British
campaign to end slavery.[45] Abolitionists disseminated leaflets and

pamphlets describing the suffering that provoked slaves to strike back at their masters in so violent a form. The scale of the 1831 Jamaican uprising and the severity with which it was suppressed gave the antislavery movement the impetus needed to pass an emancipation bill two years later. Jane may derive the proper name of slavery from the book she is reading (Goldsmith's *History of Rome*), but the analogy she makes between her own oppression and slavery relies on the historical memory of recent events in the West Indies.

Following the success of the antislavery movement, English women and workers harnessed its language for articulating their own struggles for equality.[46] The slave analogy was nothing new to the nineteenth century, but with the increased popularity of abolitionism in the 1820s, the oppression of European women was more explicitly compared to the West Indian system of slavery. "This state of the civilized wife," proclaims one defender of women's rights, "worse than that of the female West Indian slave, is termed a state of equality."[47] Women abolitionists also made the analogy between their own subordinate place in the antislavery movement and that of the slaves on whose behalf they spoke. And, members of the working class publicized the existence of "white slavery" in English factories. Yet, the social groups that identified themselves *as* slaves did not necessarily identify *with* black slaves. For instance, the working-class argument of "white slavery" was derived from the planter's defense of slavery—namely, that labor conditions in the West Indies were better than those in English factories. And, working-class organizations that lobbied for improving factory conditions were openly hostile to the predominantly middle-class abolitionists for their preferential treatment of black slaves.[48] If the analogy between race relations in the West Indies and class and gender relations in England did anything, it was to empty slavery of its racial signification. In this regard, the slave metaphor that Brontë deploys does not break with the discourse of her times. There is no character of a West Indian slave to be found in *Jane Eyre;* she remains inaccessible except through Jane's own acts of rebellion. Yet, the figure of slavery, coupled with the shadowy existence of Rochester's West Indian wife, points to the presence of a racial memory. A faint imprint of the "black slave" can be discerned in the narrative demand on Jane to disassociate herself from the anger that is so crucial in establishing her childhood resistance. In the last instance, the agency of the female as individualist cannot be enacted through the figure of a rebellious slave because slaves were not considered part of civilized society.

Abolitionist literature addresses the black slave as a human being who is less than human and as an incipient individual whose human potential is locked up in an unnatural system of slavery. Slaves are represented as the victims of cruel masters who have them fettered in body, mind, and soul *and* as a people who are active in obtaining their own freedom. The contradictory representation of the black slave as one who desires freedom but has no free will of his own (and I use the male pronoun advisedly) manifests itself in the demand made upon abolitionists to assume the voice of the black slave. The ambiguity in the famous slogan reproduced on boxes, ornaments, letterheads, and posters—"Am I not a man and a brother?"—with its iconic representation of a Negro in chains shows the double inscription of one who both is and is not a man. The rebellious slave, as one who acts but cannot cognize his actions, is a contradictory figure of resistance, as is evident in an 1824 tract entitled *The Rights of Man (Not Paines) But the Rights of Man, in the West Indies:*

> Nothing can be more evident than, that, if the slave-master will rule his slave by the law of power,—(which must ever be the case where slavery exists, for no man is a slave willingly,) the Slave has a right to make use of the law of power in return. When the master is strongest, the slave must submit; and when the slave is strongest, the master must suffer the effects of his contumacy.... Unprotected, then, as the Slave is by law;—upon the principles of natural right and justice, the allegiance he owes to the law, is *nothing*. He is out of its pale on every hand,—he is not a member of civilized society,—and, consequently, has a right to rid himself of the chains of his bondage, in whatever manner, at whatever time, and as soon as he can ... as long as his present state continues, the Slave has a right to rebel;—no moral guilt whatever, that I see, can possibly attach to him, for attempting to assert what is the universal birthright of mankind, or for claiming to himself the *right and lordship of his own body.*[49]

According to this pamphleteer, the violence slaves commit during times of rebellion would be immoral without the prior violence of the master enslaving them against their wills. Slaves are spoken of as being active in obtaining their freedom, but it is an agency predicated on their exclusion from civilized society. In other words, they do not act as "free agents" in the sense of being able to assume a moral responsibility for their actions.

Missionaries were especially disturbed by the immorality of a system in which black slaves, having no control over disciplining their bodies, were not accountable for their souls. "Every slave being compelled, under pain of corporal punishment, to yield implicit obedience to the will of the master," writes one abolitionist, "... the Negroes, as a people, are as destitute of correct morality as they are of liberty."[50] Since slave rebellions are perceived as a savage response to an even more barbaric system for extracting labor power, once blacks are free they no longer have the right to revolt.

Jane's development from a rebellious child into a self-assertive woman is represented by her movement from the instinctive rebellion of black slaves toward assuming the moral responsibility of a cognizing individual. The figure of the rebel slave, as I have already indicated, lacks the cognition on which moral agency is based. This is the mark of racial difference, a point of resistance for extending the meaning of the slave rebellions to a female agency predicated on speech. Unlike black slaves, Jane names herself as "a free human being with an independent will" (*JE*, 223). But more than that, the novel stages what constitutes an appropriate form of resistance for achieving self-autonomy within socialized space.

Since open revolt threatens the laws of civilized society, Jane's education into adulthood involves learning to control her anger and to channel her desires into a socially acceptable form of self-determination. Even though her childish explosions of anger are liberating, in retrospect, the adult Jane comments on these instances as improper conduct for a child. The rebellious female child is not quite human; she is a bad animal, a mad cat, a heathen, and a fiend. Unchecked rebellion is particularly identified as the savage response of uncivilized nations. Jane's friend at Lowood, Helen Burns, chastises her for wanting to "strike back" at those who are cruel and unjust, saying, "Heathens and savage tribes hold that doctrine; but Christians and civilised nations disown it" (*JE*, 50). The young Jane at first finds the concept of Christian endurance difficult to comprehend. She does, however, keep her humiliation to herself when Brocklehurst makes a public example of her. As she struggles to stifle her sentiments, Helen walks by and gives her the strength of self-control. "It was as if a martyr, a hero, had passed a slave or victim, and imparted strength in the transit" (*JE*, 58). For Jane, Christian endurance means being positioned as a victim to be saved; for Helen, it means suffering in this life to reap the rewards of heaven. The second stage of Jane's life ends with Helen dying of consumption, happy in the knowledge that she is going to her Maker. At this point in its narration, the novel confronts its reader with two equally undesirable alternatives for female socialization: the silent space of passive victimage or the tragic space of early death. And so the first stage of Jane's education draws to a close. Having established an irreconcilable conflict between her desire for self-assertion and her preassigned gender role of self-denial, the educational novel moves into a new phase that shows her negotiating a socialized space that does not negate a female self. And it is the civilizing mission that provides the grounds for her negotiations.

Jane Eyre charts the success of its heroine in resolving the conflict between self-determination and socialization that structures the *Bildungsroman*.[51] As a female *Bildungsroman*, however, it also stages the impossibility of such a resolution because the socialization of women means submitting to a male head of household. The difficulty the novel has in resolving this conflict should cause one to question Sandra M. Gilbert and Susan Gubar's approving description of "the astounding progress toward equality of plain Jane Eyre."[52] Brontë's novel of development is structured less as a woman's progress toward a final goal than as her negotiation of the narrow restraints of fixed gender roles. The same force of emotions that can be liberating for Jane also "masters" her good sense when she falls in love with her employer. This is why, despite the value placed on feelings, she stresses the need to subject them to a "wholesome discipline" (*JE*, 141). Jane's struggle for independence involves finding a socially acceptable form for rejecting the restrictions imposed upon poor relations, governesses, mistresses, and wives. In other words, she requires a domestic form of resistance, a language that can bring the force of political insurgency into the "woman's sphere" of the home. The doctrine of "feminine influence" and "woman's mission" provides one possible mode of articulation.[53]

The limited power available to middle-class women at the time Brontë was writing is expressed in the idea of their influential yet subordinate position vis-à-vis men. According to the doctrine of feminine influence, women do not exercise power directly in the public sphere but indirectly through their relationship to men as wives, mothers, and daughters. Sarah Lewis (who, like Brontë, was herself a governess) explains in her influential book,

Woman's Mission (1839), the far-reaching effects of women's domestic role:

> Power is principally exerted in the shape of authority, and is limited in its sphere of action. Influence has its source in human sympathy, and is as boundless in its operation.
>
> If there were any doubt which of these principles most contributes to the formation of human character, we have only to look around us. We see that power, while it regulates men's actions, cannot reach their opinions. It cannot modify dispositions nor implant sentiments, nor alter character. All these things are the work of influence. Men frequently resist power, while they yield to influence an unconscious acquiescence.[54]

Since Lewis is a woman writing a tract for other women, her problem is one of explaining to her readers that their subordination to men can be a source of power. This is why she suggests that what women lack in political authority they make up for through moral influence in their homes. Since women's influence in the public world is limitless only if its scope is restricted to the private sphere, the idea of feminine influence suggests an inherent conflict between a woman's desire for personal advancement and a disinterested duty to her family. Lewis asks whether it is possible for women to conduct their lives according to a doctrine, the object of which is "to awaken the sense of power, and to require that the exercise of it be limited; to apply at once the spur and the rein."[55] She resolves the problem by advising her readers to value their training in denial, devotion, and sacrifice—in short, female self-renunciation:

> The one quality on which woman's value and influence depend is the renunciation of self, and the old prejudices respecting her, inculcated self-renunciation. Educated in obscurity, trained to consider the fulfillment of domestic duties as the aim and end of her existence, there was little to feed the appetite for fame, or the indulgence of self idolatry. Now here the principle fundamentally bears upon the very qualities most desirable to be cultivated, and those most desirable to be avoided.[56]

Lewis's tract, which locates female self-renunciation at the heart of women's power, is a paradigmatic text of the debate within which *Jane Eyre*, as a domestic novel, finds itself. Upon devaluing the domestic virtue of self-renunciation, Brontë breaks with the position that Lewis represents. Yet, if self-denial is what reins in women's power so that moral order can be maintained, how can Brontë reassure her readers that its devaluation will not lead to moral chaos? This is the question the novel addresses in Jane's negotiations for a language in which women's power will not threaten the moral order. And, nowhere is the horror of female self-indulgence more vividly imagined than in the inordinate passions and appetites of Bertha Mason.

Rochester's first wife is commonly read as a symbolic substitute for Jane Eyre and the monstrous embodiment of unchecked female rebelliousness and sexuality.[57] Gilbert and Gubar, for instance, characterize Bertha as "Jane's truest and darkest double" that represents the rebellious passions she has been trying to repress since childhood. Hence, they see the madwoman's opposition to the forthcoming wedding as a figurative and psychological manifestation of Jane's own desires for independence that her marriage to Rochester would negate.[58] Bertha Mason is a Calibanesque figure—a cannibalistic beast who chews her brother's flesh to the bone, a fiend who spews forth obscenities, and a monster who cannot control her sexual appetites. The resemblances between Bertha and Shakespeare's monstrous figuration of the Carib native have caused some readers to identify her as a member of the colonized. In a reading that is otherwise sensitive to history, Susan Meyer understands the racial ambiguity suggested by her creole heritage and swarthy complexion as sufficient evidence that the first Mrs. Rochester is black. This reading permits her to describe Bertha as a Maroon or runaway slave even though, as the daughter of a merchant-planter, she belongs to the class of slaveholders.[59]

In Jamaica, the term creole may have designated all native-born population (both of African and European origin), but in England it was a derogatory name for the West Indian sugar plantocracy. *Jane Eyre* is a novel of the 1840s, a time when slavery was so unpopular that only those who directly benefited from it continued to defend it. Bertha Mason is a female version of the "immoral West Indian planter," a literary stereotype that, following the abolition of the African slave trade, was commonly invoked as "a useful shorthand for depravity."[60] It is clear from Rochester's description of his first wife that it is not her madness he finds so intolerable as her debauchery:

> I lived with that woman upstairs four years, and before that time she
> had tried me indeed: her character ripened and developed with

frightful rapidity; her vices sprang up fast and rank: they were so strong, only cruelty could check them; and I would not use cruelty. What a pigmy intellect she had—and what giant propensities! How fearful were the curses those propensities entailed on me! Bertha Mason,—the true daughter of an infamous mother,—dragged me through all the hideous and degrading agonies which must attend a man bound to a wife at once intemperate and unchaste.... a nature the most gross, impure, depraved, I ever saw, was associated with mine.... And I could not rid myself of it by any legal proceedings: for the doctors now discovered that my wife was mad—her excesses had prematurely developed the germs of insanity. (*JE*, 269–70)

The particular form of Bertha's insanity bears the signs of an idle plantocracy in the state of decline. Since the self-indulgence of the planter class was considered responsible for feeding its vices, it is not madness that is the cause of Bertha's moral degeneration but rather the other way around—her "excesses" have strained her minuscule mind to the point of unhinging it.

Jane often refers to her own state of mind, when consumed by her love for Rochester, as a condition of madness. Yet, it is her superior intellect as well as her recognition of the need for "laws and principles" (*JE*, 279) that separates her own excesses from Bertha's. Narratively speaking, the plantation woman is sacrificed so that an upwardly mobile English woman of an ambiguous class can replace her as Rochester's wife. The partnership in marriage that Jane achieves at the end is contingent upon the appearance of Rochester's first wife. But the narrative function of the Creole stereotype is also to disassociate a pure English race from its corrupt West Indian line.

Due to the long history of racial mixing in Jamaica, the scandal the creole presented to the British was the possibility of a white person who was not racially pure. (In defense of the creole's racial purity, Edward Long outlines in his *History of Jamaica* [1774] an elaborate classification system, according to which Negro blood can be "bred out" over five generations.)[61] As a member of the white-identified planter class, Bertha is perhaps more threatening than a free person of color, for she shows that "whiteness" alone is not the sign of racial purity.

Rather than being equated with color, racial purity is identified with an English national culture. Rochester makes a point of distinguishing himself from the planters that punish their slaves when he says that he refused to control Bertha with cruelty. And, as a true English woman, Jane embodies the new honesty and national pride that will guide England in its overseas social mission. Rochester indicates that no other woman comes close to expressing what for all intents and purposes are the signs of an English national character, "cool native impudence, and pure innate pride" (*JE*, 237). Jane provides a lengthy account of the degradation and humiliation she suffers following her flight from Thornfield when, poverty stricken and weak with hunger, she is reduced to common begging. The detailed description of her Christian endurance of these trials produces a narrative that shows her as having earned, through hard work and determination, the real source of her success—which is to say, an inheritance from a rich uncle in Madeira, a port of call on the trade route between the Guinea coast and the West Indies. An inheritance is necessary for narrowing the class difference between Jane and Rochester, while the hardships she suffers distance her from the idle class of the West Indian plantocracy. Her financial gain and his loss of Thornfield make them economically equal. But economic independence in and of itself is insufficient for female emancipation in marriage—that is, so long as the value of self-renunciation is attached to the woman's domestic role.

The famous passage from chapter 12 that extends the action of political rebellion to the "silent revolt" (*JE*, 96) of women is paradigmatic of a constant reworking of the domestic sphere in order to accommodate the social values of individualism. Since domestic women influence the public domain only in relationship to men (i.e., through their influence), they are not individuals in the sense of being moral agents. As Denise Riley explains, "If women are only to be thought *in relation*, then the status of being a woman while being a social-ethical subject is a logical impossibility."[62] It is my contention that the paradox of being an individual in the domestic sphere is resolved by defining the English woman in relation to other women instead of to men. In *Jane Eyre*, a domestic form of social agency is established through a national and racial splitting of femininity, with the creole woman serving as a figure of self-indulgence and the Oriental woman, of self-immolation.

Sati as Feminine Ideal

To say that woman is an angel ... is to imply that her specialty is self-effacement, resignation, and sacrifice; it is to suggest to her that woman's greatest glory, her greatest happiness, is to immolate herself for those she loves.... It is to say that she will respond to absolutism by submission, to brutality by meekness, to indifference by tenderness, to inconstancy by fidelity, to egotism by devotion.

—Maria Deraismes, "La Femme et le droit"[63]

Jane's life story is based on a model of self-determination that derives from social action in the public sphere. Hence, despite the marriage of equality with which the novel ends, its narrative energy goes into demonstrating the impossibility for a domestic woman to be both an individual and a wife. So long as she is a wage earner, Jane has a certain degree of autonomy at Thornfield. The first time she meets Rochester, she refuses to speak at his command but instead scolds him for assuming an attitude of superiority. Yet, the novel also makes it clear that "governessing slavery" (*JE*, 238) is no model for female emancipation. Because they were educated, governesses were not considered part of the working class, even though they were wage earners. Yet, the lower-middle-class women who earned their living as private tutors were so dependent on their employers for their keep that many ended up in the poorhouse. The discrepancy between the governess's social status and her economic class manifests itself in the difficulty a book on education has in defining her place in the home: "The real discomfort of a governess's position in a private family arises from the fact that it is undefined. She is not a relation, not a guest, not a mistress, not a servant—but something made up of all. No one knows exactly how to treat her."[64] The uneasiness this writer expresses has to do with the ambiguous position of the governess as one who both embodies the domestic ideal and threatens it. As an educator, she is a role model for middle-class children; as a domestic woman who is also a wage earner, she transgresses the separation of spheres that ensures Victorian morality.[65]

Jane especially threatens middle-class morality when she breaks with social norms by agreeing to become Rochester's wife. Drawing attention to the discrepancy in their age, wealth, and social status, Mrs. Fairfax, the housekeeper, warns her that "gentlemen in his station are not accustomed to marry their governesses" (*JE*, 233). Jane soon discovers that, despite the legitimacy of her forthcoming marriage, she is positioned as mistress rather than wife. In this regard, her ambiguous class status reveals a certain truth about the domestic woman. Rochester may think that dressing his future wife in rich silks and expensive jewelry is an expression of his love, but in her eyes he is claiming ownership over her body. Jane's suspicions are confirmed when he playfully compares her worth to the purchase price of "the grand Turk's whole seraglio" (*JE*, 236). At this moment there is a strategic shift in the slave analogy. To begin with, the master/slave relation is both gendered and Orientalized, which means that it is now a direct statement about gender hierarchies. But more important, Jane explicitly rejects the role of slave as the sign of Rochester's mastery over her. In response to his inquiry as to what she will do while he is "bargaining for so many tons of flesh," she proclaims: "I'll be preparing myself to go out as a missionary to preach liberty to them that are enslaved—your harem inmates amongst the rest" (*JE*, 237). Jane does not identify herself as a slave in order to express her desire for liberation, as she did when she was a child. Rather, she assumes the position of a missionary who will free others that are enslaved. Slavery cannot figure female rebellion because the slave in this instance is an Oriental woman who is passive and agentless. By positioning herself as a missionary, Jane empowers herself with the moral superiority of British civilizers at the precise moment that her own morality is undermined. In other words, an assertion of *racial* superiority discursively resolves Jane's class and gender inferiority in relationship to Rochester.

The Eastern references are sustained throughout the scene of their courtship, which ends with a historical figuration of the Hindu woman. After a reverie on the devotion he expects from his future wife, Rochester sings a love song in which the woman promises to live and die with her man. Jane responds with the following outburst: "I had as good a right to die when my time came as he had: but I should bide that time, and not be hurried away in a suttee" (*JE*, 240). Here, Hindu widow-sacrifice refers to the self-sacrifice that the doctrine of woman's mission requires of English women. As a proper name for a woman's submissiveness, meekness, and devotion to her husband, sati locates female passivity in Hindu women. The Eastern analogy of gender hierarchies exposes the barbarism of English marriage laws, but only inasmuch as Oriental despotism is a paradigm for such barbarism. In this regard, the metaphors of harem women and sati in *Jane Eyre* belong to a civilizing discourse that produces its own object of negation.

The moral imperative of modern colonialism to bring the colonized into civil society meant that natives had to be "made" savage before they could be civilized. The signs of this requirement are visible in W. W. Hunter's lecture entitled "England's Work in India" (1879–80), given during a more self-conscious time of imperialism than the 1840s. The force of his words does not go into describing England's civilizing work but the cruel and bloody practices of the Indians:

> The rising generation in India have been freed from superstitious terrors, they have been led to give up cruel practices, they have learned to detest and despise their forefathers' bloody rites. Widow burning, infanticide, hook-swinging, self-mutilation, and human sacrifice—these are the few familiar relics of the old bondage under which the Indian intellect cowered and the Indian heart bled. Great as has been the material progress of India during the past century, its emancipation from ignorance and priestcraft forms is, to my mind, a far more splendid memorial of British rule. Truly the people that walked in darkness have seen a great light.[66]

"Barbarism" is the truth-effect of a selective description of Indian culture as the negative pole of a civilizing influence. And, the native male appears especially barbaric in the colonial reforms intended to alleviate the condition of women. The modalities of this discourse can be discerned in the redefinition of sati as a crime during the years leading up to the Abolition Act of 1829.

In her careful reading of the official records, Lata Mani argues that the Hindu widow was neither the subject nor the object of a discourse on the abolition of sati but the grounds for colonial intervention in Indian society.[67] The British may have desired to end what they considered to be a savage practice, but not at the risk of jeopardizing their relationship with Hindus. By demonstrating that they were defending the widow's rights, they could circumvent the label of interventionists. The early legislating of widow-sacrifice was thus predicated on finding a precedent in ancient Sanskrit texts and on distinguishing "good" (voluntary) from "bad" (coerced) satis. In other words, the British effectively sanctioned widow-sacrifice so that they might abolish it. Since the *religious* sanctioning of sati was open to debate, a regulating of the practice hinged on the place of the woman's will. Magistrates carefully monitored the burnings in order to determine whether Hindu widows went willingly to their death or were coerced.

What is significant to Mani is the process by which the widow's subjectivity is effaced so that others might speak for her. The woman who speaks in the official records does so at the command of the civil servant entrusted with introducing a new moral order. And, her speech is framed in a manner that positions the civilizer as the agent of change and the native woman as an object to be saved. The magistrate mediating the widow's speech addresses her as the victim of religion if she gives her consent and of pundits and relatives if she resists. The legislative prohibition of sati thus hinges on a construction of the widow that requires men (both British and Hindu) to speak on her behalf. Mani counters this effacement of female agency by making the widow the subject of a feminist discourse. The feminist critic, however, is faced with a double bind: to address the widow as a victim is to risk representing her as an object to be saved; to introduce her agency is to open up the possibility of a voluntary suicide.[68] This is why Mani insists that we entertain "the possibility of a female subjectivity that is shifting, contradictory, inconsistent."[69] By this she means that we should refuse a discourse that reduces agency to the singular moment of a "decision" and be attentive to the contradictions between speech and action in the widow's active negotiations of death. By focusing on what eyewitness reports marginalize—the violence of being burned alive, the widow's suffering and her resistance—Mani loosens the bind between victim and passivity. She shows that in cases of so-called voluntary satis, some widows were drugged or weighed down with wood. Others, who were persuaded to commit sati for familial or economic reasons, sometimes attempted last-minute efforts to escape by jumping from the flaming funeral pyre. Since widows who declared their intention to become satis often changed their minds, a reading of their agency in terms of "voice" can only produce a narrative of female acquiescence.

An attention to the widow's shifting subjectivity is all the more necessary in view of the force of colonial explanations that freeze her image into a *tableau vivant* of death. The following description of a sati by a British magistrate is emblematic, for Mani, of how the meaning of a highly interpretable text is fixed:

> If it were desired to portray a scene which should thrill with horror every heart, not entirely dead to the touch of human sympathy, it would suffice to describe a father, regardless of the affection of his tender child, in having already suffered one of the severest miseries which flesh is heir to, with tearless eye leading forth a spectacle to the assembled multitude, who with barbarous cries demand the sacrifice, and unrelentingly delivering up the unconscious and unresisting victim to an untimely death, accompanied by the most cruel tortures.[70]

Mani explains that what the magistrate "sees" is based on unexamined presuppositions about the actors in question: the relatives are cruel and cold-blooded; the crowd is barbaric and bloodthirsty; and the widow is an unresisting victim. I would add to the cast of characters, that the European is a moral agent. The magistrate positions the horrified onlooker who is sympathetic to the widow's plight as one who is morally superior to the cruel and unfeeling crowd enjoying the spectacle. In this manner, any sympathy a Westerner might feel for the widow is expressed through the colonial construction of her as a victim to be saved.

The trope of "human sympathy" does not establish a common identity between colonizer and colonized so much as it identifies the racial superiority of the English. This same structure is visible in *Jane Eyre*. Although Jane expresses a sympathy for harem women, she does not identify herself as one but positions herself as a missionary woman who will save them. But more than that she distinguishes herself from Hindu women by declaring her refusal to burn on her husband's pyre. Rather than establishing a shared identity between the English and Hindu woman, the novel's reference to sati ranks Hindu women low on the feminist scale of emancipation. This distancing of the English woman from her Eastern sisters enables the problem of female emancipation in marriage to be resolved in what constitutes the final stage of Jane's development.

After fleeing from Thornfield following her discovery of Bertha Mason's existence, Jane enters into a relationship with a new "despotic" master. Under the tutelage of St. John Rivers, she finds herself an obedient student who is increasingly fettered to his will. He wants her to join the Indian missions, work for which she feels she has no vocation. Missionary work is guided by the spirit of self-sacrifice rather than the mutual reinforcement of self-interest and progress that characterizes the colonialism of the first half of the nineteenth century. The overseas missions, strongly evangelical in character, have a curiously feminine form. "Evangelical manhood, with its stress on self-sacrifice and influence, came dangerously close to embracing 'feminine' qualities," explain Leonore Davidoff and Catherine Hall, and for this reason manliness was reinforced through a control of emotions, the religious duty of work, and, above all else, the separation of a "woman's sphere."[71] The enforced masculinity of evangelicalism is evident in the coldhearted, duty-bound St. John, who considers his labor for God to be above the petty concerns of humankind.

Unlike colonial civilizers, the missionary was willing to sacrifice his life for the greater good of humanity, an act of martyrdom that placed him squarely within a Christian allegory.[72] St. John expresses his "hopes of being numbered in the band who have merged all ambition into the glorious one of bettering their race—of carrying knowledge into the realms of ignorance—of substituting peace for war—freedom for bondage—religion for superstition—the hope of heaven for the fear of hell" (*JE*, 329). Missionary wives, however, did not have the same access to the heroic discourse of self-sacrifice as their husbands. An English woman who joined the Christian missions was obliged to efface herself on two counts, one religious and the other sexual. Living and working with Indian women, they ranked low in a rigidly hierarchical Anglo-Indian society that disapproved of religious conversion and European contact with poor and low-caste natives (the primary group that converted to Christianity). The thought of working with Indian women appeals to Jane, for it is only when St. John raises this possibility that she agrees to become his helpmate. But she also does not want to be a missionary wife, saying: "I am ready to go to India, if I may go free" (*JE*, 356). This option is not available to her because, as St. John informs her, single women are not allowed to join the Christian missions.

Even though Jane cannot be the missionary that she once declared she would become, that does not mean she is in the same position as Indian women. St. John's desire makes no lesser demand on her than her life because she knows she lacks the stamina to work under the hot Indian sun. Yet, her premature death is also spoken of as voluntary on her part, for she understands her obedience to be an act that is "almost equivalent to committing suicide" (*JE*, 364). The unspoken text of Jane's being "grilled alive in Calcutta" (*JE*, 366) is a colonial discourse on Hindu women who were burned alive on their husbands' pyres.[73] Unlike the Hindu women who are "hurried away in a suttee," Jane exercises her free will and voice-agency. Prying her own desires away from the hypnotic power of St. John's, she reverses her former passivity and, upon doing so, names him as the agent of her death. She enunciates the oppressiveness of marriage customs that demand a wife's devotion to her husband when she declares that the sacrifice St. John demands of her is nothing short of murder: "If I were to marry you, you would kill me. You are killing me now" (*JE*, 363). He, in return, calls her words "violent, unfeminine, and untrue." With this act of resistance Jane finally comes into her own, thereby proving her passionate outburst to be both feminine and true.

What often passes unnoticed in feminist readings of Jane's final ascendancy into power is that her agency is underwritten by a male voice. She is able to refuse St. John only after hearing Rochester call out her name; her future husband, in effect, names the new assertive female. The male voice behind Jane's assertion of her power means that she is not an individuated self in the sense of being autonomous from her husband. Instead of defining Jane as a social agent, the novel reorders the doctrine of "female influence" so as to grant women agency in the domestic sphere. Yet, the domestic individual is a condition of possibility for women's entry into public life. In the decades following the publication of *Jane Eyre*, middle-class English women interpreted the domestic ideal in a manner that permitted them to take their duties outside the home. By redefining prostitution, alcoholism, and child-labor laws as domestic issues, moral crusaders were able to win control over certain sectors of the public sphere. *Jane Eyre* is a novel that hovers on the horizon of middle-class English women's bid for social power.

Yet, the domestic individual creates a conflict for the novel's romantic plot, which works toward its own utopian vision of female emancipation in marriage. The conflict between marriage and passionate love, a woman's duty to her family and her self-determination cannot be resolved so long as the separation of spheres is left intact. In terms of its final reconciliation, the novel does not alter the domestic sphere so much as it asserts that a woman can find self-fulfillment in devotion to her family. As Carol Ohmann observes, Brontë's "radicalism was always in tension with conservative tendencies, and she was better, even in *Jane Eyre* and *Shirley*, at posing social problems than at sighting ways to solve them."[74] The problem of self-determination for the domestic woman is resolved through a linguistic power capable of making the feminine virtue of self-sacrifice represent self-fulfillment. "Sacrifice! What do I sacrifice?" Jane declares in anticipation of her marriage to Rochester as her story draws to a close; "famine for food, expectation for content.... is that to make a sacrifice? If so, then certainly I delight in sacrifice" (*JE*, 392).

The almost magical metamorphosis of feminine self-sacrifice into its polar opposite is impossible within the constraints of a marriage plot; it requires the burning body of the Hindu widow as an icon for the angel in the house. In this regard, it is not simply a case of the "native female" being excluded from a discourse of feminist individualism, as Spivak suggests.[75] Rather, Jane's appeal to the moral mission of colonialism for asserting her own autonomy indicates a triangular relationship whereby English women's bid for domestic power passes through the racial hierarchy of colonialism. In short, the silent passivity of the Hindu woman is the grounds for the speaking subject of feminist individualism.

Brontë's first novel gives us the faint glimmer of a discursive relationship between the domestic virtue of self-renunciation and Hindu widow-immolation that becomes more explicitly articulated during the post-Mutiny period. Following the trajectory of Jane's narration that ends with St. John sacrificing his life for the Christian missions, I take the English woman's story overseas to India. Barred from the noble work of the civilizing project, the English woman enters a colonial iconography of martyrdom only in the capacity of victim. Unlike her male counterpart, it is her brutalized corpse rather than her body of good deeds that is of significance to the moral mission of colonialism.

Massacre of English officers and their wives at Jhansi. From Charles Ball's *History of the Indian Mutiny* (1858).

3

The Civilizing Mission Disfigured

In *Mrs. Dalloway*, Virginia Woolf paints a portrait of Clarissa's old aunt that I take to be an allegorical picture of the English woman in India. Helena Parry did not fight brave battles or rule over the natives, as did soldiers and civil servants. Her memories of the raj are not the stuff history books are made of, "for at the mention of India, or even Ceylon, her eyes (only one was glass) slowly deepened, became blue, beheld not human beings—she had no tender memories, no proud illusions about Viceroys, Generals, Mutinies—it was orchids she saw, and mountain passes and herself carried on the backs of coolies in the 'sixties over solitary peaks; or descending to uproot orchids (startling blossoms, never beheld before) which she painted in water-colour."[1] To view the past with the singular vision of Helena's good eye is to presume that both art and English women do not participate in the business of colonialism. It is a vision that is contingent upon the native's invisibility, for scarcely do we begin to see them than the picture is suddenly transformed. There is something disturbing about the image of an English woman being carried up mountains on the backs of Indians for the sole purpose of finding rare orchids. If one considers that the 1860s was the decade following one of the largest anticolonial revolts, Woolf's portrait of Helena Parry is all the more telling. It was through the sacred image of English womanhood—thus elevated, she appeared to transcend colonial relations—that British strategies of counterinsurgency were introduced.

The tenth of May 1857 has entered colonial records as a day of infamy for the British in India. It was on that fateful day in Meerut that sepoys mutinied against their officers, setting fire to the cantonment before marching on to Delhi and naming the Mogul king, Bahadur Shah II, emperor of Hindustan.[2] The idea that the company was a generous master and the sepoy a loyal servant was so firmly fixed in the colonial mind that initial news of the mutiny was met with disbelief. "The Sepoy army is not in revolt; it does not even appear that it is discontented,"[3] reported the Calcutta correspondent for the London *Times*. A few days later, on 23 June 1857, the centennial of British rule in India, the initial denial was replaced with the following words of warning: "An Imperial interest is at stake—nothing less than our dominion in British India."[4] The extraordinary scene at Meerut—its burning bungalows, smashed prisons, and slain Europeans— would become a familiar sight in the months ahead. During that year of social upheaval, colonialism was in a state of crisis. It was a year when to be a European meant almost certain death, and the end of British rule appeared imminent.

When the uprisings erupted in 1857, the British found themselves without a script on which they could rely. The racial typing of the "mild Hindoo" explained the long history of India as a conquered nation even as it permitted the new conquerors to cast themselves as mere players in a prewritten script. According to this script, the European colonizers were saving the natives from Eastern despotism by teaching them the laws of self-government. This is not to suggest that the civilizing mission was a fiction the British created for themselves or the Indians whom they governed. Rather, it performed the ideological work of producing a native desire for Western knowledge and, by extension, for British rule. Armed with an English education and access to the publishing business, a Bengali urban elite represented for all intents and purposes the "native public opinion" in the 1830s.[5] And, the colonized who spoke the master's language did not curse like Caliban but praised Prospero for extending Europe into Asia. It is in this capacity that the upper-class/caste Hindu served as an ideological alibi for colonialism. One is not surprised to discover that the paradigmatic colonial subject openly opposed the 1857 revolt.

The absence of consent that the anticolonial uprisings represented could not be understood according to the racial stereotype of Hindu passivity or the logic of British rule by native consent. A new racial typing was required, and this is where the figure of Oriental barbarism comes into play. The following lines from Alexander Duff's *The Indian Rebellion* (1858) show the effort to make the preexisting stereotype of the "Asiatic" accommodate the violence of anticolonial insurgency: "Throughout all ages the Asiatic has been noted for his duplicity, cunning, hypocrisy, treachery; and coupled with this . . . his capacity of secresy and concealment. But in vain will the annals even of Asia be ransacked for examples of artful, refined, consummate duplicity, surpassing those which have been exhibited throughout the recent mutinies."[6] The British regarded the Hindu male to be cruel, yet physically weak, duplicitous rather than savage. In the absence of a stereotype for the "savage Hindoo," the "blood-thirsty Musselman" was often identified as the perpetrator of the worst crimes. All Muslims were believed to be rebels, and the popular base of the uprisings was rationalized as the desire of an enslaved race for the despotic rule of a Mogul emperor. However, the "Great Revolt" (as the 1857 rebellion came to be known among Indians) was fought on several fronts that were relatively autonomous from the plan to restore Bahadur Shah II to the throne.

The Indian Mutiny or Sepoy Rebellion was not quite the military insubordination that its name suggests but rather a wave of uprisings in which Indian soldiers, princes, religious leaders, and peasants all played a role.[7] As the rebellions spread across northern India, so did the prophecy that the *firinghis* (a derogatory name for Europeans) would be driven out on the one hundredth anniversary of the Battle of Plassey, the beginning of British rule in India. While acknowledging the seriousness of the revolt, English and Anglo-Indian newspapers dismissed such predictions as the lies of the marketplace. Their dismissals belong to an official truth that delegitimates the language of dissent by classifying word-of-mouth transmissions as rumors. "To regard rumour as lying," writes Ranajit Guha, "is a measure of the distance between a typical site of collective discourse and an ideal seat of official truth—between the bazaar and the bungalow."[8] Guha understands rumor to be an oral form of transmitting information in preliterate societies. In 1857, for instance, riots in one village were often initiated by the news that peasants in a neighboring village had reclaimed their bonds from the *banias* (moneylenders). Guha situates the mobilizing power of rumor in the ambiguity of its signification; as an anonymous, verbal message whose source is unknown, it can be rearticulated at any point along its line of transmission.[9]

Colonial historiography considers the Indian Mutiny to have been started by a rumor. Suspecting the British of converting them to Christianity, sepoys believed that the cartridges of a new Enfield rifle had been greased with beef and pork fat. Faced with the choice of breaking their religious faith or disobeying their commanding officers, good men, who were otherwise loyal, trustworthy, and "true to their salt,"[10] believed the lies about the greased cartridges and refused to follow orders. Narratives like the one I have just recounted give the impression that native soldiers, in a sudden fit of religious fervor, went on a rampage of slaughter and destruction. By attributing the origins of rebellion to the fear of technology, colonial explanations represent the Mutiny as a war between religious fanaticism and Reason.

Stories of British plans to sabotage the religious proscriptions of both Hindus and Muslims are less the signs of superstitious fears than the expression of a distrust and dissatisfaction with colonial rule and, more important, the statement of communal alliance.[11] The far-reaching effects of rumor can be seen in the ease with which the news of a British ploy to violate the sepoy's religious faith was translated into a language that affected the general population, as, for instance, the belief that food had been polluted with animal extracts such as ground-up bones in flour and animal fat in ghee.[12] Colonial historiography downplays the pervasiveness of anticolonial sentiment by coding social unrest as the frenzy of *badmashes*, the thievery of *dacoits*, or the mob violence of an unruly rabble. Contemporary historians perform a similar negation when they repeat the official version that delegitimated the popular base to the rebellions. In his recreation of the events at Meerut, Christopher Hibbert, author of the most respected popular history of the Mutiny, describes the sepoys as being "misled by rumours," instigated by prostitutes "taunting them with their failure," and joined by "badmashes from the bazaar" and "bands of marauders . . . from the surrounding villages."[13] It is here, in the unsavory characters of rumormongers, whores, rascals, and ruffians, that we can read the signs of subaltern insurgency. But even as the official version negates the popular base of the uprisings, it is forced to acknowledge that the insurrections were not confined to the military. This is because a British faith in sepoy loyalty could not be restored without situating the origins of the story of the greased cartridges in the bazaar rather than the barrack.

While native predictions of the end of colonialism were dismissed as rumor, stories the English told each other were presumed to be true. To regard the rumors circulating among

Indians as lies is to read the signs of rebellion according to the narrative demands of the official records. To ignore the legitimating function of rumors in the Anglo-Indian communities is to negate the ability of fiction to generate the effects of truth. As a means of emphasizing the relations of power in the historical distinction between fact and fiction, I include as part of the colonial production of knowledge on the 1857 rebellion the disreputable evidence of journalism and popular histories. I consider these narratives as the British effort to comprehend, on the one hand, a native refusal of foreign rule where there should be consent, and, on the other, colonial coercion where there should be benevolent guidance.

The Truth-Effects of Fiction

> But why follow these details—why wonder that our country people cannot comprehend the full barbarity of these unprovoked massacres, when those who saw them recall the scenes more as a dream than as a reality—an enduring impression left by a hideous vision?
> —Mrs. Muter, *Travels and Adventures* (1864)

During the early days of the Mutiny a strange and horrifying tale took hold of the colonial imagination, spreading throughout Anglo-India and all the way back to England. Mutineers, the story went, were subjecting "our countrywomen" to unspeakable torments. Natives, the story continued, were systematically raping English women and dismembering their ravished bodies. The rumors had scarcely been started before they were discredited as having no factual basis. Yet the events of 1857 went on record as nothing less than the barbaric attack of mutinous sepoys on innocent women and children. "Fortunately the actual occurrence of these horrors was seldom proved," reports Pat Barr in *The Memsahibs: The Women of Victorian India*, "but they served to inflame public opinion in England and Anglo-India—particularly because the principal victims were said to have been women."[14] English newspapers, journals, and pamphlets that printed stories without investigating their sources effectively transformed rumor into information. Thus was a reading public made to share in the terror—and revenge—as the letters, stories, and news reports slowly made their way from the embattled regions of India.

Operating behind a screen of decency that demanded it withhold details, the English press generated a narrative desire around what it did not say. The editorials divulged information in hints and innuendos, while the stories accompanying them were pieced together from the testimonies of eyewitnesses who were often not present at the scenes they describe. What these so-called eyewitnesses "saw" was invariably seen by a friend; what they heard always seemed to have happened elsewhere. One officer later recalled that at Delhi he heard about the terrible events at Cawnpore, and at Cawnpore he heard the same stories about Delhi.[15] Carried from town to town by a mobile avenging army, the tales of terror had no known origin. Although discrepancies did not always pass unnoticed, the general tenor of the Mutiny reports showed a strong desire to represent rumor and hearsay as fact and information. Imagination was an authorized trespasser in the fact-finding mission of the newspapers, which invited readers to visualize the unspeakable acts that could only be disclosed in fragments. A story that appeared during the early stages of the Mutiny established the "fact" that women and children were killed at the palace in Delhi by first declaring little knowledge of events, then appealing to the imagination as a privileged source of information, before finally reporting what had only been heard: "We know little of the exact scenes which transpired, and imagination hesitates to lift the veil from them. We hear, however, that about 50 helpless women and children who had hid themselves in the palace on the outbreak were subsequently discovered, and the whole murdered in cold blood."[16] As the mystery that imagination will uncover from behind the veil of ignorance, rumor has already been declared a truth.

Our perception of the Mutiny has been colored by the years of myth making that have gone into forming a racial memory about its events. Bloodshed and massacre, the common tropes for thinking about 1857, overshadow the less dramatic effect the rebellion had on everyday life. English women's writings are especially valuable for their descriptions of the domestic disorder in a colonial world turned upside down.[17] Maintaining a household was no easy task for members of a class that was completely dependent upon native labor. The number of servants working in a European home ranged from ten to fifty.[18] With news of the end of British rule in the air, servants ran away, leaving their masters and mistresses to fend for themselves. In their journals the wives of high-ranking officers complained about the insolence of even the most menial of workers who remained behind. Others wrote of how they were unable to perform domestic chores in the Indian heat. One of these high-ranking women, Mrs. Coopland, commented on overhearing her punkah pullers saying that they would soon be masters, as the English were only superior in cold climates. "I could not help fancying," she wrote, "they might have made us punkah and fan *them,* so completely were we in their power."[19] Her reading of her servants' insubordination as the sign of their absolute power reveals the precariousness of a racial superiority that is so taken for granted by the British that it is presumed to be a universal truth.

Once the racial and moral superiority of the British is undermined, the incredulity expressed by Macaulay some twenty-five years earlier returns with more ominous significance:

> That we should govern a territory ten thousand miles from us, a territory larger and more populous than France, Spain, Italy, and Germany put together, a territory, the present clear revenue of which exceeds the present clear revenue of any state in the world, France excepted; a territory, inhabited by men differing from us in race, colour, language, manners, morals, religion; these are prodigies to which the world has seen nothing similar. Reason is confounded. We interrogate the past in vain.[20]

Macaulay can indulge in such rhetorical flourishes because his faith in the superiority of the British is unshaken. One cannot say the same about 1857, even though it was not the first case of an anticolonial rebellion. Mutinies, peasant revolts, and border disputes span the history of the British in India; just two years earlier some thirty thousand to fifty thousand Santal tribals rebelled.[21] What is different about 1857 is that it was the first instance of sepoys killing officers and their families. In addition, the revolt could not be rationalized as the discontent of one group of Indians; it lasted for more than a year and revealed that the army itself could not be relied on.

The experiences of colonialists in a state of exhaustion, terror, and confusion have since been sealed with the stamp of authenticity that guarantees all eyewitness reports. Since the legitimation of colonialism was premised on the presumed passivity of the colonized, the killing of even one European took on the exaggerated proportion of a massacre. Yet, most of the British who died were not massacred in cold blood but lost their lives during the protracted battles that involved maneuvers and countermaneuvers for control of strategic towns scattered across northern

India. Different factions of rebels (sometimes armed with heavy artillery) laid siege to the cities, while loyal soldiers (both British and Indian) were marched back and forth to reclaim fallen territories. Mrs. Coopland writes of how many more lives might have been saved if the British had evacuated women and children from the outlying stations instead of keeping them there to avoid arousing suspicion.[22] Trapped in towns with diminishing supplies of food, water, and medicine, Anglo-Indian communities faced the added risk of dehydration, cholera, and dysentery. The image of death by disease or bullet wound is far less noble than that of helpless women and children being cut to pieces by leering sepoys with swords in hand. It is the latter image, however, that was fixed on canvas and in ink for posterity. The primary referent for this emblem of barbarism was Nana Sahib, the Hindu leader responsible for the massacre of British civilians at Cawnpore (*Kanpur*) on 15 July 1857. Upon retreating from Cawnpore before an approaching British army, he ordered the execution of his hostages. Around two hundred English women and children were put to death in the Bibighar, or "House of the Ladies." Their bodies were concealed in a well at the back of the house or else thrown into the Ganges River. Although Nana Sahib's actions were the exception rather than the rule, the occurrence of even one massacre such as Cawnpore endowed all the terrifying tales with their truth-effects.

Commissioners and magistrates entrusted with investigating the rumors could find no evidence of systematic rape, mutilation, and torture at Cawnpore or any place else. The official reports, however, came too late, as the sensational stories had already done their work. Rebels were perceived as sadistic fiends, and Nana Sahib was especially vilified for the unforgivable crime of desecrating English womanhood. Barr exhibits a predictable understanding of the Cawnpore massacre when she writes that there, "one of the most revered of Victorian institutions, the English Lady, was slaughtered, defiled and brought low."[23] When the massacre of women is reported as the destruction of an institution, we know that the sacred image of English womanhood has outlived the story of the women's lives.

The Bibighar, which also came to be known as the Slaughter House, was preserved with its dried blood and rotting remains as a kind of museum for passing troops to visit. Accounts of what had transpired there were reconstructed from the remains of the dead women. Any nakedness was interpreted as the sign of rape and not, as was more often the case, the theft of jewelry and clothing from the women's bodies after they had been killed. British soldiers cut locks of hair from the dead women's heads as mementos that were passed from hand to hand as fetish objects of a pornographic nightmare. Thus began the mythic invention of the murdered women's torments, as soldiers covered the walls with bloody inscriptions in the hands of the "Mutiny ladies" directing their men to avenge their horrible deaths.[24] Sir John Kaye, whose history of the Mutiny is a definitive Victorian account, makes a point of indicating the inaccuracy of the stories recounting what had transpired at Cawnpore. Nana Sahib did not force English women into his harem (as was popularly believed) but made them cook for and wait on him and his entourage. "Our women were not dishonoured," concludes Kaye, "save that they were made to feel their servitude."[25] His words are telling about what is at stake in the invented stories of rape and torture— namely, the rebels had unsettled a colonial order to the degree of reversing its hierarchy of mastery and servitude.

A representation of English women as the innocent victims of anticolonial rebellion was instrumental both in reestablishing preexisting structures of colonial authority and in preparing the grounds for new ones. The iconic value of the English woman-as-victim is nowhere more evident than in the claims that rebels had crucified their female prisoners like Christ the Savior.[26] Other easily recognizable topoi from the great tradition of Western civilization familiarized the unfamiliar and rendered imaginable the unknown. The tales of terror drew on a stockpile of horrors more likely to be encountered in the pages of Dante, Ovid, and Shakespeare: Children roasted alive in boxes or force-fed the flesh of their fathers, babies cut from the bellies of their mothers, women dismembered. The difficulty of associating such images with the "mild Hindoo" is visible in the contradictory language of a Bombay letter writer who exclaimed: "But, oh, the *savage* mind never yet conceived the atrocities which these *civilised* savages have committed. . . . The exquisite nature of the torture they inflict has something awful in it."[27] The term *atrocity*, which pervades the Mutiny reports, condemns the rebellion to the annals of morally reprehensible crimes. Yet, the acts they describe are more telling of the European rather than the Oriental mind. While a classical and biblical tradition provided the British with their charged plots of martyrdom, heroism, and revenge, an elaborately crafted body of writing endowed the mythic plots with their historical efficacy.

The sensationalist stories, which are to be found in private letters, newspapers, and popular histories, all circle around a single, unrepresentable center: the rape of English women. Upon declaring the sepoy crimes to be "unspeakable," the Mutiny reports offer a range of signification that has the same effect as the missing details. In other words, they "speak" the violence of rape. Following Monique Plaza's characterization of rape as a violence "which has the bodies of women as its object of privileged appropriation,"[28] I want to suggest that, in the Mutiny reports, the *representation* of rape violently appropriates English women as "the sex." This appropriation takes place through an objectification of the women as eroticized and ravaged bodies.

The eyewitness reports all plot the women's deaths as the culmination of the same sequence of events: they are stripped naked, sexually abused, and then tortured. A particularly notorious version of this plotting is to be found in a letter from a clergyman that made its way into several newspapers. It first appeared in the *Times*, which reprinted the following report from a man of God as a God-given truth:

> They took 48 females, most of them girls of [sic] from 10 to 14, many
> delicately nurtured ladies, — violated them and kept for the base
> purposes of the heads of the insurrection for a whole week. At the
> end of that time they made them strip themselves, and gave them up
> to the lowest of the people to abuse in broad daylight in the street of
> Delhi. They then commenced the work of torturing them to death,
> cutting off their breasts, fingers, and noses, and leaving them to die.
> One lady was three days dying.[29]

The letter from the clergyman codes the anticolonial rebellion as a sex crime. In addition, the fetishization of body parts objectifies the female corpse over and above any value the women might have in life. Inasmuch as the women do have any value, it lies in their moral purity, which is established for the sole purpose of being negated. Implied here is that each time a native so much as touches one English woman, he desecrates all of English womanhood. Karl Marx, reporting for the *New York Daily Tribune*, noticed what should have been obvious to others—that the letter was written by "a cowardly parson residing at Bangalore, Mysore, more than a thousand miles, as the bird flies, distant from the scene of the action."[30] The clergyman's letter was included in a collection of fictitious reports published the following year, as the effort of one Edward Leckey to begin "the task of discriminating between truth and fiction."[31] Yet, it also made its way into the numerous histories and novels that were so popular after the crisis had ended. Variations on the basic structure of, in this case, an invented story recur again and again in the newspaper reports. As speech acts, they position English women as innocent victims and Indian men as sadistic sex criminals; insurgency is thus represented above all else as a crime against women.

Upon characterizing the stories of sexual violence as fictions, I do not wish to suggest that no English woman was raped—that is, to perform the reverse of colonial accounts that denounce the rumors of British soldiers raping Indian women. Even one instance of a rape is a sobering reminder of the sexual violence directed against all women during times of war. What I am suggesting is that there is no evidence pointing to a *systematic* rape and mutilation of English women, and that the Mutiny reports reenact that absent violence in its place. The fear-provoking stories have the same effect as an actual rape, which is to say, they violently reproduce gender roles in the demonstration that women's bodies can be sexually appropriated.[32] In this regard, the meaning of rape cannot be disassociated from its discursive production.

Only by considering the invented stories in terms of their effects do we see that a focus on the terrifying crimes against women displaces attention away from the image of English men dying at the hands of the insurgents. The reports contain no elaborate descriptions of men being dismembered, since such a fragmentation of the male body would allocate British men to the objectified space of the rape victim—a status that would negate colonial power at the precise moment that it needed reinforcing. I do not mean to say that this absence is a willed operation but rather that it is a structured silence that has to do with the conditions of possibility of what can and cannot be said. From the perspective of the colonizer, once a European man is struck down, then anything is possible; in death, his mortality is exposed and sovereign status brought low. A discourse of rape—that is, the violent reproduction of gender roles—helped manage the crisis in authority so crucial to colonial self-representation at the time.

Since the contradictions of gender and race are articulated

within the signifying system of colonialism, a discourse of rape is overdetermined by colonial relations. It is helpful, when unpacking this economy of signs, to consider Elizabeth Cowie's important insight into the cultural production of women not only as exchange objects but also as signs.[33] According to Cowie, the reproduction of women's gender roles constitutes a transaction that also gives value to a particular signifying system. In all those stories of "Sepoy atrocities," I would argue, the *English lady* circulates as a sign for the moral superiority of colonialism under threat of native insurrection. The slippage between the violation of English women as the object of rape and the violation of colonialism as the object of rebellion permits the moral value of the domestic woman—her self-sacrifice, duty, and devotion—to be extended to the social mission of colonialism. The signifier may be *woman*, but its signified is the value of colonialism she represents. This might explain why, despite the narrative energy generated around the sign woman, the stories of the women themselves escape the frame of the narrations.

Reports that stage the ravaged white female body as a public spectacle reduce English women to the vulnerability of their sex. As the following text from Campbell's *Narrative of the Indian Revolt* indicates, such accounts bypass the mutilation of men to linger over the details of what was done to the women. What is noteworthy about this particular narrative is that the agent of the torture is missing; it could be any native or every one. We will later see why no Indian—male or female, young or old—escapes suspicion:

> Tortures the most refined, outrages the most vile, were perpetrated upon men, women and children alike. Men were hacked to pieces in the presence of their wives and children. Wives were stripped in the presence of their husbands' eyes, flogged naked through the city, violated there in the public streets, and then murdered. To cut off the breasts of the women was a favourite mode of dismissing them to death; and, most horrible, they were sometimes scalped—the skin being separated round the neck, and then drawn over the head of the poor creatures, who were then, blinded with blood, driven out into the blazing streets. To cut off the nose, ears and lips of these unhappy women (in addition, of course, to the brutal usage to which they were almost invariably submitted), was merciful.[34]

Campbell fragments the female body in the most explicit way he knows how. He provides a hierarchy of tortures, the "most horri-

ble" of which is a woman's loss of identity through the effacement of her facial features. By the time he has finished with her,
there is nothing left to the English woman but her brutalized
body. We do not know what it means for the women to see their
husbands killed, even though men are included among the victims. Rather, we are forced to view the women's rape and mutilation through their husbands' eyes. In this manner, the reader is
invited to experience the horror of sexual violence from a male
perspective. What is significant to Campbell is that it is not just
any women who have been subjected to the native's "brutal
usage" but women *who are the property of English men.* In short,
there is no place for inserting female agency in this account.

Since the signifying function of "woman" depends on a role
that restricts English women to the "innocent space" of the domestic sphere, their command of colonial authority is of little interest to the Mutiny reports. There exists, as a consequence, a
fracture between the colonial woman's positioning within the
sensational stories as a helpless victim or violated body and her
own sense of "self."

Judith of Cawnpore

> She pulled the head out of the bag and held it for them to see.
> "This is the head of Holofernes, general-in-chief of the Assyrian
> army; here is the canopy under which he lay drunk! ... My face
> seduced him, only to his own undoing; he committed no sin
> with me to shame me or disgrace me."
>
> —Judith (13: 16)

The English women who describe their Mutiny experiences in
diaries, journals, and memoirs do not always respond to the
threat of rape and torture from within their socially constructed
gender roles. There is no question that they believed the terrifying stories, which made the thought of capture all the more
frightening. And there are those who say they kept poison in
case of an attack and instructed their husbands to avenge their
deaths. Yet, on the whole, the women primarily express a concern for staying alive rather than, as is the case with the newspaper reports, saving their honor. One memoir writer remembers
that she owed her life to her mother's ability to negotiate their
escape:

My mother remained below to "put them off the scent" she said should any come to seek us. This she did by seating herself on the *charpai* and drawing the skirt of her dress over her head *"chudder* fashion" as the native women do, completely hiding her face. She made the *chowkidar* stay near her, telling him that my father was watching from the roof and had his guns loaded, and should he any way betray us, my father would shoot him *first.* My father was entirely guided by her judgement, for he knew she was better able to understand the natives than he was, and he trusted her steady determined manner of dealing with them. He knew little of the language and had not long been out in India, therefore his clashing in any way with the natives would have been utterly fatal to us, for he would never have put up with their insolence (much of which was completely lost on him) and either abused them or struck them.[35]

In this account, the English man is still the fearful figure of colonial authority; however, the English woman, as one who is used to handling a household of servants, is more adept at strategies of self-survival. Other women express their reliance upon a language of colonial authority, claiming to have scared off hostile villagers by speaking to them authoritatively. This tactic sometimes failed, as is evidenced by the occasional mention of female friends who were killed for attempting to intimidate rebels with their commanding voice. By appealing to their own sense of domestic authority under conditions that did not always guarantee its success, Anglo-Indian women demonstrated a modicum of faith in their ability to command the natives.

The authority with which these women speak is a sign of their class standing as much as their racial superiority. This is because the Mutiny narratives preserved in the archives or in print all belong to the wives of army officers and civil officials. These upper-middle-class women had greater contact with the natives who served them than they did with their own working class. They rarely mention working-class English women, except as the source of a particularly lurid tale, which, as gentlewomen and ladies, they often refrained from discussing. Officers' wives were especially notorious for treating the wives of low-ranking soldiers with contempt. Since the working-class English woman who came over to India was considered "more like an animal than a woman,"[36] one cannot presume that the category of "English woman" in the Mutiny reports included her. Rather, these women appear only as an absence, between the interstices of a chivalrous code that demanded the victim be a lady.

There are instances when English women were praised for

their heroism, endurance, and bravery; however, it was always in the service of *moral* fortitude. One of the most famous stories reenacted in playhouses and lecture halls across England described a youthful captive who slew several sepoys with a sword before drowning herself. The woman is known to us only as the youngest daughter of General Wheeler, the commander-in-chief at Cawnpore before it fell to Nana Sahib. Miss Wheeler was presumed dead, when news arrived that a *sowar* (cavalry man) had carried her off as his mistress. According to the following narration, the Bibighar women would have fared no better if not for young Wheeler's heroism:

> The poor creatures (the women and elder girls) were sought to be tempted by an emissary of the Nana to enter quietly into his harem; but they one and all expressed a determination to die where they were, and with each other, rather than yield to dishonour. They were then destined to be given up to the sensual licence of the sepoys and sowars who had aided in their capture; but the heroic conduct of Sir Hugh Wheeler's daughter is said to have deterred the ruffians. What this "Judith of Cawnpore" really did, is differently reported. Her heroism was manifested, in one version of the story, by an undaunted and indignant reproach against the native troops for their treachery to the English who had fed and clothed them, and for their cowardice in molesting defenceless women; in another version, she shot down five sepoys in succession with a revolver, and then threw herself into a well to escape outrage; in a third given by Mr. Sheperd, this English lady, being taken away by a trooper of the second native cavalry to his own hut, rose in the night, secured the trooper's sword, killed him and three other men, and then threw herself into a well; while a fourth version, on the authority of the ayah, represents the general's daughter as cutting off the heads of no less than five men in the trooper's hut. *These accounts, incompatible one with another, nevertheless reveal to us a true soldier's daughter, an English gentlewoman, resolved to proceed to any extremity in defence of her own purity.* (emphasis added)[37]

Even in an account of female bravery such as this one, what is at stake is a woman's moral strength. Like Judith, Miss Wheeler is remembered for her courage and patriotism, but above all else her chastity. The place of female agency—the determination of the female prisoners and the resolution of the soldier's daughter—lies in a woman's choice of death over dishonor. On the basis of this decision, Miss Wheeler has no option other than to take her own life, even though she has already assumed the masculine role of punishing the sepoys. What is unusual about the Wheeler story is the conflicting evidence that prevents the author from presenting one, true report. Yet, the absence of a singular narration, which demands that he ground his own authority in "what was said" rather than "what happened," adds to the force of his conclusions. In other words, whatever the discrepancies, the four versions all reconfirm that Miss Wheeler was an English lady and gentlewoman.

Seven years after the Mutiny had ended, George Trevelyan (who was Macaulay's nephew) denounced the stories of Miss Wheeler's heroism as fictions all. According to the evidence he presents in his best-selling book, *Cawnpore*, a sowar kidnapped her and then bribed native witnesses to spread the news of her death so that he would not be forced to give her up.[38] After extensive police inquiries, Miss Wheeler was discovered as having converted to Islam and was "living quietly" with the sowar's family. The contradictory evidence to the Wheeler story has invited contemporary historians to speculate about her own designs and motives. Hibbert's version of what happened resembles Trevelyan's, except that he finds a place in the story for the English woman to exercise her free will. "Many years later," he writes, "a Roman Catholic priest in Cawnpore came upon an old lady in the bazaar who told him on her deathbed that she was Miss Wheeler. She said that she had married the sepoy who had saved her from massacre, that he had been good to her and that she did not want to get in touch with the British authorities."[39] The version Hibbert reports shows that the present-day desire to establish sympathy or romantic love between English women and Indian men is perhaps as strong as the Victorian one to negate it. Yet, it also reveals that such counternarratives can only be complicit with the colonial documents from which they are derived.

Given the limits of the historical records, there is no place for women's sexual desire in the captivity stories. It is impossible to determine whether Miss Wheeler was happily married to the man who saved her life or, having crossed the forbidden boundary of conjugating with the enemy, was unable to return to her own people. What we can be certain of is that an English woman who cohabited with rebels during the Mutiny could not reenter Anglo-Indian society without confessing her weakness, expressing horror over her decision, and demonstrating the extremity of her coercion. A sixteen-year-old survivor of the Cawnpore massacre (whose name was withheld from her published narrative to protect her identity) records the circumstances of her captivity and escape. Her confession becomes increasingly contradictory as she explains the conditions of her survival, recounting how her prayers for death soon changed into a desire to live. "The effect of the ill-treatment I had endured tended to make me a downright hypocrite," she writes. "I could have been made to do anything, and I played my part as a convert to the Mahommedan creed in a style at which I feel astonished now."[40] A second survivor at Cawnpore, Amelia Horne, also converted to Islam; she, however, underscores her resistance to religious conversion.[41] Narrating her story some thirty years later, Horne refrains from giving the details of her month-long residence in the home of a sowar, other than saying that she was kept there against her will.

Since Miss Wheeler did not return to her family, a similar confession is unavailable to us. What does get restored along with the evidence of her sexual desire is a racial origin that is open to inquiry. Having disclosed that Miss Wheeler renounced her Christian faith and married a Muslim man, Trevelyan concludes that "she was by no means of pure English blood."[42] The woman who was once a heroic English lady and true soldier's daughter is now revealed to be Eurasian. In other words, her racial construction changes to the precise degree that her badge of honor is now a sign of her disgrace. As the case of the general's daughter demonstrates, what determines her membership to the English race is less her class or racial origin than her "choice" of death over dishonor; female moral fortitude is the sign of racial purity. A class-specific term such as the English lady, and the ideal of womanhood it implies, thus produces racial divisions over and above those of class. The expression of race through gender and class categories indicates the emergence of a more explicitly race-oriented idiom being put into place through a semiosis of "woman."

The Rani of Jhansi

Among the fugitives in the rebel ranks was the resolute woman who, alike in council and on the field, was the soul of the conspirators. Clad in the attire of a man and mounted on horseback, the Rání of Jhánsi might have been seen animating her troops through the day.
—Kaye's and Malleson's History of the Indian Mutiny (1898)

To consider the discursive elements of sexual violence in the Mutiny reports is to see that the feminized space of what it means to be rapable also bears the racial inscriptions of what it means to be an *English* woman. By contrast, Indians are not gender-identified in colonial accounts of the administration of punishment. *Villager, insurgent,* and *nigger* are the non-gender-specific terms used interchangeably for all natives who were punished. Even the most telling narratives, which are to be found in private correspondences rather than public records, do not identify Indian women as the targets of British attacks. English and Anglo-Indian newspapers are equally silent on the matter. The only mention of Indian women exists in reports on the fall of the rebel stronghold at Delhi—the most glaring example of the rampant looting, murder, and destruction conducted in the name of restoring law and order. Some reports make a point of saying that, unlike treacherous sepoys, British soldiers showed great restraint and did not assault or murder defenseless women.[43] Such denials are of the order of a *disavowal*, that is, a negation that places such acts within the realm of possibility. Responding to the outcry from Irish and Quaker newspapers regarding the army's behavior at Delhi, the *News of the World* confirms that "not one of them appears to have been molested," even though British soldiers knew "the native women were active instigators of the Sepoys in their worst atrocities."[44] This is the closest the press comes to representing the sexual assault of Indian women. Yet, the mere mention of native women inciting mutineers to commit their bloodiest deeds overwrites any possibility of their sharing with English women the status of "innocent victim." Upon demonstrating the race and class exclusiveness of colonial constructions of woman-as-victim, I do not mean to suggest that such a construction should be extended to other women. Rather, my purpose for showing the overdetermined object of rape is to demonstrate some of the problems that arise when the social positioning of the rape victim serves as the basis for theorizing the sexual oppression of women.[45]

Contrary to Western stereotypes of the passive Oriental woman, Indian women are spoken of in the Mutiny reports as the worst offenders of the rebel crimes. Hags, she-fiends, or bazaar whores—these are the cruel women behind the barbaric acts of rape and mutilation. The most infamous of these women was the warrior queen of Jhansi, who was both admired for her bravery and despised for her treachery.[46] Considered responsible for a massacre second only to that at Cawnpore, she was known to the British as the Jezebel of India. Despite the Rani's notoriety, her role in the massacre at Jhansi is widely disputed. Some say she was held captive by mutineers; others, that she was persuaded to join them; and still a third group, that she was a power-hungry queen. She was killed while riding into battle attired in men's clothing. Sir Hugh Rose, the officer responsible for the Rani's defeat, was reported to have said of her that "the Indian Mutiny has produced but one man, and that man was a woman."[47] This and other colonial constructions of the Rani, particularly those that describe her cruelty and lasciviousness, cast her in a decidedly masculine role. The following report that appeared in the *Bombay Times* depicts her as the chief instigator of the abuse of prisoners. As the one who orders her men to rape, humiliate, and torture their female victims, the Rani of Jhansi exercises a power of speech that is capable of violating English womanhood even though, as a woman, she herself cannot perform that violence:

> Shortly after, the whole of the European community, men, women, and children, were forcibly brought out of their homes; and, in presence of the Ranee, stripped naked. Then commenced a scene unparalleled in historical annals. She, who styles herself "Ranee," ordered, as a preliminary step, the blackening of their faces with a composition of suet and oil, then their being tied to trees at a certain distance from each other; and having directed the innocent little children to be hacked to pieces before the eyes of their agonised parents, she gave the women into the hands of the rebel sepoys, to be dishonoured first by them, and then handed over to the rabble. The mal-treatment these poor creatures had received was enough to kill them, and several died ere the whole of the brutal scene had transpired; but those who still lingered were put to death with the greatest cruelty, being severed limb from limb. The death the men were subjected to was by no means so intensely cruel as that which our countrywomen received at the hands of their ravishers.[48]

Before the Rani can exercise her will over the lives (and deaths) of Europeans, she must first break their code of racial superiority. The English are consequently transformed into natives through a darkening of their faces. The difficulty in representing a stereotypically passive Indian woman as the perpetrator of sexual abuse is overcome by the double move of sexually positioning the Rani as the instigator of rape and torture (an action that semantically places the sepoys in a passive role) and racially positioning her victims as lowly natives. Even in an instance of gender role reversals such as this, the mutilation of English men cannot be represented. The effect the role reversal has on the Rani, however, is to exclude her from the "class of women," which is the sexual positioning of the rape victim. The closest the Mutiny reports come to depicting the rape of native women is in the description of *English* women with their blackened faces. In this masquerade of race and gender roles, we are presented with the fantastic image of an Indian woman behind the rape of other "native" women. In this manner, the women who are the victims of sexual violence are still in essence English. The category of woman-as-victim is racially coded because the ideal of Victorian womanhood is a *sign* for the colonial civilizing effort.

The representation of the English lady as an institution that had been desecrated plays into a code of chivalry that called on Victorian men to protect the weak and defenseless. Soldiers charged into battle with the cry of "Remember the Ladies! Remember the Babies!" on their lips. Presupposing their women to inhabit a domestic space that was safe from colonial conflict, these men responded as good soldiers, fathers, and husbands. They reasserted claim over what was rightfully theirs by protecting the victims and punishing the offenders. And the victims' honor was defended by making the punishment fit or (as was more often the case) exceed the crime. In this manner, the knightly virtues of honor, a veneration of women, and protection of the weak were invoked so that the army *as an institution* could act as a punishing avenger.

Mutiny historiography understands the brutality with which the uprisings were suppressed as the uncontrollable rage of Victorian men responding to the knowledge that the sanctity of their homes had been violated. Hibbert's is a contemporary version of this colonial understanding: "To the mid-nineteenth century British mind, this ruthless murder of women and children was a crime of unspeakable, blasphemous enormity. Englishmen regarded women in a light quite different from that in which Indians did, as creatures not merely of another sex but almost— if they were not mere drudges—of another form of creation, as (in T.H. Huxley's phrase) 'angels above them.' "[49] Because it appeals to the separation of spheres that was so crucial to safeguarding the moral value of colonialism, this explanation gives back to colonialism its own alibi. In short, it sees the punishment of rebels as a momentary fit of rage rather than the exercise of a power licensed by martial law. Shortly after the initial mutiny at Meerut, British army officers were issued a summary power that was quickly replaced by the even more extreme Act of 6 June. "Under that last Act," records one officer in his memoirs, "such powers were given wholesale to all and sundry, and barbarities were committed with a flimsy pretext of legality."[50] The British campaign of terror was thus already long under way before the news of the massacre at Cawnpore on 15 July reached the ears of British soldiers. What confirmed the "Sepoy atrocities" against English women were the punishments that reflected them.[51] Conducted as highly ritualized affairs, such punishment served as a model for the horrifying images the British saw in the bodies of their own dead women.

One can see in the fictions of the mutilated female bodies colonial strategies of counterinsurgency designed to maximize native terror. The execution of mutineers by tying them to the front of cannons and exploding them into minuscule pieces mirrored the death of the English women whom they had allegedly dismembered. At Cawnpore, rebels were made to lick dried blood from the Bibighar floor before being taken to the gallows. "To touch blood is most abhorrent to the high caste natives," writes Brigadier-General James Neill, engineer of the more elaborate punishments. "They think by doing so they doom their soul to perdition. *Let them think so.* My object is to inflict a fearful punishment for a revolting, cowardly, barbarous deed, and to strike terror into these rebels."[52] The rituals of punishment that were exercised acccording to what Neill calls a "strange law" stages the power of the colonizers (often invoked as the hand of God) beating down upon rebellious natives even after death through the torment of their souls.

The contradiction to seeking to restore a colonial order through physical torture is dramatized in the demand on British officers to maintain a facade of civility while administering punishment. "We made the Nana Sahib's (the Fiend's) Collector prisoner," writes an officer under Neill's command. "We stuffed pork, beef and everything which could possibly break his caste down his throat, tied him as tight as we could by the arms and told the guard to be *gentle* with him."[53] These are no men driven mad at the thought of "unspeakable crimes" committed against their women but ones who are engaged in issuing and executing military orders. In retrospect, Lieutenant-Colonel Maude, an ex-officer of Havelock's column, admits that "our feeling was not so much of revenge as a desire to strike terror into the hearts of those natives who were in any way either sympathising with or had been aiding and abetting in these horrors."[54] And, by virtue of being punished, every native was retroactively a rebel. In a report on how the punishment of a single villager got out of control and ended with the entire village being burned to the ground, an officer admits, "Though not intended ... [the destroyed village] may prove a salutary example and was not undeserved, as every inhabitant of the place is believed to have been implicated in the late disturbances."[55] J. W. Sherer, the magistrate of Fatehpur, who accompanied the army on its march toward Cawnpore, describes the scene of utter decimation that met his eyes. His is an eyewitness report not to be encountered in the pages of fiction or historiography:

> But many of the villages had been burnt by the wayside, and human beings there were none to be seen. A more desolate scene than the country we passed through can scarcely be imagined. The swamps on either side of the road, the blackened ruins of huts now further defaced by weather stains and mould; the utter absence of all sound that could indicate the presence of human life or the employments of human industry (such sound being usurped by the croaking of frogs, the shrill pipe of the cicala, and the under-hum of the thousand-winged insects, engendered by the damp and heat); the offensive odour of the neem trees; the occasional taint in the air from suspended bodies, upon which before our very eyes the loathsome pig of the country was engaged in feasting: all these things,— appealing to our different senses,— contributed to call up such images of desolation, and blackness, and woe, as few, I should think, who were present will ever forget.[56]

Despite the explicitness of this description and the care with which Sherer reconstructs the memory of what he saw, the agent of destruction remains hidden. He gives no indication as to which side is responsible for transforming the country into a wasteland—except that Neill's regiment is a few days ahead of him, and hanging, after all, is a British practice. The homologies Sherer establishes between the decaying tropical landscape and decimated native villages—the blackened swamps and the charred remains of huts, the monotonous buzz of insects and the absent hum of human activity, the repulsive scent from the neem trees and their "fruit" of rotting bodies—make the unnatural acts of retribution part of an even more unnatural terrain. The identification of a colonial system of terror with the Indian landscape suggests that torture is the only language the native understands.

The excessiveness of the punishment in relationship to the crime, the ritualized form of the executions, the ceremony of pain and death—these are the colonial strategies of counterinsurgency designed to "strike terror" in the rebellious native. They are also attributes of the "great spectacle of physical punishment" that, according to Foucault in his well-known study of prison reform, ended in the early nineteenth century. *Discipline and Punish* traces the disappearance of public execution in Europe and the United States and its replacement with the corrective technology of the penal system.[57] Although Foucault acknowledges the "trace of 'torture' in the modern mechanisms of criminal justice,"[58] physical punishment drops out of his discussion altogether once it loses its spectacular form. Yet, it is the spectacle of punishment in the exercise of sovereign power that interests me here. Because Foucault derives his theory of disciplinary power from a Eurocentric model of prison reforms, it cannot be used to address the colonial situation, in which technologies of discipline are overdetermined by imperial structures of power.

The punishment of the 1857 rebels reduces them to the corporeality of their bodies, and, as such, it expresses a right of sovereignty out of Europe's own "barbaric" past. Foucault's description of the tortured body of the condemned as "a body effaced, reduced to dust and thrown to the winds, a body destroyed piece by piece by the infinite power of the sovereign [that] constituted not only the ideal, but the real limit of punishment"[59] could just as easily describe the British punishment of the mutineers and rebels. Ranking the severity of insurgency in a way that simple hangings could not, the native's tortured body served as a sign for the institution of a new imperial order.

Colonial historiography does not censor the excessive force used to suppress the 1857 rebellions so much as record it as a lapse in British authority that permitted the abuse of power. I, on the other hand, would argue that the physical punishment meted out during the Great Revolt defined the limits of the power that a handful of foreigners could exercise over millions of natives in their homeland. The incredulity that Macaulay expressed over the possession of India in 1833 is now made credible through a fixed hierarchy of domination and subordination, superiority and inferiority inscribed upon a racially marked colonial body.

Contrary to what the grand narrative of the civilizing mission suggests, the liberal rule of colonial law and the exercise of sovereign power were not mutually exclusive. India was not only the place where British administrators experimented with Bentham's ideas of Panopticonism but also was the place where torture was an everyday practice for extracting revenue from an Indian peasantry that had no legal recourse.[60] In the years immediately preceding the 1857 uprisings, peasant representatives brought charges of torture against British officers.[61] The company responded to such complaints with investigations that did not trace the chain of command beyond the local level of native collectors and police officers. As a consequence, no European officer was ever charged with a violation. Upon holding local landlords responsible for violating a colonial law, the company could present itself as an enlightened ruler committed to protecting the Indian peasantry from cruel *zamindars*. In his essay, "Dominance without Hegemony and Its Historiography," Guha describes local forms of power and punishment as being structured by colonial relations. He characterizes colonial authority as a two-tiered system in which a British order interacted with an Indian idiom of *Daṇḍa*, which was "an *ensemble* of 'power, authority and punishment.' "[62] The British both took over precolonial coercive techniques at the local level and introduced new ones on a global scale. Indian landholders in outlying areas were expected to provide forced labor for visiting colonial officials as they had done for hill rajas in the past, and the sexual exploitation of servant women continued to be treated as the master's right. A new practice the British introduced was that of pressing the martial races of northern India into one of the largest imperial armies in the world.[63] Another transformation was the economic impoverishment following the collapse of the indigenous textile industry and the Permanent Settlement of Bengal that prompted a peasant migration overseas.[64] Indian men and women began to replace black slaves as "coolies" on West Indian plantations, while those who remained behind were hired locally to cultivate cotton dye in a system historians have since called "indigo slavery."[65] These are just some of the new coercive techniques that tied local, precolonial practices into the global economy of the British Empire.

India was officially named the *Indian Empire* in the Queen's Proclamation of 1 November 1858 that transferred the administrative duties of the East India Company to the British Crown. The contractual relationship between British official and Indian subject was now replaced with Mogul rituals of power and authority.[66] And so began a new era of imperial rule in which the monarch of Great Britain became the sovereign, or raj, of India.

The Queen's Proclamation was but the official seal on a text that had already undergone secondary revision. The English women's ravaged bodies were the retroactive effect of a terror-inducing spectacle that ushered in a new imperial authority in which a feudal hierarchy was rearticulated as a relationship of race. When posited as a cause, the stories of rape and torture allow colonial strategies of counterinsurgency to be represented as the aberrant response of otherwise civilized men driven mad at the thought of their tormented women. Thus adhering to the logic of colonialism as a civilizing influence, this explanation reconfirms the morality of the civilizers. An alternative way to read the invented stories is as the effect of the organized violence of colonialism. In this reading, we see that the sexual signification of the Mutiny reports preserves the tenets of the civilizing mission by coding the British use of physical violence as the extension of a *moral* influence. A petition from the Anglo-Indian residents of Calcutta, requesting that the administration of India be transferred from the East India Company to the British Crown, makes clear the connection between force and moral influence: "Throughout India the Native belief in the prestige of British Power has been destroyed and where the Asiatic has no dread of physical force he has no respect for moral influence."[67] Europeans who died at the hands of rebels were recorded in history books as martyrs, much in the same way missionaries were described as sacrificing their lives for the greater good of humanity. In this manner, the social mission of colonialism came to be increasingly represented as an immense sacrifice to stamp out the last vestiges of savagery. Suturing the rupture of rebellion back into the grand narrative of the civilizing mission, the tales of atrocities served as a screen discourse for the savage methods used to ensure that natives knew their proper place—but also for the vulnerability of colonial authority.

The civilizing mission was disfigured in the sense that it now incorporated the mutilated bodies of English women and the scars of insurrection. But it was also disfigured in the sense that the figure of the dark-skinned rapist was made literal. The racial typing of the weak and effeminate Indian male does not give itself over to the sexually aggressive image of a rapist in the absence of a regularity in representation. An emergent discourse of rape closely imbricated with the racial coding of insurgency constitutes a discursive regularity of this sort. What the colonizer had previously considered unthinkable—that is, an Indian man raping an English woman—was now eminently possible.

Miss Wheeler defending herself against the sepoys at Cawnpore. From Charles Ball's *History of the Indian Mutiny* (1858).

4

The Rise of Memsahibs in an Age of Empire:
On the Face of the Waters

The stories of "Sepoy atrocities" formed a racial memory of the 1857 uprisings as the barbaric attack of Indian savages on innocent English women and children. This memory was kept alive through pilgrimages to all the major sites where Europeans had been killed. At Cawnpore a plaque was placed on the well into which the bodies of the Bibighar inmates had been thrown. The inscription on the plaque—"Sacred to the perpetual memory of a great company of Christian people, chiefly women and children"—designated the well as a shrine.[1] Like the imaginary writing on English women's bodies, these monuments were spectacular signs of Indian savagery to be read by future generations. The terrors and triumphs of 1857 also became legendary in the countless poems, plays, novels, and children's stories that were written. "Of all the great events of this century, as they are reflected in fiction," observes a reviewer forty years after the uprisings, "the Indian Mutiny has taken the firmest hold on the popular imagination."[2] Convinced that the great Mutiny novel was yet to be written, the author of the review essay anticipates Rudyard Kipling taking up the task. As it turns out, Kipling never did write the epic work expected of him, and the numerous works that appeared simply replayed the same hackneyed set of imperialist plots that predominated Anglo-Indian fiction.[3]

Through a curious act of reversal, Mutiny fiction transformed the fictitious stories of rape and mutilation into factual evidence. In *First Love and Last Love* (1868), James Grant quotes liberally from the most sensationalist of the stories, not failing to include the infamous letter from a clergyman, which he takes the liberty of attributing to "a native eye-witness."[4] Other novels, under similar pretensions of historical faithfulness, confront their readers with the faithfulness of their sketches. "Reader of mine, do you think all this wildly exaggerated?" queries the narrator of *Maurice Dering* (1864). "Perchance you fancy that all the incidents of that awful time were set down in official reports and recorded by special correspondents. I speak only from hearsay; but I believe there lives a man on the full-pay of our army who saw these things done very much as I have here described them."[5] What is significant about such statements is that they share with the newspaper stories and popular histories the effort to establish the truth-telling power of rumor. But more than that, Mutiny fiction embellishes the "eyewitness reports" with Orientalist stereotypes of Asiatic depravity and licentiousness. The Rani of Jhansi appears as an Eastern beauty whose cruelty and treachery exceed her sensuality; Nana Sahib is depicted as a fat, lazy, and depraved man who kills his female hostages because they will not enter his *zenana*. Thus propagating fantasies of Oriental men desiring white flesh, Mutiny fiction enhances the sexual coding of anti-colonial insurgency that is latent in the historical narratives.

I submit the Mutiny reports as the beginnings of a racial discourse on Indian men sexually assaulting colonial women. Prior to these documents, there exists no stereotype produced on the scale of the sepoy fiend who expresses an aggressive Indian male sexuality. Anglo-Indian literature thus found its mythic brown-skinned rapist in the rebellion of 1857. And so the fictional status of rape was actively forgotten as the stories discredited as untrue made their way into fiction where they became the irreproachable evidence of history. Yet, the issue at hand is not whether an English reading public turned to such novels for a historical understanding of the uprisings. The question that needs to be asked is why there was such a compulsion to repeat the "red year" and the "red revenge."[6]

Mutiny fiction does not belong to the more serious kind of literature written for social edification. "No one needs to teach what everyone knows," observes Fredric Jameson about Victorian novels of social commentary, "and ethical doctrines are in this sense to be understood as symptoms of a social situation which calls out for the supplement or the corrective of the doctrine in question."[7] With regard to the racial memory of 1857, there was no moral or ethical decision to be made; the taken-for-grantedness of the official version foreclosed the possibility for any other frame of reference. There was, however, one novel written to remedy the "bloodthirsty tone" of those stories that caused its author, along with countless other children, to have "burnt and hanged and tortured the Nana Sahib in effigy many times."[8] This work is Flora Annie Steel's *On The Face of the Waters* (1896), and it was the most popular Mutiny novel of them all.[9] Avoiding the sensationalism of the newspaper reports, Steel set out to write a historical novel that would give poetic expression to a moment of profound social transformation. Her obsession with recording the accuracy of events has been well documented by herself and others.[10] She was able to gain access to a sealed box of confidential papers, but only on condition she exercise the patriotism and discretion expected from a woman of her rank and prestige.[11] Steel immersed herself in her research, living on a rooftop like her heroine, roaming the streets of Delhi, and pouring over official records and histories. She considered the highest praise to have come from the stranger who informed her that her book allowed him to forgive Indians for the murder of his wife during the uprisings.[12]

Despite such testimonies from her English readers, Steel does not break with an imperialist understanding of the rebellion. She explains the anticolonial uprisings in terms of a British failure to command authority and, for this reason, shows sympathy for loyal and obedient Indians alone. Echoes of the white man's burden can be heard in the novel's narrative voice, which claims that the British army fought on behalf of "the millions of peasants plowing their land peaceably in firm faith of a just master who would take no more than his due" (*OFW*, 338). Nor does Steel's Mutiny novel question a colonial historiography that records the massacre of English women as yet another example (besides sati and female infanticide) of the Indian male's disregard for women's lives. In her historical fiction, native discontent with British rule is understood as a religious revival ranging from sepoy furor over greased cartridges to a more pervasive resentment over the 1829 abolition of sati and passage of the Widow Remarriage Act in 1856. Although this Mutiny novel is written by an English woman, it shares with popular histories the tendency to represent Indian women as the chief instigators of sepoy crimes. The Queen of Delhi is depicted as stirring her devoted followers into a frenzy. And, the catalyst for the rebellion is a bazaar whore who taunts sepoys into proving their manhood: "The speech which brings more than speech had come from the painted lips of a harlot" (*OFW*, 190). The narrative function of the harlot—who, like the Rani of Jhansi, speaks violence into being—is to delegitimate the religious discourse of prophecy that was so crucial for spreading the revolt. Steel is not interested in redefining the gender role of Indian women so much as finding a place for English women's agency in the racial memory of the Mutiny.

On the Face of the Waters deviates from the standard fare of Mutiny fiction by telling the story of an English woman who actually survives the fall of Delhi. Its heroine, Kate Erlton, lives for three months inside the city walls disguised as a Persian woman, until she finally manages to escape to the cantonment on the Ridge. Her strategies of self-survival are described as both heroic and courageous. Given the racial memory that enforces a forgetting of the English women who survived, Steel makes a point of ensuring that her narrative not be dismissed as a woman's fancy. "Regarding my fiction," she explains in the preface, "an Englishwoman was concealed in Delhi, in the house of an Afghan, and succeeded in escaping to the Ridge just before the siege. I have imagined another; that is all. I mention this because it may possibly be said that the incident is incredible" (*OFW*, v). Although Steel restores English women to the colonial historiography from which they are absent, she writes her story according to gender issues that were current at the time of the novel's writing. She tells the story of an English woman who not only survives the fall of Delhi but, more important, also benefits from the rebellion. Kate takes away from the experience a lesson in self-dependency and thus is "rescued" from the domestic life that had previously stifled her. Steel came under criticism for the modernity of the women's issues she addresses in her historical novel. "It is this obtrusion of the sex-problem and not the mingling of history and fiction" writes the reviewer in search of the great Mutiny novel, "that spoils her book."[13] My own interest in Steel's Mutiny novel lies less in demonstrating a faithfulness to the past than in reading how the past is made to accommodate the "New Woman" of the post-Mutiny era. Thirteen years prior to its publication, English women once again found themselves the center of a racial discourse ensuring that natives knew their proper place—except that this time they contributed to its making.

New Woman in the Colonial Text

I now have the honour to make an urgent yet humble appeal
to you English women—I may say English sisters. I sincerely
and earnestly call upon you to do all in your power to effect
the elevation of the Hindu women.... A noble mission
decidedly it is, to go across the ocean and scale hills and
mountains, to surmount difficulties and to risk health, in order
to wipe the tears from the eyes of weeping Indian sisters.

—Keshub Chandra Sen,
"Speech to the Victoria Discussion Society" (1870)

English women's initiation into issues of colonial government occurred over the Ilbert bill controversy, also known as the "white mutiny."[14] On 9 February 1883, Courtnay Peregrine Ilbert introduced a bill granting Indian magistrates criminal jurisdiction over Europeans in the rural districts. The bill's most vocal opponents were the tea and indigo planters in Bengal, who feared that Indian judges would be more likely than British judges to prosecute them for mistreating their workers.[15] Their fear, however, was expressed in terms of the mistreatment English women would suffer under the new law. There was an outcry over the humiliation English women would have to undergo if native judges were to hear cases of rape. And rumors circulated about Indians, encouraged by the liberties of the proposal, attempting to rape an English woman in Calcutta.[16] Three thousand Calcutta residents met to approve a resolution claiming that the bill would give "rise to a feeling of insecurity as to the liberties and safety of European British subjects in the mosfussil,—also of their wives and daughters; and it has already stirred up on both sides feelings of race antagonism and jealousy such as have never been aroused since the Mutiny."[17] The bill was passed the following year but in such a weakened form as to be ineffective.

The Anglo-Indian women who organized a Ladies Committee to protest the bill played a strategic role in lending credence to the opinion that liberal reform violated the sanctity of English womanhood. The unprecedented nature of the women's participation in public affairs is evident in the resistance they encountered from the men whose opinion they shared. Yet the numerous letters to newspaper editors that were written by men under female pseudonyms show the strategic value in having the opposition to the bill assume a female voice.[18] One of the more scathing indictments of the bill appeared in a Calcutta daily under the title

"A Lady's View of Mr. Ilbert's Bill."[19] Its author was no man but Annette Ackroyd Beveridge, an English woman who went to India in 1872 in response to the request of the Bengali reformer Keshub Chandra Sen for female educators in Bengal.[20] Upon arriving at Calcutta, "for the first time [she] realised how uncivilised are their notions about women."[21] Disassociating herself from Sen, Ackroyd opened her own Anglicized boarding school for Bengali girls. After struggling with diminishing enrollments, she retired from teaching and married Henry Beveridge. Although she was married at the time she wrote her letter to the *Englishman*, her position cannot be read as an expression of the "incorporated" status of a colonial wife.[22] Her husband, Henry Beveridge, was one of the few British civil servants who was in favor of the bill. Annette Ackroyd Beveridge may have belonged to the liberal camp of Anglo-Indians who socialized with the natives, but she was an unabashed colonialist when it came to issues of government. Here is an excerpt from her infamous letter to the *Englishman* (6 March 1883):

> Englishwomen have been forgotten while their rulers are busied in adding a new terror to their lives in India.... Six-and-twenty years do not suffice to change national characteristics ... I am not afraid to assert that I speak the feeling of all Englishwomen in India when I say that we regard the proposal to subject us to the jurisdiction of native Judges as an insult. It is not the pride of race which dictates this feeling which is the outcome of something far deeper—it is the pride of womanhood.... In this discussion, as in most, *"il y a question de femmes"*—and, in this discussion, the ignorant and neglected women of India rise up from their enslavement in evidence against their masters. They testify to the justice of the resentment which Englishwomen feel at Mr. Ilbert's proposal to subject civilised women to the jurisdiction of men who have done little or nothing to redeem the women of their own races and whose social ideas are still on the outer verge of civilisation.

By opening her letter with an allusion to the racial memory of the Mutiny, Ackroyd suggests that English women, like their Indian "sisters," have suffered indignities at the hands of Indian men. The assertion of a shared oppression (in which gender takes precedence over race) permits her to invoke Indian women who speak up for their own rights to be also speaking on behalf of English women who oppose the Ilbert bill. Since she herself rejects the bill on the grounds that "civilised women" cannot be subjected to the jurisdiction of men who enslave their own women, an emptying out of the racial content of woman-hood has the effect of deepening racial difference. Statements like Ackroyd's letter have contributed to the stereotype of the racist memsahib.

Although best known through Forster's merciless caricature in *A Passage to India*, the memsahib is a notorious female figure who comes into her own during the post-Mutiny period. Historically, *memsahib* is a class-restrictive term of address meaning "lady master," which was used for the wives of high-ranking civil servants and officers.[23] Stereotypically, she is a small-minded, social snob who tyrannically rules over a household of servants and refuses to associate with Indians. I want to suggest that this stereotype is none other than that of the defenseless "Mutiny lady" stripped of her innocence. In the jingoistic discourse of the Mutiny, English women were represented as abused victims so that English men could be their heroic avengers. During a post-Mutiny era of reform, the women themselves were held responsible for the excessiveness of the military action. "It is a fact," declares Wilfred Scawen Blunt in *Ideas about India* (1885), "that the Englishwoman in India during the last thirty years has been the cause of half the bitter feelings there between race and race. It was her presence at Cawnpore and Lucknow that pointed the sword of revenge after the Mutiny, and it is her constantly increasing influence now that widens the gulf of ill-feeling and makes amalgamation daily more impossible."[24] Blunt is suggesting that if English women had not come out to India, they would not have been massacred by the rebels. And if not for the massacres, British soldiers would not have committed the atrocities they did.

The blame placed on English women for the deterioration of race relations belongs to what Margaret Strobel calls "the myth of the destructive female."[25] This myth posits an idyllic past of racial mixing prior to the arrival of white women. Although early Indo-British relations were not quite so friendly as proponents of the myth suggest, there are historical reasons for associating the deterioration of colonial relations with the presence of English women in India. The arrival of large numbers of upper- to middle-class women not only coincided with the 1818 expansion and consolidation of colonial territories but was also considered as a means of alleviating the problem Eurasians presented to the East India Company's hiring procedures.[26] When racial mixing was further discouraged in the aftermath of the 1857 revolt, the restriction of Anglo-Indian women to the domestic sphere was all the more a sign of the racial and moral superiority of the ruling race.

The stereotype of the memsahib is not simply a false representation of real women but also a sign of the domestic lives they lived. The Anglo-Indian version of the domestic ideal resembles its English counterpart inasmuch as the restriction of middle-class women to the home is the sign of national virtue and moral superiority.[27] But it is also different in the sense that the domestic sphere is a space of racial purity that the colonial housewife guards against contamination from the outside. During the post-Mutiny years, the value of the domestic ideal was extended to the civilizing mission to protect the ethical and moral principles of colonialism. A discourse of domesticity, as it is bound up with that of racial superiority, is manifested in the duty of colonial women to maintain a separation of the races. It is in this domestic role of the Anglo-Indian woman that the stereotype of the memsahib is to be located. The "innocent space" of the home ceases to be innocent once racial segregation is considered part of domestic work. Because of her strategic positioning within an enforcement of the racial hierarchy, the memsahib is spoken of as embodying the worst evils of the Empire. She is a scapegoat for imperialism, the remedy and poison that both ensures racial segregation and threatens to undermine race relations.

Colonial women protested their preassigned gender roles by demanding a more public life that would take them outside the racially segregated space of the home. Steel herself was an independently minded Scotswoman, who married a civil servant and accompanied him to India in 1868. Her own social status as a *burra mem*, or "big lady," was derived from her husband's rapid advancement up the ranks of the Indian Civil Service. While in India, she learned to read and write several languages, assumed the post of inspectress of mission schools, and was vice-president of the "Victoria Female Orphan Asylum." Much to the consternation of the ICS, she lived apart from her husband for a year so that she might complete the term of her own public appointment in a different part of the country. Steel claims, in her autobiography, to have known Indian women intimately and that when she left India, three hundred assembled at the railway station to say good-bye. Her knowledge of Indian women and their culture, however, expresses the colonial benevolence of the elite class to which she belonged. Hence, even though she supported limited suffrage for Indian and English women alike, she looked down on native women because, in her opinion, they were hopelessly caught up in perpetuating their own oppression. The signs of colonial benevolence are also visible in the expectations she had of her countrywomen. Steel censured English women for not being able to speak the vernacular languages but also for not conducting themselves with the dignity of the ruling race. "We do not wish to advocate an unholy haughtiness," she writes in her best-selling guide for Anglo-Indian housewives, "but an Indian household can no more be governed peacefully, without dignity and prestige, than an Indian Empire."[28] This explicit statement of racial superiority in a household manual dramatically stages how *race* is not a transparent category of self-representation for domestic authority in post-Mutiny India. Household duties themselves are now implicated in the government of Empire.

Flora Annie Steel, perhaps more than anyone else, embodies the memsahib in all of her contradictions. These contradictions are ignored by those feminists who explain the racist memsahib as a male-generated image that misidentifies the relative powerlessness of white women. One approach of this argument is to show how European women are the victims of a system not of their own making.[29] Hence, any benefit they might derive from colonialism is characterized as the burden of their responsibility for upholding the prestige of the race. Other studies reconstruct the everyday lives of colonial wives in order to show that mothering and domesticity involve more complicated work than the stereotype of the idle mistress might suggest.[30] This approach reconstructs European women's lives from their own writings, thus giving us a limited vision of colonial relations as *they* saw it. Or else they retrieve the histories of those invisible women of the Empire—the educators, nurses, missionaries, and social reformers—who were dedicated to improving the lives of native women. The effort to demonstrate that women contributed a nurturing, sympathetic, and maternal alternative to the masculine ethos of Empire ignores the centrality of such feminine values to the discourse of the civilizing mission. Helen Callaway, for instance, suggests that European women were responsible for improving race relations in Nigeria and commends them for what she calls a "feminisation" of Empire—the shift from paternalism, authority, and control to sympathy, understanding, and greater equality.[31] By replacing the presupposed racism of memsahibs with their sympathetic understanding, she fails to contend with how white women were instrumental (both as signs and agents) in maintaining colonial hierarchies of race. Jane Haggis pinpoints the problem when she writes that "in the ways in which white women have been brought to the fore of the historical and analytical stage, colonialism is no longer a problem of power, exploitation, and oppression, but rather of the gender identity of the rulers."[32]

The problematic needs to be reversed so that we can explain not how European women transformed colonialism but how colonialism has left its indelible mark on European women. This is indeed the approach that a second group of feminists have taken. In her essay "The White Woman's Burden," Antoinette Burton shows how Victorian and Edwardian feminists turned to the racial hierarchy of imperialism for advancing their own demands for emancipation. They enhanced their gender position by establishing themselves as authorities on Indian women, whom they ranked as inferior to women of civilized nations. "Both in practice and in theory," writes Burton, "the Indian woman acted as a foil against which British feminism gauged its own progress. Thus, not only did British feminists of the period reproduce the moral discourse of imperialism, they embedded modern western feminism deeply within it."[33] She concludes that the middle-class English women who assumed a moral responsibility for their less-fortunate Indian sisters became the agents of imperialism. This proposition is further supported by the work of Janaki Nair and Geraldine Forbes, who track the favorable response among British women to the demand for the social reform of native women.[34] Female education was one area of reform that particularly opened up opportunities for European women reformers. The "Ladies Association for the Promotion of Female Education Among Heathen" was formed in 1866, and even the Indian missions that had previously discouraged single women from joining began to recruit women missionaries for educating secluded upper-caste/class zenana women. The infrastructure established during the post-Mutiny period made India safe for single women. Missionary work now had a greater appeal for British women, who considered teaching zenana women more prestigious than working with poor and low-caste native converts (which missionary wives continued to do as before). The unmarried, middle-class women who were hired as governesses, zenana, and missionary school teachers generally

found the higher wages and professional status overseas prefer-
able to employment in England.[35] India might have figured more
prominently in Brontë's first novel if the life of her heroine had
been imagined some twenty years later.

Yet, Anglo-Indian women were not permitted the same liberties as their English sisters who came over as social reformers. In
a polemical two-part essay defending the "*right* to work for
India," J. E. Dawson requests that the same compassion and sympathy shown toward the cloistered "Indian native lady" be extended to her Anglo-Indian counterpart.[36] She proceeds to paint
the dismal picture of a lonely and bored housewife confined to
her home with nothing to occupy her mind but idleness. The
English woman who marries an Indian civil servant is not only
forced to leave her family behind in England but is also separated from her husband and children in India. Dawson explains that
women are sent to live alone in the cooler hill stations six
months of the year, and, as soon as their children are of age,
they leave their parents for schooling in England. The colonial
wife is not permitted to engage in philanthropic work or even
learn an Indian language because it is believed that she needs to
be sheltered from a culture that shows little respect for women.
The absence of social duties other than "calling" or preparing for
balls, she concludes, forces Anglo-Indian women into a superfi-
cial life-style centering on fashion, flirtations, and frivolities. In
this manner, Dawson demonstrates that the stereotypical memsahib is the product of social restrictions placed on the typical
colonial wife. She ends the first part of her essay with the reminder that the frivolous memsahib who leaves the care of her
children to the *ayah* (Indian nursemaid) risks producing a gener-
ation of Anglo-Indians that are more Indian than English. In the
second part of her essay, Dawson again begins by comparing
English to Indian woman, but this time she testifies to the "indis-
putable superiority" of "our domestic institutions" (*WI*, 359).

The place of the native woman in each part of Dawson's essay
dramatizes the movement of her argument from the suggestion
of a resemblance between the condition of Indian and English
women to the assertion of racial difference. Alluding to the mis-
erable existence of Hindu women who enter arranged marriages
at an early age and spend the rest of their lives in seclusion, she
explains that if they practice female infanticide or sati themselves, it is only to alleviate the misery the future holds for them
and their daughters. Rather than presuming that Indian women

act out of ignorance or religious delusion (which is what colonial officials did), she shows them to be conscious of their actions. Evidence of such consciousness, however, only establishes the need for English women to serve as moral examples for native women to imitate.

The impulse behind Dawson's essay is to make the English woman's moral agency, rather than her moral value, serve as the sign of civilization and progress. What kind of moral example, she inquires, does an idle woman whose life revolves around lawn tennis and parties provide for the natives? And why should Indian men not consider the colonial wife to be worse off than zenana women, who are not so isolated as to inhabit an alien land with no knowledge of its languages? Dawson argues that nothing short of the emancipation of Anglo-Indian women will encourage Indian men to improve the status of their own women. She concludes with the hope that English women will one day be mothers of the Empire:

> In this way we think our daughters may cherish a confident ambition that they will prove worthy of their great country, their higher culture, and their ennobling faith. Thus they may aspire to become pioneers not of civilization only, but of religion. And thus they may with hope expect the day when India's daughters as well as sons will, with some shew of reason, call them their *"cherishers"* —their *"protectors"* and their *"mothers."* (*WI*, 370)

Dawson draws attention to a resemblance between the domestic woman's restriction to the home and that of Indian women, not in testimony of their shared oppression, but to show that there is a need for English women to participate in the civilizing mission. Yet the paradox of an argument based on demonstrating the shared sexual oppression of English and Indian women is that any resemblance between the two patriarchal systems threatens to collapse the East-West difference on which the social mission of colonialism is based. This is why the greater emancipation of the Anglo-Indian woman also relies on demonstrating her superiority to Indian women. Dawson's essay shows that a rejection of the gender hierarchy the domestic ideal enforces does not similarly negate the racial superiority it implies. It may, in fact, reinforce it. Steel's Mutiny novel makes similar discursive moves in its effort to intervene in the domestic role of white women.

I want to consider *On the Face of the Waters* as a novel that reworks the racial memory of the Mutiny to reflect the greater visibility of Anglo-Indian women in public life. In this regard, I read it as a feminist intervention that was missing from the public debates on the Ilbert bill. Inasmuch as the Anglo-Indian Ladies Committe legitimated the idea that English women need to be protected from Indian men, the position it took on the Ilbert bill failed to question the racial memory of the Mutiny. What interests me about Steel's novel is the way in which her story finds a place for English women's agency in the Mutiny narratives by interrogating their presumed gender role. The objective of this chapter is to demonstrate less how Anglo-Indian women reproduce a dominant discourse of colonialism than it is to show how they negotiate gender power within it.

Reading for Feminist Plots

A "home" if it can bear the name, whence the presiding genius of home,—the wife and mistress is absent half the year—is at best a hollow pretence.... Could such a woman be brought face to face with her future as above depicted, and see her likeness there, and were some seer, as of old, to pronounce on her the sentence "Thou are the woman," might we not hear her indignant rejoinder as she disclaims it and asks: *"Am I a dog?"*
—J. E. Dawson, "Woman in India" (1886)

The feminist plotting of *On the Face of the Waters* lies in its undoing of the domestic ideal that confines women to the protected space of the home. The reader is introduced to Kate Erlton as a paradigmatic Anglo-Indian woman who possesses "the innate repulsion of the alien" (*OFW*, 10) for everything native and makes a religion of "her cult of home" (*OFW*, 22). Yet the futility of her life is summed up in her passionless marriage to Major Erlton, her absent son at school in England, and her inability to improve her situation. Kate devotes her life to maintaining a semblance of respectability in the face of her husband's dishonesty and unfaithfulness. The story opens with her attempting to bribe James Greyman (alias Jim Douglas) so that he will not press charges against her husband for cheating at horse racing. Although Jim sees no point in forestalling the inevitable, he decides to give her the chance to save her marriage. Despite his wife's devotion, Herbert Erlton is in love with Mrs. Gissing, a character modeled after the stereotypical memsahib of Anglo-Indian fiction. Pat Barr describes this stereotype, which is to be found in the writings of Kipling and other male authors, in the following manner: "She was frivolous, vain, sometimes adulterous, a heartless bitch with an ever-tinkling laugh and the occasional soft spot for a handsome subaltern."[37] As the plot develops, it becomes clear that Kate is unable to make her husband happy precisely because she is the ideal wife who devotes her life to her family. Having no dreams or ambitions of her own, "all she asked from fate was that the future might be no worse than the past; so that she could keep up the fiction to the end" (*OFW*, 14). Yet the novel also reveals that her spirit of self-denial is the manifest form of unfulfilled desires stemming from her marriage of convenience. In this manner, it undoes the opposition on which the value of feminine virtues is based. Upon being confronted with divorce, Kate realizes that the difference between self-denial and self-interest is "a question between different forms of enjoyment; the one as purely selfish as the other. More so, in a way, for it claimed more and carried the grievance of denial into every detail of life" (*OFW*, 223). Kate comes to this realization at the onset of the 1857 rebellion, which wrenches her out of the insularity of her English-style home.

The personal crisis of Kate's marriage is woven into the political crisis of anticolonial insurrection. It is the Christmas of 1856, nine months after her meeting with Douglas, when she hears that Alice Gissing will be moving to Delhi only a few miles from the cantonment where Kate and her husband live. Realizing that her marriage is threatened, she prays that she might have a final chance at saving it. What she does not know is that Alice is pregnant with Herbert's child, and, because of this, he plans to divorce her so that he might marry his mistress. Kate does get her chance to save her marriage, but from the unexpected quarters of the Indian Mutiny. Major Erlton is attending an inspection at Meerut when he sends his wife the letter requesting a divorce. Shortly behind his letter marches a regiment of mutinous sepoys that attacks Delhi just as Kate is confronting her rival about the affair. Alice is struck dead by a lance while attempting to save a little boy from a rebel who is chasing him. Her untimely death solves the problem of Herbert leaving Kate but not of their loveless marriage—that is resolved by a stray bullet that kills him after Delhi has been retaken. The major's accidental and narratively contrived death can be read as the novel's dispensing with a character whose sole narrative function is to establish the unhappy conditions of Kate's domestic life. The tragic and heroic end of Alice Gissing, on the other hand, transforms her into the figure of English womanhood that British soldiers carry into battle. By having the adulterous yet courageous Alice Gissing serve as the feminine ideal that soldiers are willing to die for, Steel wrests the "English lady" away from a sacred image in which a woman's chastity is the sign of her moral value. In this manner, she implicitly questions the narrative conventions of the genre to which her fiction belongs.

Given the centrality of the veneration of womanhood to a Victorian understanding of the uprisings, it should come as no surprise that Mutiny fiction is dominated by romance, a genre devoted to the knightly virtues of honor, valor, and the protection of women. The Mutiny romance is predictable in its approach. One strand of plotting tests the ability of an interracial relation (always between an English man and Indian woman) to withstand the antagonisms of war. The Indian woman typically betrays her beloved, or else, if she is essentially good, the novelist is forced to kill her so that the hero can be free to marry a true English woman. Another popular theme concerns the fate of English women who are separated from their menfolk. Upon falling captive to sepoys, they are either murdered or else rescued before the rebels have a chance to violate them. One of the most sadistic interpretations of the captivity story appears in G.A. Henty's *Rujub the Juggler* (1893). Upon being captured by Nana Sahib for his zenana, the heroine, Isobel, burns her face and upper body with acid so that he will interpret her blisters as the sign of a contagious disease. She applies the acid so liberally that she is scarred for life. That a woman's honor should be saved at any cost is voiced by Isobel herself, who calmly explains to her friends: "I was so anxious to disfigure myself that I was determined to do it thoroughly."[38] The novel describes the agony of her self-mutilation but only to the effect of commending her for her heroic and noble deed. Her disfigurement has the desired effect on Nana Sahib, who sends her away in a hurry. By showing English women to speak the same discourse that objectifies them as brutalized bodies, Mutiny fiction makes the moral value of English womanhood into a site of feminine desire.

Bithia Mary Croker's *Mr. Jervis* (1895) gives us the rare glimpse of a woman who bargained for her life. However, her depiction provokes the sentiment that "fiction has few more pathetic figures than this renegade Englishwoman."[39] The woman appears in the story just long enough to confess her error in judgment thirty-four years before, when a sowar offered to spare her life and she took it. She recounts how she was subsequently married to "a half-witted, feeble creature" who died, leaving her "a native widow." Having suffered the living death of Indian widowhood, she now lives alone and works with lepers. "I *ought* to have died long ago," she proclaims, "but it is those who are good and beloved who die."[40]

Mutiny fiction, like the newspaper reports, invests English womanhood with such extraordinary value that the lives of the women themselves are devalued. Alternatively, Steel does not destroy the sacred image of womanhood but, upon giving value to the English woman in life, recodes it. Mrs. Gissing sacrifices her life to save a child rather than her honor, and, when Kate Erlton finds herself in the palace that is the rebel stronghold, she is not once confronted with the possibility of a sexual assault. As such, *On the Face of the Waters* works within, rather than against, the code of chivalry that is so crucial to a Victorian understanding of the Mutiny. Steel gives us a version of the romance plot (the hero risks his life to save a woman while she nurses him back to health) but with a twist: The English woman in question is not saved by a man but by her own ingenuity. Arriving too late to save Alice, Jim Douglas leaves Kate with a garrison that is subsequently attacked. She manages to escape by concealing herself behind a wood pile because she "knew that her hope lay only in herself" (*OFW*, 262). After the skirmish dies down, she disguises herself as a native woman by wrapping a blanket around herself sari-style and returns to the Gissing house. Jim discovers her there and brings her to live with Tara Devi, a high-caste Rajput widow whom he rescued from the flames of her husband's funeral pyre eight years earlier, when she was but sixteen years old. Kate spends three months in Delhi with Tara, who teaches her how to speak and act like a native so that she will not arouse suspicion.

The English woman in hiding can be considered as a female counterpart to Jim, who, being employed as a spy for army intelligence, practices the same skills of disguise to travel back and forth between the city and the garrison. However, being a woman, Kate is not free to transgress the borders that a British army spy does.

Jim considers it too risky to take her out of the city, and, as a consequence, he is haunted by the need to rescue her, especially since he arrived too late to prevent Mrs. Gissing's death. For him, it is not a question of losing one woman but of contemplating the hundreds that must have died because men like himself were unable to save them. He takes very seriously the orders General Nicholson issues to him: "Save Kate, or— *kill somebody*. That was the whole duty of man" (*OFW*, 395). The narrator, speaking against a masculine discourse of revenge, informs us that "Kate, however, had already been found, or rather she had never been lost." Steel's heroine is so concerned with ensuring that Jim not return to Delhi to save her that she places her own life in danger in order to save him. He does come back for her, but only to discover that she has already made her escape with the help of Tara and other Indians. In a resolution designed to give narrative closure to the novel's romantic plot, Kate confirms in a declaration of her love for Jim Douglas that she has been "saved." Nonetheless, the energy of Steel's narration goes into demonstrating that English women need neither protection nor saving. Although she refuses to represent them as defenseless victims, she shows a greater ambivalence toward the revenge motif also bound up with a Victorian code of chivalry. This ambivalence has to do with the strategic role the idea of woman-as-victim plays in instituting an imperial authority and in safeguarding the morality of colonialism.

The novel does not break with a colonial logic that explains the British retribution as a response to the massacre of innocents. On the whole, it is critical of the desire for revenge that looms large in the minds of its characters, but it also hesitates to denounce the severity with which the rebellions were suppressed. When British soldiers kill unarmed peasants, including a woman, the narrator questions "the right of revenge pure and simple" (*OFW*, 326) but stops short of condemning the act. The cruel and authoritarian John Nicholson (the general responsible for retaking Delhi) is depicted as a heroic, almost mythical figure, whose obsessive desire to punish rebels is rationalized as a tragic flaw.[41] The final image with which the novel ends is that of Nicholson dying in the battle to retake Delhi as a "symbol of the many lives lost uselessly in the vain attempt to go forward too fast" (*OFW*, 469). The fuller implications of his obsession with punishment are spelled out by Douglas, who fears that the exaggerated reports of rape and torture will produce a panic capable of undermining British authority. His fears are confirmed in scenes of soldiers blundering into battle as they hasten to avenge the "Mutiny ladies." The question Douglas poses to Major Hodson is one that Steel invites her reader to entertain: "Is the crisis so desperate that we need levy the ladies?" (*OFW*, 391). In turn, the narrator passes judgment on an eyewitness report that praises Hodson for killing the three Mogul princes on the very spot where English women had been violated. "A strange perversion of the truth," we are told, "responsible, perhaps, not only for the praise, but for the very deed itself" (*OFW*, 458).[42] The novel thus questions the accuracy of historical evidence that blames women for the violence conducted in their name.

In the preceeding chapter I explained how the terror-inducing tactics of the army were no insane acts of revenge but a display of British sovereignty over India. Upon exposing the masculinist coding of the racial memory of the Mutiny, *On the Face of the Waters* risks delegitimating explanations that sanction the colonial campaigns of terror. In addition, by exposing the oppressiveness of the domestic woman's life, it threatens to collapse the racial difference that the Victorian feminine ideal safeguards. The same chivalry that calls on Victorian men as avengers requires women to save their honor and chastity over and above their lives. A code of conduct that sanctions female suicides during times of war thus comes dangerously close to the orthodox Hindu position on sati, namely, that a widow's self-immolation is her sacred duty. Both British and Hindu codes venerate womanhood as an institution to the extent of devaluing women's lives.[43] The resemblance is all the more evident if one considers that a legitimating narrative for Hindu widow-sacrifice was the Rajput martial custom of aristocratic women taking their own lives to avoid being taken captive by conquering Muslims.[44] This resemblance might explain why Steel's story of an English woman who survives the Mutiny requires the figure of sati as a space of death. Whereas in *Jane Eyre* the figure of sati resolves the problem of reconciling female self-determination with self-renunciation, in *On the Face of the Waters* it resolves the problem of finding a place for female self-survival within Mutiny historiography. The tropological value of sati lies in its efficacy as an icon for domestic subjugation. It permits Steel both to establish English woman's agency and to protect the domestic model through which the racial superiority of the colonizers was reaffirmed.

The Subject of Sati

The Martyr Saints at the stake or on the rack, however terrible
their sufferings, were enabled to rise above them, and even to
rejoice and sing in the midst of their anguish ... Somewhere,
half way between the Martyr Saints and the tortured "friend of
man" the noble dog, stand, it seems to me, these pitiful Indian
women, girls, children, as many of them are. They have not
even the small power of resistance which the western women
may have, under the tyranny of the executive of this base
system.

—Josephine Butler, *The Storm-bell* (1898)

The plotting of Steel's novel resembles that of Brontë's in several
important respects. Each romantic plot is guided by a feminist individualism in which true love is the just reward for female
courage, self-awareness, and independence. *On the Face of the
Waters* is more conservative than *Jane Eyre*, as Kate moves from
a loveless marriage of convenience into a relationship not of
economic and intellectual equality but of reciprocal love. Yet the
clearing of a new domestic space in each novel requires the sacrifice of a colonial Other. In *Jane Eyre*, Bertha Mason goes too
far in one of her nocturnal roamings. The mad creole woman
sets fire to Thornfield and then jumps off the roof to her death.
In *On the Face of the Waters*, the Rajput widow, Tara Devi, is so
consumed by her jealousy for Kate that her already "unstable
mind" (*OFW*, 467) is driven over the brink of sanity. She finally
consummates the sati that was denied her eight years earlier by
climbing onto the roof of a burning building. The image of Tara
on a burning Delhi rooftop calls to mind that of Bertha above
the flaming battlements of Thornfield. Here are the death scenes
in each of the two novels:

"And then they called out to him that she [Bertha Mason] was on the
roof; where she was standing, waving her arms, above the
battlements, and shouting out till they could hear her a mile off; I saw
her and heard her with my own eyes. She was a big woman, and had
long black hair: we could see it streaming against the flames as she
stood. I witnessed, and several more witnessed Mr. Rochester ascend
through the skylight on to the roof: we heard him call 'Bertha!' We
saw him approach her; and then, ma'am, she yelled, and gave a
spring, and the next minute she lay smashed on the pavement."
    "Dead?"
    "Dead? Ay, dead as the stones on which her brains and blood were
scattered." (*JE*, 377)

"My God!" came an English voice, as something showed suddenly upon the roof. "I thought you said it was empty—and that's a woman!"

It was. A woman in a scarlet, tinsel-set dress, and all the poor ornaments she possessed upon her widespread arms. So, outlined against the first sun-ray she stood, her shrill chanting voice rising above the roar and rush of the flames.

"Oh! Guardians eight, of this world and the next. Sun, Moon, and Air, Earth, Ether, Water, and my own poor soul bear witness! Oh! Lord of death, bear witness that I come. Day, Night, and Twilight say I am suttee."

There was a loud roar, a sudden leaping of the flames, and the turret sank inwardly. But the chanting voice could be heard for a second in the increasing silence which followed. (*OFW*, 467–68)

As readers, we are made to view both acts of suicide through the eyes of a witness—the servant who reports the incident to Jane Eyre and the soldier who points out Tara Devi's sudden appearance on the roof. Each novel presents us with the image of a deranged woman with arms outstretched against the burning sky in a spectacle of death.[45]

The resemblance between the two scenes is so uncanny that the different figuration of each is at first not discernible. The description of Bertha's broken body on the pavement marks the violence of her fall. In Steel's novel, on the other hand, we see Tara engulfed in flames and hear her voice; her unfaltering chanting suggests, however, that she feels no pain. The description of her burning differs little from the orthodox Hindu position, which claims that, at the point of death, the good widow is possessed by *sat*, a trancelike state by which she transcends the pain of her burning.[46] A glorification of sati that aestheticizes widow-burning to the degree of negating the widow's pain has led Rajeswari Sunder Rajan to address the widow as a subject in pain. As a means of countering the glorification of sati, she suggests reading the widow's subjectivity according to the terms of present-day agitprop and activist art in India, where "the sati is not a dead woman, but a burning woman seeking to escape, not a spectacle but the subject of action and agency."[47] How might the feminist critic of an Anglo-Indian novel consider the assignment of subjectivity that is in this related text of gendering? In other words, how can one use Indian feminists' replacement of sati-as-death with sati-as-burning to unravel the plotting of *On the Face of the Waters*? I shall address this question by retracing the steps Steel takes to write a life for a Rajput widow who has been saved from being burned alive on her husband's pyre.

From the very start, Tara Devi expresses her disappointment that the honor of sati was denied her. Yet it is not clear whether she speaks out of a devotion to her husband or a rejection of the lowly status of widowhood that awaits her in life. We do know that she resisted having her head shaved (as was required of Hindu widows) and was drugged before being placed on the funeral pyre. Because his intervention makes her an outcaste in her own society, Jim Douglas offers to employ her as a servant for his Persian mistress, Zora, whom he purchased (also eight years earlier) from a house of prostitution. Tara's decision to leave her community, we are told, comes out of a refusal to accept "the life of a dog" (*OFW*, 30) that is her punishment for disgracing her family and polluting her village. While in Jim's employ, she continues to wear her jewelry even though it is forbidden for a widow to do so. The contradictory sentiments pulling her in two directions are described as "the mingling of conscious dignity and conscious degradation, gratitude, resentment, attraction, repulsion, [that] made her a puzzle even to herself at times" (*OFW*, 29–30). These words locate the enigma that sati presents to Victorian women in the widow's own consciousness. However, they also refuse to reduce Tara's subjectivity to her decision to become a sati. The inconsistencies in her actions permit the reading of a more complicated subjectivity than that of female obedience and passivity.

As one who is rescued from her husband's funeral pyre only to face the degradation of Hindu widowhood, Tara Devi is a character out of the feminist intervention in sati. The colonial effort to abolish sati was not a women's issue because it failed to address the conditions of death imposed upon the Hindu widow in life—her prolonged fasting, enforced celibacy, and perpetual state of mourning. While officials addressed the widow's decision to burn as the sign of her blind devotion, English women argued that the Hindu widow who chose to burn did so out of a *knowledge* of the life that awaited her. In the same essay claiming colonial women's right to work for India, Dawson accused the British government of further restricting the widow's options by abolishing sati in the absence of legislating more extensive reforms regarding widowhood:

> Nor can we wonder at the eagerness with which the young and ardent
> widow embraced her only chance of escape from misery, *viz.*, the
> brief but for her glorious agony of Suttee. We, ourselves, can only
> marvel that all that a beneficent and enlightened Government has
> been able to do on her behalf, is to close to her this, her sole door of
> hope, and leave her the helpless victim of a fate, than which none
> more harshly cruel has ever stained a nation's annals. The Hindoo
> widow is as practically beyond the reach of the law, as the Pariah dog
> of which, in her degradation, she is but the human antitype. Hunger,
> thirst and weariness are her lifelong companions. In sickness, as one
> under the bann of the gods, none will tend her: in health, she is the
> despised drudge. In the midst of the family, she lives alone, shunned
> and unpitied. When at last starvation, sickness, and sorrow have done
> their work, and she gathers up her poor shrivelled form to die on the
> cold stone floor, none will weep for her or lament! (*WI*, 360–61)

By extending the meaning of sati to widowhood, Dawson shows
that the choice between death and the conditions of death in life
are limited options indeed. This argument was not made by
British women alone. The same year that Dawson's essay appeared in Calcutta, the Hindu reformer, Pandita Ramabai, published *The High Caste Hindu Woman* in the United States. While
condemning the practice of widow-sacrifice, Ramabai also concludes that the abolition of sati deprived the widow of an option
to end her suffering.[48] Nonetheless, the nineteenth-century argument made by British and Indian women alike inevitably produces the dilemma of rationalizing the widow's decision as a
choice *for* death and of introducing the possibility of sati as a
voluntary suicide. This is what Dawson does in her sympathetic
description of the widow's plight. It is also what restricts the possibilities of Steel writing a life for a widow who escapes dying on
her husband's pyre.

The subplot of Tara's story opens with Zora dying, an event
that anticipates the termination of her services. Having repaid her
debt to Douglas by serving Zora, she dons the white sari of a
widow, shaves her head, and goes down to the Ganges to drown
herself. The next time we hear of her, she has become a saint.
While praying for death at the holy river, she is struck by fire that
leaves the "sacred scars" (*OFW*, 112) of sati on her upper and
lower limbs. The miracle places her in a liminal state of being
both a widow who survives her husband and one who dies with
him. She is simultaneously an outcaste and a saint, a lowly
widow and heroic sati. Indicating that a delayed immolation is a
logical impossibility, an Indian admirer of Steel explains that the

author seems to have mistaken the Hindu widow for a saintly woman also known as a sati.[49] I would argue that it is not simply a case of Steel's mistaking one for the other but of her giving her character a life according to the narrative demands of sati-as-death rather than sati-as-burning. Because she presumes that Tara's declaration to become a sati is the expression of her desire, she does not tell a story that is critical of the spectacle of death but one that writes a life for the widow on the basis of her choosing death. In other words, Steel reconstructs the subjectivity of the widow *in life* from her decision to die. This might explain why Tara Devi's life is figured as a deferred sati. The words she continuously proclaims—"I am *suttee!*"—make a state of death into a state of being. The spectacle of death, with which the novel concludes, overwrites the inconsistencies and contradictions of the widow's subjectivity presented in the opening pages of the novel.

As much as Steel attempts to tell Tara's story, she is unable to because she can only understand female subjectivity in terms of the free will of the individual. The problem this presents might explain why even her contemporaries found the character of the Rajput woman to be unsatisfactory. The *Saturday Review*, which otherwise holds the novel in high esteem, complains that "the Rajputani, Tara, goes through the entire book very close to the main actors, and apparently invested in the author's mind with a unique interest; but to the reader she is a complete mystification."[50] Rajan's telling observation can perhaps explain the reviewer's befuddlement: "An exclusive focus on choice and motivation in constructing the subjectivity of the sati in some representations leads either to mystification or to cognitive closure."[51] Steel's novel dramatizes the logical impasse of reconstructing the subjectivity of a sati from her decision to burn.

Yet the place of the free will of the sati is crucial for resolving the threat that the story of an English woman's self-survival during the Mutiny poses to a colonial discourse of racial superiority. When Tara does make a choice for life, it is a choice for Victorian domesticity, as there is one thing she desires more than the glorification of sati, and that is to become an English housewife like Kate. The presence in the rooftop quarters of an Anglo-Indian woman attired in native dress and jewelry reminds Jim of the idyllic corner of an Eastern paradise he shared with Zora, his Indian mistress. But he also enjoys the touches of Western culture that Kate adds to their rooftop residence. It is this essential difference between the English woman and the Indian life she lives that the novel pursues in the sexual rivalry between Kate and Tara. Excluded from the scene of action, Tara is depicted as always hovering at the edge of an idyllic picture of domesticity: Kate and Jim playing chess as equals or singing Sonny (the boy that Alice saved) to sleep. The Rajput is "the other woman, crouching in the corner, [who] watched all three with hungry, passionate eyes. Here, in this group of man, woman, and child, without a personal claim on each other, was something new, half incomprehensible, wholly sweet" (*OFW*, 364). As Dawson's essay makes clear, the nuclear family that serves as a referent for the fictional kinship of Jim, Kate, and Sonny is itself a fiction. In Steel's novel, however, the problem of the Anglo-Indian family is resolved through the native woman's desire.

The narrative function of the Rajput widow is to stabilize the Victorian ideal of womanhood so that the Mutiny role of the English woman might be realigned. Determined to prove that she is the better woman of the two, Tara urges Kate to disguise herself as a sati, which involves removing her jewelry, wearing a widow's shroud, and shaving her head. Kate agrees to do whatever Tara wishes in exchange for the assurance of Jim's safety. Much to the Rajput woman's astonishment, because even she was shaved against her will, Kate begins hacking away at her hair and actually enjoys it, "for, in truth, she was becoming interested in her own adventures, now that she had, as it were, the control over them" (*OFW*, 400). These words make clear the racial difference between the English woman, who has agency over her actions even when she enters the space of sati, and the Indian woman, who is a slave to her domestic role. In my reading of *Jane Eyre*, I explained how the doctrine of woman's mission is made to accommodate the domestic individual through a racial splitting of femininity in which sati serves as a paradigmatic figure of female self-immolation. Here, the free will of the domestic individual is demonstrated through a reverse tropological move in which the English woman occupies the space of the Hindu widow.

The ability of Kate to enter and leave the space of death (a masquerade that repeats the movements of the military spy across enemy lines) binds the sati all the more to her burning as a voluntary suicide. When Jim falls ill a second time (after Kate has made her escape to the Ridge and he returns to Delhi to rescue her), Tara repeats Kate's earlier actions. She makes a pitiful attempt to re-create an English-style room and struggles to nurse him back to strength with chicken broth. Realizing her failure when he does not respond to treatment, she fetches Kate to help Jim. The Rajput widow increasingly recedes out of the picture, until she is but a "poor ghost" (*OFW*, 466), watching the English woman save the man they both love. At this point of the narration, Tara climbs up onto the burning roof, finally consummating the aborted burning on her husband's pyre.

The explanation Steel gives for the title of her Mutiny novel is symptomatic of the limits of the imperial frame of reference in Anglo-Indian women's writings. "I have chosen it," she writes, "because when you ask an uneducated native of India why the Great Rebellion came to pass, he will, in nine cases out of ten, reply, 'God knows! He sent a Breath into the World.' From this to a Spirit moving on the face of the Waters is not far" (*OFW*, v–vi). Her translation of the religious discourse of peasant insurgency into a Christian allegory for the righteousness of British rule delegitimates the native voice in the act of invoking it as an authoritative text. This move is reiterated in the letter with which the novel concludes. "Truly the whole thing was a mystery from beginning to end," remarks Captain Morecombe about the uprisings. "I asked a native yesterday if he could explain it, but he only shook his head and said the Lord had sent a 'breath into the land'" (*OFW*, 475). In its final judgment, the novel stages the mystery that the revolt presents to the British as an event that escapes the comprehension of the rebels themselves. When located in the Indian consciousness, "mystery" no longer points to a problem; rather, it takes the place of an answer. The rhetorical move of making a question its own answer requires a native informant at the point at which a colonial logic breaks down. This is how I understand the narrative function of the Rajput widow in Steel's reworking of the Mutiny narratives. Despite the novel's questioning of the value domesticity places on female self-immolation, the superiority of English domestic institutions is maintained through the demonstration that the Hindu woman, unlike the memsahib, is unable to exercise her free will. In this regard, Tara, who is a mystery even to herself, holds together Anglo-Indian domesticity precisely where it begins to unravel. *On the Face of the Waters* does not critique the domestic work of enforcing racial segregation so much as it redefines the place of the

Anglo-Indian woman in the home. It was not until the emergence of an Indian national movement in the early twentieth century that the racial memory of the Mutiny came under direct attack.

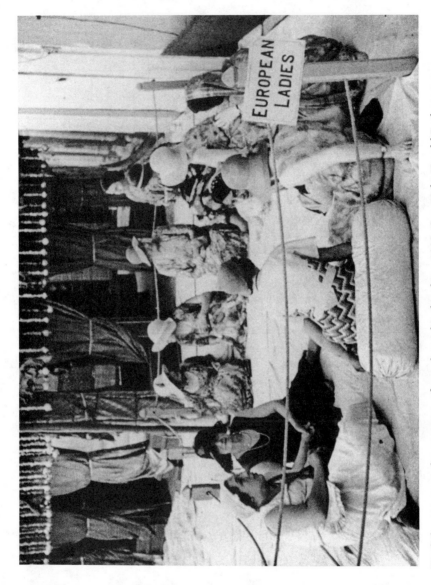

English women at the marriage of a maharajah's daughter, 1932. Copyright Harold Lechenperg. Reproduced by permission.

5

The Unspeakable Limits of Civility:
A Passage to India

Eighteen fifty-seven may have been remembered by the British as the savage attack by rebels on defenseless women and children, but it was known to Indians as the First War of Independence.[1] In 1909, Vinayak Savarkar published *The Indian War of Independence: 1857,* a polemical study of the Mutiny as a heroic anticolonial struggle.[2] The controversial book, which was intended to rouse Indians into armed insurrection, was widely circulated despite its proscription. On the other side of the colonial divide, the demonstrations, *hartals* (general strikes), and civil disturbances reverberating throughout India reminded the white minority of those earlier crisis-ridden times. The years between the two world wars, what Allen Greenberger aptly calls the "Era of Doubt," were shot through with anxiety about the British Empire.[3] The death of Queen Victoria in 1901 served as a reminder that the Empire too was not permanent, and the numerous memorials built in her honor represented the effort to capture the permanence of Empire in stone. Besieged by demands from its colonies for home rule, the British Crown declared Ireland a free state in 1922 and granted Egypt nominal independence. In the case of India, no dominion status was granted. The following remark by Lord Curzon (Viceroy from 1899 to 1905) might explain why: "As long as we rule India we are the greatest power in the world. If we lose it, we shall drop right away to a third-rate power."[4] During the early years of decolonization, the Mutiny was a particularly charged signifier for the British to reconfirm the permanence of Empire—but also for Indian nationalists to anticipate its demise.

The struggle over the meaning of 1857 is evident in the opposing explanations given for the army's massacre of unarmed Indians at Amritsar. The events leading up to the massacre started in March 1919, when Indians demonstrated against the Rowlatt bill, which permitted political prisoners to be tried without a jury or right to appeal. On 9 April, the same day that Gandhi was arrested, the lieutenant-governor of Punjab ordered the arrest and deportation of two political leaders from Amritsar. The next day, amidst rioting, looting, and burning, a missionary woman was dragged off her bicycle and beaten with sticks. The woman, Miss Sherwood, was left for dead but later was found by Hindu shopkeepers who tended to her injuries. On 15 April, martial law was declared for the first time since the Mutiny. Four days later, under the sanction of martial law, General Dyer issued his infamous "crawling order," which required Indians to crawl on all fours through the street on which the missionary woman had been attacked. Two days before the declaration of martial law on 13 April, he ordered his men to fire on unarmed Indian protesters attending a banned meeting. Trapped within the walled assembly place known as the Jallianwala Bagh, the demonstrators were easy targets for the soldiers, who shot a total of 1,650 rounds. According to the official report, 379 were killed and 1,200 wounded.[5] Indian estimates were much higher. For Indians, the name of Amritsar was synonymous with massacre much in the same way that Cawnpore resonated among Europeans with the slaughter of innocents.

The massacre, at which British soldiers mercilessly killed defenseless women and children, transformed the colonizers into the object of their own emblem of barbarism. The tendency of British historiography, even today, is to treat Dyer's order to shoot as "singular and sinister" rather than a military action authorized by a civil sector, which included the lieutenant-governor, Michael O'Dwyer.[6] The British waited eight months before conducting an investigation, and then only in response to Indian protests. The English press largely ignored the incident, while Anglo-Indian newspapers expressed greater horror over the attack on Miss Sherwood. In his memoirs, *India As I Knew It*, O'Dwyer keeps returning to the threat rioters posed to English women as a touchstone for reconstructing the Punjab disturbances.[7]

Dyer's random punishment of Indians for the attack on a single English woman resembles the strategies of counterinsurgency deployed during the Mutiny. Of course, the punishments were not conducted on the scale of the 1857 retributions; however, they did assume a similar form. The crawling orders, salaaming orders, and public floggings[8] were intended to dramatize colonial authority much in the same way as the punishments administered according to what General Neill in 1857 called a "strange law." It should come as no surprise, then, that in his deposition to the Hunter Committee responsible for investigating the disturbances, Dyer claimed to have averted a second mutiny.[9] Leading English newspapers confirmed that he did indeed face a situation as serious as the early stages of the Mutiny. And Anglo-Indian supporters rallied to defend his actions as a necessary measure against a European bloodbath. An article in *Blackwood's Magazine*, anonymously signed "by an Englishwoman," states the case all too plainly: "No European who was in Amritsar or Lahore doubts that for some days there was a very real danger of the entire European population being massacred, and that General Dyer's action alone saved them."[10] A committee of thirteen Anglo-Indian women was formed to raise money for the Dyer Appreciation Fund. In Bengal, 6,250 women signed a petition protesting the inquiry and claiming that the general's actions had prevented them from being subjected to "unspeakable horrors."[11] There was a small minority among the British, on the other hand, who held the racial memory of 1857 itself responsible for the massacre at Amritsar. "What is immediately relevant," writes historian Edward Thompson in *The Other Side of the Medal* (1925), "is for us to note that at Jallianwalla and during the outcry which our people made afterwards we see the workings of imperfectly informed minds obsessed with thought of Cawnpore and of merciless, unreasoning 'devils' butchering our women."[12]

Thompson claims he wrote *The Other Side of the Medal* in response to Indian protests over the distorted picture of the Mutiny in British historiography. A primary target for the protesters was *The Oxford History of India*, which records the British retributions as "a few acts on both side which it is painful to recall."[13] Thompson considers the Indian rejection of moderate reforms to stem from the one-sidedness of colonial history. Unless the representation of 1857 be corrected, he sees no hope for a reconciliation. "Right at the back of the mind of many an Indian," he writes, "the Mutiny flits as he talks with an Englishman—an unavenged and unappeased ghost" (*OS*, 30). Because he regards it as his mission to speak on behalf of Indians who, lacking the skills of a historian, are unable to displace the official version themselves, Thompson proceeds to recount the atrocities on the British side and, like the historiography he opposes, cites one tale of horror after another—except this time it is British officers and not mutinous sepoys who are the perpetrators. By presenting the barbarism behind the military badge of honor, Thompson hopes to placate the terrifying memory that haunts Indians. Citing the outcry over Amritsar as proof of colonial goodwill, he defends an administration that will no longer conceal its wrongdoings behind a wall of silence. Yet, by presuming the investigation of Dyer's actions to be a response to British rather than Indian protests, Thompson silences the people he claims to represent. His constant shuttling between colonizers and colonized—looking at "ourselves" to represent the "other"—points to a specularity that reveals the true subject of his book. It soon becomes clear that the ghosts that need appeasing are not the ones haunting Indians but those that cast doubt on the benevolence of colonialism. Thompson is disturbed by the execution without trial of the Sikh rebels who were blown from cannons in 1872, the rampant pillaging, burning, and hangings in Kabul in 1879, and finally, the Amritsar massacre itself. He explains these actions as momentary fits of madness brought on by the memory of 1857: "The Mutiny—that nightmare of innumerable savage hands suddenly upraised to kill helpless women and children—has been responsible for . . . deeds that would have been impossible to English men in their right frame of mind" (*OS*, 87). By treating violent strategies of counterinsurgency as a deviation from the noble intentions of colonialism, his study reproduces the effects of the historiography it opposes. But more than that, it extends a Victorian understanding of the retributions against Indian rebels to the 1919 massacre at Amritsar.

Failing to see the attack on English women as anything other than a desecration of womanhood, Thompson considers the penalties for the assault on Miss Sherwood to be justified. He also condemns, as a crime greater than Nana Sahib's at Cawnpore, the "Ravishment Proclamations" in which Indian nationalists called for the "dishonor" of English "ladies." The incendiary posters (as they are cited in the Hunter Committee's report and O'Dwyer's memoirs) use the racial signification of the native rapist as a weapon against the British.[14] By playing on a colonial fear of rape, they perform a reversal that nonetheless conforms to a colonial discourse in which the sexual humiliation of women is an indirect attack on British men. Thompson, however, does not interpret such threats as evidence of an intimate knowledge of the European mind; rather, he interprets them as signs of an insurmountable difference:

> But my impression at the time, and now, is that even the most sensitive and noble Indians failed to realise the depth of British feeling on this matter, or to see why we consider that dishonour and suffering is so much worse when inflicted on a woman than when inflicted on a man. . . . it may be, as we are often told to-day, that our sentiment is a sham and hypocrisy, a false glamour flung about women by an age of barbarism which we call the age of chivalry. But it will not be easy to dispel from the European mind the conviction that this sentiment is the most precious gift to us from the confused and often mistaken thinking of our mediæval forefathers, and that it has done infinitely more to purify and ennoble life than all the *satis* that ever took place. (*OS*, 109)

Although Thompson identifies the veneration of womanhood as the legacy of Europe's barbaric past, he reminds his readers of the even greater barbarism of Hindu men. His defense of chivalry relies on a colonial logic that posits the prior violence of the native men whom the colonizers must civilize. The impetus behind Thompson's revision of Mutiny historiography is not to clear the mutineers of such labels as "fiends" and "demons," but to clean the English character of the stain of "savagery" and "barbarism."

The Other Side of the Medal represents a liberal response to the Amritsar massacre that E. M. Forster, disillusioned with liberalism, is careful not to repeat. Unlike Thompson, who saves the English character by showing its monstrous side to be "unreal" (*OS*, 132), Forster is more deeply troubled by the massacre that he calls one of those indefensible "examples of public infamy."[15] When he began writing *A Passage to India* (1924), after a stay in India from 1912 to 1913, he conceived of an illicit romance between an Indian man and an English woman.[16] By the time he completed the manuscript after a second visit in 1921, the country had undergone such radical changes that he admits to having been unable to finish his novel until he returned to England, because "the gap between India remembered and India experienced was too wide."[17] The story of an interracial love mired in cultural differences must have seemed out of step with the events of history. The story of an interracial rape, more explosive by far, plays out the tensions between a dissenting native population and a defensive white minority. Forster's final novel bears

117

the imprint of the years during which it was written. Although he does not refer to the Punjab disturbances by name, the events that transpire in the fictitious town of Chandrapore closely parallel those at Amritsar.[18] I am interested in the appearance of the Jallianwala Bagh massacre in *A Passage to India* not so much as a historical fact but as a ghostly presence that guides its plot.[19]

The Indeterminacies of Rape

> The unspeakable attempt presented itself to her as love: in a
> cave, in a church—Boum, it amounts to the same.
> —E. M. Forster, *A Passage to India*

A Passage to India holds up for public scrutiny the racialization of colonial relations by generating its narrative desire through the indeterminate status of a rape. Adela Quested, who is English, accuses an educated Muslim, Dr. Aziz, of molesting her in one of the Marabar caves. Since the reader is not privy to what happened, we are faced with the contradictory evidence of Adela's accusation and Aziz's denial. Her accusation sets off a judicial machinery that condemns Aziz before he is even brought to trial. Victimized by an unjust colonial system, he becomes a *cause célèbre* for Indian nationalists. The plot then undergoes a strategic reversal. The accuracy of Adela's judgment is undermined during the trial when, upon interrogation, she claims that she was mistaken. The roles of assailant and victim are now dramatically reversed as the novel reveals the "real crime" to be an abuse of power that can only lead to the demise of colonialism. Forster's staging of the court scene around the reversal of a rape charge disrupts the taken-for-grantedness of the racially motivated assumption that, to use the words of the prosecution, "the darker races are physically attracted by the fairer, but not *vice versa*" (*PI*, 218–19). Yet it is never revealed whether the attempted rape was real or imagined, and the question of what happened in the Marabar caves continues to intrigue readers. Whereas earlier inquiries investigated the mystery for what it revealed about Forster's narrative technique or Indian metaphysics, recent criticism has shifted the terms of the debate toward issues of race and gender.

Forster's critical look at colonialism presents a problem that is particularly vexing for feminists. Upon questioning whether the real crime is Adela's accusation or Aziz's assault, *A Passage to India* sets up an opposition between the English woman and Indian man. If one decides, in keeping with its anti-imperialist theme, that the crime lies in a system capable of reducing an Indian man to his pathological lust for white women, then even the slightest hint of an actual rape cannot be entertained. Conversely, a defense of Adela's accusation involves condemning the Indian patriarchy and Aziz's objectification of women as sex objects. The ambiguity surrounding the alleged rape thus forces the critic to defend either the native man or the white woman against his/her opponent. It is this either/or decision (but never both) that has divided readings of *A Passage to India* along gender lines.

Critical opinion tends to favor Adela's hallucination as the most likely explanation for what happened in the caves.[20] Offering her sexual repression as evidence, such accounts discredit her charge against Aziz as not only mistaken but also misguided. Even those readings that critically engage the problems of colonial representation treat Adela's cry of rape as the sign of her repressed desire. Although *A Passage to India* does suggest the imaginary nature of the attack, it does not provide sufficient evidence for presupposing that Adela's musings on Aziz's handsome appearance should translate into a sexual fantasy of rape.

In his screen adaptation of the novel, David Lean legitimates this common reading by adding a scene that eliminates any doubt that, on at least one other occasion, the unattractive Adela suffered a bout of sexual hysteria. The scene shows her leaving the safety of the European compound to venture out on a bicycle alone. She chances upon an ancient Hindu temple, whose sexually explicit carvings arouse her curiosity and interest. The threatening aspect of her sexual arousal is figuratively represented in the aggressive monkeys that swarm over the statues and scare her away. Adela returns to Chandrapore breathless, pale, and sweating. Having just broken off her engagement to Ronny Heaslop, she now says she will marry him. His query—"What happened?"—and her response—"Nothing"—are emblematic of the film's message regarding the cave scene. In a flashback of Adela staring fixedly at Aziz's silhouetted shape looming in the cave's entrance, Lean repeats the image of her pale and frightened face after her encounter with the monkeys. The conclusion to be drawn is so obvious that he provides no further elaboration.

A masculinist explanation of the mystery in the cave (such as Lean's) is based on the "common knowledge" that frigid women suffer from sexual hysteria and that unattractive women desire to be raped. This interpretation works backward from the imaginary rape, metaleptically positing the effect of an effect as its cause. The argument consequently produces its own tautology: Adela hallucinated the rape because she was sexually repressed, the proof of which lies in her hallucination. Feminist criticism of *A Passage to India* has dismantled this tautology by revealing the "making into meaning" of its assumptions. Rather than discounting the imaginary nature of the attack, feminists respond to the critical verdict against Adela by retracing her hallucination to a "first cause" of patriarchal authority instead of sexual hysteria. Elaine Showalter, for instance, reads the hallucination in terms of Adela's apprehensions about committing herself to a loveless marriage that is nothing short of "legalized rape."[21] Brenda Silver also links the imaginary rape to the gender roles suggested by marriage. Since Adela enters the cave disturbed about her forthcoming marriage to Ronny Heaslop, she is forced to acknowledge her social status as a sex object and thus to confront "the material and psychological reality of what it means to be rapable."[22]

Although they are correct to situate the alleged rape within the larger frame of women's oppression, Showalter and Silver fail to address the historical production of the category of rape within a *system of colonial relations*. Feminist criticism has thus replaced one tautology with another. The feminist tautology goes something like this: Adela experiences the conditions of rape because she is objectified as a woman, the proof of which lies in her experience of rape. What does it mean for an English woman's experience of her oppression to be staged as a scenario in which she is the potential object of a native attack? In other words, how does the feminist critic negotiate the either/or opposition between the colonizing female and the colonized male that the novel sets up? I would begin by insisting that Adela's confrontation of "what it means to be rapable" is framed by race relations that cannot be understood as yet another form of patriarchal oppression.

What is immediately noticeable about gender hierarchies in *A Passage to India* is the discrepancy between Adela's social positioning and that of Anglo-Indian women. From the early pages of the novel there are suggestions that, due to racial segregation, colonial women are protectively cloistered behind an anachronistic code of chivalry and honor. "Windows were barred lest the servants should see their mem-sahibs acting," the narrator informs us, "and the heat was consequently immense" (*PI*, 24). Fielding's refusal to be "lively and helpful" toward women "would have passed without comment in feminist England" (*PI*, 62) but not in Anglo-India. Unfamiliar with their customs, Adela is surprised that club members have chosen to perform *Cousin Kate*, a play that Showalter reminds us is "a mildly antifeminist comedy."[23] Thus establishing an opposition between the emancipated women of England and the stalled liberation of mem-sahibs, *A Passage to India* plots Adela's movement from one side of the East-West divide to the other.

It is not just that Adela enters the cave contemplating a marriage that will subsume her identity into that of her husband. More important, she recognizes the danger of assuming the Anglo-Indians' racist assumptions about India and its inhabitants. "Well, by marrying Mr. Heaslop, I shall become what is known as an Anglo-Indian," she says to Aziz as they make their way toward the caves:

> He held up his hand in protest. "Impossible. Take back such a terrible remark."
> "But I shall! it's inevitable. I can't avoid the label. What I do hope to avoid is the mentality. Women like———" She stopped, not quite liking to mention names; she would boldly have said "Mrs. Turton and Mrs. Callendar" a fortnight ago. (*PI*, 145)

Adela's inability to identify Mrs. Turton and Mrs. Callendar as the insensitive colonialists that they are, demonstrates her newfound loyalty to Anglo-Indian women. Her transformation into a mem-sahib was already under way the moment she agreed to marry Ronny Heaslop. "She was labelled now" (*PI*, 94), she thought to herself at the time. If the label is inevitable, the mentality is inescapable. A disregard for Indians to the degree of rendering them invisible is an offense that Anglo-Indian women repeatedly commit. Mrs. Turton addresses Indian women in the third person, as if they do not exist, and Mrs. Callendar stares right through Aziz when she takes his carriage. Forster has justifiably been taken to task for situating the evils of colonialism in the attitudes of Anglo-Indian women. What I am attempting to do

here, however, is to read the strategic deployment of the memsahib in colonial discourse, one that demands her scapegoating
in the anti-imperialist message of *A Passage to India*.

By the time Adela enters the cave, her self-consciousness
about what it means to be an Anglo-Indian is forgotten. After
presuming that, as a Muslim, Aziz has more than one wife, she is
oblivious to having offended him and, being so wrapped up in
her own thoughts, is not even aware of his presence. "Quite unconscious that she had said the wrong thing, and not seeing him,
she also went into a cave, thinking with half her mind 'sight-see-
ing bores me,' and wondering with the other half about marriage" (*PI*, 153). Only half of Adela's mind is on thoughts of marriage; the other half expresses a boredom with Aziz's elaborate
efforts to show her "the real India." Her divided mind reveals a
tension between the double positioning of the English woman—
as inferior sex but superior race. It is a contradiction that must be
addressed in any discussion of the alleged assault.

When Adela emerges from the cave accusing Aziz of rape, she
consolidates the identity she would rather deny. Which is to say,
she reconfirms the racist assumption that, given the slightest opportunity, the native will revert to his barbaric ways. In her haste
to escape, she flees through cacti, lodging thousands of minuscule spines into her flesh. Her mutilated condition confirms the
violence of the attack, but it also reduces her sensibility to her
tortured body. "Everything now was transferred to the surface of
her body, which began to avenge itself, and feed unhealthily"
(*PI*, 193). Her fellow expatriates react to the news of the sexual
assault from within a code of chivalry; they treat Adela as a mere
cipher for a battle between men. "Miss Quested was only a victim, but young Heaslop was a martyr; he was the recipient of all
the evil intended against them by the country they had tried to
serve; he was bearing the sahib's cross" (*PI*, 185). The term
sahib's cross is a parody of the idea of the white man's burden
that represents colonialism as an act of martyrdom. It is also an
indictment of the masculinist perception that the sexual humiliation of English women is an indirect attack on men. The objectification of Adela into a passive victim denies her an entry into
the great narrative of the white man's burden even as it confirms
the self-sacrifice of the men who serve that mission. *She* cannot
save the natives from their depravity, but neither can she save
herself. Adela, the memsahib, the Anglo-Indian woman, has
strayed far from the borders of feminist England. She may have

entered the caves with some semblance of her former identity, but she leaves it as a violated body bearing the visible signs of the native's ingratitude. Behind the novel's reference to Adela's tortured body are the Mutiny reports on the rape and mutilation of English women.

The racial memory that echoes across the Mutiny novels as a horrific nightmare is also silently constitutive of *A Passage to India*. The (mis)representation of the object of the 1857 uprisings is so closely imbricated with the racial stereotype of brown-skinned men desiring white women that the Mutiny serves as a convenient name for expressing colonial fears and fantasies over the intermingling of two races. The Anglo-Indian residents of Chandrapore think of Aziz's "crime" as "the unspeakable limit of cynicism, untouched since 1857" (*PI*, 187), while the district superintendent of police, Mr. McBryde, advises Fielding to "read any of the Mutiny records" (*PI*, 169) for evidence of the Indian criminal mind. By alluding to the Mutiny as *the* representative crime of a sexual assault, the Anglo-Indians not only invoke the memory of those earlier "unspeakable crimes" but also reproduce its effect. I take from Forster's presentation of the alleged rape within the frame of 1857 the license to read his novel as a critical intervention in a discourse that codes anticolonial rebellion as the assault of English women. By intertwining the lives of individuals with the history of decolonization, his plotting of sexual violence contends with the ideological effect of a colonial discourse of rape.

The drama surrounding Aziz's arrest reenacts the precariousness of the colonialist mission under threat of native insurrection. It is a vulnerability that hides behind a representation of the Indian male's sexual desire for white women as the cause of colonial conflict. As the court case draws nearer, the novel recreates the explosive atmosphere of 1857 and 1919 in a scene showing club members who debate what they should do about the hostile mobs demanding that Aziz be released. Their discussion centers on defending their women and children, a particularly charged phrase for eliciting cries of revenge. One young, golden-haired woman, whose husband is away, is afraid to go home "in case the 'niggers attacked'" (*PI*, 181). Her fellow Anglo-Indians invest the image of "her abundant figure and masses of corn-gold hair" with the full value of colonialism; for them, "she symbolized all that is worth fighting and dying for" (*PI*, 181). Parodies of this sort can be read as sobering reminders of the retributions against a rebellious Indian population that were committed in the name of English womanhood. If, as de Man informs us, "all true criticism occurs in the mode of crisis,"[24] Forster's parody is critical in the sense that it revives the racial memory of the Mutiny not in order to manage the crisis of the 1920s in colonialism but to force it.

Instead of invoking "the protection of women and children" as an excuse for police and military action (which is what Thompson does), *A Passage to India* shows that the catch phrase conveniently exculpates English men from any wrongdoing. "They had started speaking of 'women and children,'" comments the narrator, "that phrase that exempts the male from sanity when it has been repeated a few times" (*PI*, 183). The novel is also critical of the tendency to blame English women for racial violence. Upon being confronted with protests in his district the Collector directs his anger and frustration at Adela: "'After all, it's our women who make every thing more difficult out here,' was his inmost thought, as he caught sight of some obscenities on a long, blank wall, and beneath his chivalry to Miss Quested resentment lurked, waiting its day—perhaps there is a grain of resentment in all chivalry" (*PI*, 214). Here, Forster shows that a colonial cult of chivalry excuses military action; elsewhere, he draws attention to the role of a discourse of rape in the management of anticolonial demonstrations. The major's uncontrollable outburst that they should "call in the troops and clear the bazaars" (*PI*, 187) is reminiscent of General Dyer's directive at Amritsar. And Mrs. Turton's command that every native who dare look at an English woman should crawl from Chandrapore to the Marabar caves echoes the infamous "crawling order." An ironic restaging of British honor and punishment, however, does not overturn the Mutiny narratives but merely questions their premises. What does reveal the fictionality of colonial truth-claims is the indeterminacy introduced to the certainty of a sex crime confirming the native's depravity.

By generating its narrative desire through the indeterminate status of a sexual assault, *A Passage to India* drives a wedge of doubt between a colonial discourse of rape and its object. During the trial, Adela delivers a verdict that throws the courtroom into chaos. "Dr. Aziz never followed me into the cave," she declares. "I withdraw everything" (*PI*, 229). When situated within the racial memory of the Mutiny, Adela's extension and withdrawal of the charge interrupt a plotting that establishes a causal relation between the native assault of English women and British suppression of rebellion. Forster does not replace the certainty of an attack with its negation; rather, he replaces it with a narrative suspension that opens up the space for a mystery. Upon addressing this "space," we should keep in mind the historical usage of "mystery" in a colonial discourse of power. "Mystery" not only names the place where the logic of colonialism breaks down but also resolves a contradiction by making a question serve as its own answer.

After the trial, Fielding explores with Adela four possible explanations for what happened: Either Aziz did molest her, she claimed he did out of her own malice, she hallucinated the attack, or someone else followed her into the cave (the guide and a Pathan are offered as two likely assailants). Although Fielding rules out the first two possibilities, Adela gives no indication to him (or the reader, for that matter) whether she reacted to a real or an imaginary assault. She finally admits that the only one who knows for sure is Mrs. Moore, who she claims acquired her knowledge through a telepathic communication. As he keeps forcing Adela to return to the question of what happened in the caves, Fielding soon realizes that the very multiplicity of explanations offers no easy resolution to the mystery: "Telepathy? What an explanation! Better withdraw it, and Adela did so.... Were there worlds beyond which they could never touch, or did all that is possible enter their consciousness? They could not tell.... Perhaps life is a mystery, not a muddle; they could not tell" (*PI*, 263). As readers, we are perhaps less satisfied than Fielding with the "life is a mystery" response. Critics have and still do search their imaginations for an explanation.

Forster himself imagined one outcome of the attempted rape that did not appear in the published version of his novel. The deleted scene contains such a detailed description of the assault in the cave that it would be practically impossible to read what transpired there as Adela's hallucination. Here we have no helpless woman seeking the protection of others, but one who calculates the right moment to make her move and fights off her attacker:

> At first she thought that <she was being robbed,> he was <holding>
> \taking/ her hand \as before/ to help her <out>, then she realised,
> and shrieked at the top of her voice. "Boum" <went> \shrieked [?]/ the
> echo. She struck out and he got hold of her other hand and forced her
> against the wall, he got both her hands in one of his, and then felt at

her <dress> \breasts/. "Mrs. Moore" she yelled. "Ronny—don't let him, save me." The strap of her Field Glasses, tugged suddenly, was drawn across her throat. She understood—it was to be passed once around her neck, <it was to> she was to be throttled as far as necessary and then . . . [Forster's suspension points] Silent, though the echo still raged up and down, she waited and when the breath was on her wrenched a hand free, got hold of the glasses and pushed them at \into/ her assailant's mouth. She could not push hard, but it was enough to <free her> hurt him. He let go, and then with both hands \on her weapon/ she smashed <him to pieces> \at him again/. She was strong and had horrible joy in revenge. "Not this time," she cried, and he answered—or <perhaps it was> the cave \did/.[25]

Like the behavior of the English women who survived the 1857 uprisings, Adela's act of self-defense is at odds with a dominant discourse that constructs her as a passive victim. As a consequence, one cannot help but notice a resemblance between the absent text of her struggle and an official discourse that erases colonial women's agency. In fact, feminist critics have submitted Forster's deletion of this scene as the sign of a more pervasive silencing of women in his novel.[26] What remains unacknowledged, however, is that the deleted script replaces woman-as-victim with woman-as-agent, but only at the risk of confirming the alleged rape. A clearing up of the mystery in favor of Adela's guilt or innocence consequently adheres to the terms of a discourse that displaces racial signification away from colonial relations onto narratives of sexual violence. We see that a restoration of the silenced stories of English women in itself does not unravel a colonial plotting of rape.

If we are to study literature for its disruption of a discourse that prevents social change, we can no longer afford to restrict readings to the limits of the literary text. The racial and sexual signification of rape in *A Passage to India* does not issue from Adela's experience in the cave; the answer is not to be found there. Like Fielding and Adela, who confront the mystery in a multiplicity of explanations, we should recognize that there are no easy answers. To clear up the mystery of what happened by searching our imagination for the missing details means reading Forster's novel according to the narrative demands of the Mutiny reports. To read the mystery itself as an effect of that colonial history, however, is to see in its indeterminacies the imprint of a racial memory. In the place of "what happened in the caves?" I offer a different kind of question, one suggested by Adela's cry in the deleted assault scene. Managing to free herself from the grip of her attacker, Adela screams, "Not this time." What are the other times, the other assaults to which her triumphant cry alludes? I think I have already answered that question.

Other Plottings, Stories Not Told

> If we rely on history to tell us what happened at a specific time and place, we can rely on the story to tell us not only what might have happened, but also what is happening at an unspecified time and place.
>> —Trinh Minh-ha, *Woman, Native, Other*

I have been describing the historical specificities that need to be addressed in any discussion of colonial constructions of the Indian male as rapist. This is because a critical reading that uses race or gender as transhistorical categories is forced to understand racial and sexual stereotypes according to their own truth-effects. Stereotypes are essentializing tropes of difference that make social constructions appear natural by cutting them loose from the histories in which they were produced. For this reason, I consider the historical production of a racial type to be crucial to understanding the particular form of racism it articulates. One place to begin writing the history of a stereotype is to show its emergence, retreat, revival, and transformation. In other words, we need to demonstrate that racial and sexual typing has no meaning outside of its conditions of existence. The historical nuances and shifts of a particular "type" show that the *perception* of difference does not precede its social construction. Yet the unchanging aspect of a stereotype each time it is repeated gives it the appearance of having no history. This apparent absence of history might explain why Silver does not turn to a colonial past for demystifying the racial construction of Aziz; rather, she relies on the myth of the black rapist in the United States. Silver invokes Frantz Fanon's discussion of the "black man as penis" to explain the positioning of the Indian sexual offender as one who is both symbolically castrated and raped by the accusation of rape.[27] The singularity of "race" in her discussion of "the Negro" in the place of "the Oriental" suggests a continuity between the divergent histories of slavery in the United States and colonialism in India.

Because "race" is overdetermined by other contradictions,

Stuart Hall calls for theorizing different racisms operating under the specific historical conditions of colonial conquest, slavery, imperialism, postemancipation, and decolonization.[28] To read stereotypes according to different histories of racism is to recognize that they do not simply exaggerate a characteristic that is perceived by a "white" eye. Rather, the exaggeration of one trait over another has to do with the ideological alibi a typology provides. Eugene Genovese points to such an alibi in racist constructions of black male sexuality in the United States when he writes that "the violence-provoking theory of the superpotency of that black superpenis, while whispered about for several centuries, did not become an obsession in the South until after emancipation, when it served the purposes of racial segregationists."[29] The nineteenth-century black activist Ida B. Wells has carefully documented how the image of the "Negro rapist" sanctioned an upsurge in violence against black men, women, and children that was aimed at reversing their political and economic gains.[30] Her findings are further supported by contemporary feminist studies of the relationship between rape and lynching (which was often accompanied by castration) in the South from the 1880s to the 1940s.[31] The myth of the black rapist presupposes even as it reproduces the Negro's lustful bestiality; the Oriental male, by contrast, is constructed as licentious rather than lustful, duplicitous instead of bestial.

In keeping with the perceived decadence of the Mogul Empire that sanctioned a British colonization of India, the sexuality of the Oriental male is typically decadent. This stereotyping is present in the licentious sensuality of Aziz, who visits prostitutes in Calcutta and offers to arrange for his friend, Fielding, "a lady with breasts like mangoes" (*PI*, 120). Like the men identified as the most savage mutineers, the man who stands accused of rape in *A Passage to India* is a Muslim, and one who indulges in Orientalist fantasies about his Mogul ancestors at that. Forster does not create in Aziz a character that ennobles the Indian male; rather, he places his male protagonist squarely within the Orientalizing discourse of the Mutiny novels. Although comparisons can be useful, the myth of the Negro rapist cannot be used to discuss the topos of interracial rape in *A Passage to India* without cutting its sexual and racial signification loose from the history that produced it.

In the absence of its colonial constructions, a critic is forced to discuss the racial codings of *rape* on a level of generality that effaces geopolitical differences. It is an erasure that permits Silver to write the condition of the colonized under the name of *woman*. By understanding rape to be a discourse of power that castrates, Silver suggests that the accusation of rape positions Aziz as both rapist and rape victim:

> When spoken of as Indian within the discourse of English and Indian, sahib and native, he himself is objectified; he enters the "category" of woman and becomes rapable. From the moment of his arrest, from the moment the door of the carriage is thrown open and the power of the state intrudes, Aziz is absorbed into a discourse that simultaneously defines him as penis and castrates him, equating castration and rape.[32]

Given the conditions of possibility of literary representation at the time Forster was writing *A Passage to India*, I would argue that Aziz cannot enter the category of *woman* and become rapable. As my reading of the Mutiny reports demonstrates, colonial narratives of rape are so invested with the value of English womanhood that they strategically exclude Indians, men and women alike. It would be difficult for an Anglo-Indian novel written in the 1920s to extend rape even metaphorically to Indian men.

Although Silver expresses that she is "aware of 'feeling privileged *as a woman*' to speak to and for third-world women (and in this case third-world men as well),"[33] it is her problematical reading of Third World men as occupying the space of First World women that permits the latter to serve as a model for all oppressed peoples. By the end of her essay, we see that Adela's cry of rape also voices the oppression of Indian women:

> Being English, she [Adela] has the power to speak the position of otherness denied to the Indians in general and doubly denied to the invisible and silent Indian woman, whose resistance resides in absence and negativity, and she uses this power to unsettle the dominant discourse. . . . For Adela, then, to speak rape becomes an act of resistance. Her double discourse brings into representation woman's experience, the unspoken, or unspeakable, that is left out of namings and ideologies even as it refuses the rhetoric of power that denies individuality and speech.[34]

Silver understands colonial structures of power as a doubling of a sexual oppression that Adela as an English woman has the power to speak. By subsuming different oppressions within the experience of the European, she allows *a discourse on the native assault of white women* to serve as a model for theorizing Indian subjugation and resistance to colonial rule.

Rather than resolve the contradictory positioning of the Western sexed subject as inferior sex and superior race, we need to hold onto that contradiction as a moment of theoretical productivity. *A Passage to India* addresses a discourse of power capable of coding anticolonial struggle as the violation of white women. Adela serves the narrative function of undermining the racial assumptions of this understanding of anticolonial rebellion, but then, having served her narrative function, she is no longer of interest to the novel. The "girl's sacrifice" (*PI*, 245) remains just that, a sacrifice for advancing a plot centered on the impossibility of a friendship between men across the colonial divide. As feminists, we should not reverse the terms of the "sacrifice"; rather, we should negotiate between the sexual and racial constructions of the colonial female and native male without reducing one to the other. Since Silver is attentive to the dangers of substituting gender for race, I do not dismiss her essay as misinformed. Rather, I regard her informed reading as symptomatic of the persistent difficulty academic feminism has with dislodging the (white) woman as a privileged signifier for Otherness. It is a privilege that can be unlearned, but only through attention to the historical production of our categories for class, race, and gender relations. If feminism has anything to teach us, it is that an official history has produced a category of *woman* that keeps women, to invoke Sheila Rowbotham, hidden from history. By deploying *rape* as a master trope for the objectification of English women and natives alike, Silver produces a category of Other that keeps the colonized hidden from history.

A reading of Adela's speech as an agency that is denied to Indians puts to rest (in the interest of the Western sexed subject) the problematical appearance of Indian women in Forster's novel. The "invisible and silent" women on whose behalf others speak would lead a First World reader to believe that Indian women, having lived for generations under unchanging conditions of oppression, are passively waiting for Indian men to liberate them. In fact, the 1920s saw the rise of an Indian women's movement that fought its battle for emancipation on two fronts: sexual equality and national liberation.[35] Even those women who were not active in feminist organizations, which spoke more directly to the concerns of urban, middle-class women, participated in anticolonial demonstrations and acts of civil disobedience.

The signs of these battles do not appear in *A Passage to India*, except in the one reference to Muslim women who are on hunger strike in protest of Aziz's arrest: "And a number of Mohammedan ladies had sworn to take no food until the prisoner was acquitted; their death would make little difference, indeed, being invisible, they seemed dead already, nevertheless it was disquieting" (*PI*, 214). Despite the criticism of the Anglo-Indian mentality that these words hold, they also work to contain Indian women's noisy resistance within the figure of the silent and hidden purdah woman. If colonized women do not speak in *A Passage to India*, it is not because they do not have a historical voice as such but because the novel cannot deliver their agency.

Although Forster has been praised for his sympathetic rendering of Indian voices, a search for the native who speaks invariably leads to the educated colonial.[36] A privileging of speech-agency can thus cause us to overlook the roles of less vocal actors that protest Aziz's arrest—the sweepers who refuse to clean the toilets and Muslim women who go on hunger strike. It also risks effacing the role of a silent yet pivotal figure that frames the important trial scene in which Adela withdraws the rape charge. He is the punkah wallah, who controls the fan that cools the courtroom, and he is an untouchable. Shunned because they threaten to pollute, members of the untouchable caste exist at the margins of Indian society. Contrary to popular belief, British colonialism did not destroy the Hindu caste system but articulated an emergent class hierarchy with the older form of occupational status in what might be called class-caste relations. The issue of caste hierarchies came under greater public scrutiny during Gandhi's efforts to end untouchability and to bring the *harijans*, or "children of God" (which was the name he gave them), under the umbrella of Indian nationalism. Gandhi did not, however, oppose untouchability as a fixed occupational status, which was in keeping with his belief in moral duty. The caste system is still very much in place today, and militant untouchables reject harijan as a name given out of upper-caste obligation.[37]

As a figure made visible only at the moment of decolonization, the untouchable tells a national rather than a colonial story of modernization. Admittedly, the educated native is the hero of Indian nationalism; decolonization would not have been possible, however, without a mobilization of even the most marginalized sectors of the Indian population. If the Western-educated colonial is the privileged subject of modern Indian history, the subaltern is exorbitant—an exteriority that is irreducible. Jacques Derrida explains the ex-orbitant as that which exceeds a metaphysical orb and thus represents the attempt of the critic to get outside the orbit of the traced path she is following.[38] With regard to this project, she necessarily fails. The two implications of what is exorbitant, the subaltern as an irreducible exteriority and the critic's necessary failure, are bound up with each other.

Forster's framing of the trial scene with a description of a lowly untouchable provides a possibility for tracing a path that can break the native male/white female opposition belonging to a colonial discourse of rape. Feminists often point out that Adela's withdrawal of the rape charge shows her refusal to participate in a racist colonial machinery. What often passes undetected, however, is that her refusal is contingent upon her catching sight of an untouchable man. For this reason, I propose yet another reading of Adela's extension and withdrawal of the rape charge—one that goes against the grain of Forster's representation of the English woman as a sacrificial scapegoat. Adela may be the "cause" of racial tensions when she cries rape, but she is also the one member of the colonizing race who recognizes the oppressiveness of colonial hierarchies. I now turn to that moment as one in which an English woman and an untouchable man are complicit in exposing the racist tenets of colonialism.

Exorbitant to the action of the courtroom drama, the punkah wallah is both peripheral and crucial to its outcome. Although we are told he has "no bearing officially upon the trial" (*PI*, 217), he is strategically positioned on a raised platform across from the assistant magistrate, who is also seated on a platform as the sign of colonial authority. The assistant magistrate is everything the punkah puller is not; he is an educated Indian. The untouchable was produced not through his contact with Western knowledge but with the filth and garbage of the city. Whereas the Indian civil servant is "cultivated, self-conscious, and conscientious" (*PI*, 217), the punkah wallah does not participate in the trial but is there merely to operate the hand-pulled fan. But the menial worker, rather than the representative of colonial justice, is the one who elicits the truth about the misjudged Aziz. Adela sees the lowly punkah puller when she first enters the courtroom, and it is his unassuming yet dignified presence that provokes her into questioning the presumed superiority of her race:

Almost naked, and splendidly formed, he sat on a raised platform near the back, in the middle of the central gangway, and he caught her attention as she came in, and he seemed to control the proceedings. He had the strength and beauty that sometimes come to flower in Indians of low birth. When that strange race nears the dust and is condemned as untouchable, then nature remembers the physical perfection that she accomplished elsewhere, and throws out a god. . . . This man would have been notable anywhere: among the thin-hammed, flat-chested mediocrities of Chandrapore, he stood out as divine, yet he was of the city, its garbage had nourished him, he would end on its rubbish heaps. . . . Something in his aloofness impressed the girl from middle-class England, and rebuked the narrowness of her sufferings. In virtue of what had she collected this roomful of people together? Her particular brand of opinions, and the suburban Jehovah who sanctified them—by what right did they claim so much importance in the world, and assume the title of civilization? (*PI*, 217–18)

The threads of the conflicting evidence Adela gives under cross-examination can be traced back to this initial interrogation of the ethics of colonialism. She eventually revokes her charge against Aziz, causing the courtroom to explode into chaos. This moment of disruption in the place of law marks a narrative turning point for Aziz's transformation from a "good" colonial subject into an anti-British agitator. After the trial he assumes a nationalist posture that enables him to say, "I am an Indian at last" (*PI*, 293). The punkah puller, however, remains silent. As an actor who does not participate in the court proceedings he appears to govern, the untouchable is marginal to a story that centers on the educated colonial. At the same time, his silent yet disquieting presence in the place of English law denotes a theater that exceeds the official records. What causes Adela to question the racial hierarchy of colonialism is her rejection of a *caste* stereotype. Instead of associating the untouchable with filth and pollution, she sees him as a vision of perfection and beauty. Upon noticing the silent dignity of the punkah puller, she begins to unlearn the lessons of colonialism. Only a similar unlearning will allow us to see what she sees when she confronts a member of the untouchable caste in the place of law.

The untouchable, as one who prompts Adela into revoking her charge, functions as a condition of possibility for disrupting the taken-for-grantedness of agent and object of interracial rape. This disruption is contingent upon a homosexual desire that is exorbitant to the heterosexual economy of the rape. Although channeled through the more socially acceptable medium of a woman's eyes, the glance that fixes the punkah wallah is identifiably homoerotic. The look may be female, but a feminization of the male body indicates a masculine desire at work.[39] It is an indication of this exorbitant signification that, in his film adaptation of *A Passage to India*, Lean does not eliminate the punkah puller but further marginalizes him. His heterosexist lens replaces Forster's "beautiful naked god" (*PI*, 231) with a fully dressed old man who sits, not at the center of the courtroom, but in a corner at the feet of the assistant magistrate. Aziz's anxious face, rather than the beautifully formed body of an untouchable man, is the image that guides Adela along the paths of truth. Lean's interpretation subordinates both the subaltern and homosexual instances of the court scene to a dominant discourse favoring the class-native and heterosexuality.

In Forster's novel, the "scene of fantasy" over which the god-like figure presides also stages the desire for a homosexual relation that can overcome social inequalities.[40] The punkah puller occupies a mythological space, a fantasy world that is removed from historical time and untouched by the norms of society. Although homosexuality is a subordinate culture in Anglo-Indian society, it is not outside the hierarchies of race, class, and caste. In other words, the loving glance that fixes the punkah wallah as a figure of truth and beauty is itself in place because of colonialism. And it is a sign of the vast distance between the European and the lowly untouchable that the latter can only be the object of a Western gaze. The punkah puller has no access to the truth he elicits, for he cannot cognize what is transpiring around him, not even his own activity of fanning: "He scarcely knew that he existed and did not understand why the Court was fuller than usual, indeed he did not know that it was fuller than usual, didn't even know he worked a fan, though he thought he pulled a rope" (*PI*, 217–18). Failing to inhabit the mind of a character that can perhaps reveal to us the "real India," Forster does not speak in the place of a subaltern who cannot speak for himself. Upon doing so, he risks representing the untouchable man as nothing but the object of Western desire. Yet, in *his* desire to represent the other side, Thompson ends up silencing the Indians on whose behalf he claims to speak. Forster's literary depiction of a subaltern man is not only inadequate but visibly so. The untouchable is a figure of truth to the precise degree that he is the object of a Western (homoerotic) gaze, for the aloofness that provokes Adela into reversing the rape charge is also the sign of an absent consciousness. This is the "blind spot in [Forster's] text, the not-seen that opens and limits visibility."[41] Although blind to its own structures of violence, the homosexual desire in the novel brings a subaltern man into a trial scene that centers on the educated Indian. The disruptive presence of the untouchable in a place of law reminds us that the violation of colonialism is not restricted to the drama unfolding in the court-room scene. The punkah wallah both breaks the opposition be-tween the Indian male and English female, and points to a scene of exploitation that exists at the limits of Western representation. Taking my cue from Forster, I want to pursue the possibilities of dispersing sexual violence into a scene of exploitation and, upon doing so, to shift the terms of a colonial discourse of rape.

Jayaben Desai, a Grunwick strike leader, attempting to talk to supporters outside the factory in June 1977. Copyright Aubrey Nunes. Reproduced by permission.

6

The Ruins of Time:

The Jewel in the Crown

My interest in *A Passage to India* and Paul Scott's *Raj Quartet* lies in the strategic role they have played in establishing the terrain for recent revisions of Britian's imperial past.[1] The popularity of *The Jewel in the Crown* (the television series if not the novel), coupled with the film adaptation of Forster's novel, places the figure of rape at the center of the raj revival. In fact, I would go so far as to argue that the tropological function of sexual violence in anti-imperialist fiction of this sort sanctions an academic use of rape as a concept-metaphor for imperialism.[2] There is sufficient evidence to support a reading of imperialism as rape, particularly in those representations that authorize a European claim of ownership through a feminization of the colonial body. As a critical intervention, the carrying across of meaning from a sexually violent act to colonial conquest draws attention to the gendering of Western authority. Although Forster does not suggest an analogous relation between sexual violence and imperialism, he opens up the possibility for such a reading in his staging of the court scene around the reversal of a rape charge. Paul Scott, on the other hand, spells out in a way Forster could not that an Indian man falsely accused of raping an English woman is himself violated by a racist government. The only crime Hari Kumar has committed is to befriend a white woman, Daphne Manners. Upon his arrest at his home in Chillianwallah Bagh, he is subjected to a punishment that exceeds his "crime." In prison, the district superintendent of police, Ronald Merrick, forges a sado-masochistic relationship of colonial mastery and native dependency through a physical and psychological torture designed to break his prisoner's will. The mistreatment of Hari in prison is representative in Scott's quartet of a white superiority that has emasculated the Indian nation.

Yet, the sexual abuse of an educated Indian man is not the incident that sets the stage for the sequence of events to be understood as the metaphoric rape of India. Hari's prison experiences are only briefly mentioned in the first book, with his own detailed testimony not appearing until the second novel, which was published two years later. Rather, the event that stages the violence of imperialism is that of Indian peasants assaulting two English women. On the morning of 9 August 1942, an agnostic, missionary school teacher, Edwina Crane, is attacked by a gang of Indian nationalists on the road from Dibrapur to Mayapore. Mr. Chaudhuri, the Brahmin teacher traveling with her, is denounced as a traitor and beaten to death because, as his assailant mockingly explains, "no self-respecting Indian male would ride with a dried-up virgin memsahib who needed to feel the strength of a man inside her" (*JC*, 55–56). Later that day, the verbal abuse against Miss Crane is reenacted in the sexual abuse of a younger Anglo-Indian woman. A gang of peasants who are in Mayapore for the rioting and looting triggered by the arrest of Congress party members chance upon Daphne and Hari in the act of consummating their unspoken love in the pavilion of an abandoned Indian-style house known as the Bibighar. With the taboo of racial segregation momentarily broken, the peasants repeat what they have just seen, while Hari is forced to watch. The two images of sexual intercourse follow in quick succession: one of love and the other of racial contempt (there is a similar contempt exhibited in the attack on Edwina Crane). The Anglo-Indian community, failing to distinguish between the two, can only code the relation between a brown man and a white woman as rape. Hence, they hold Hari responsible for what happened in the Bibighar. The object of the first novel in the quartet, *The Jewel in the Crown*, is to provide us with an interpretative text for distinguishing interracial love from rape. On the basis of this distinction, Hari enters the feminized space of rape by becoming the innocent victim of a racial attack.

To return to the question I posed at the opening of this book: How does the image of Indian peasants raping a white woman come to signify the racial and sexual violence of imperialism? The difficulty in reversing the direction of the rape is evident in a recent reading of *A Passage to India:* "Allegorically, Adela is Britain, which has raped India; the guilt at the base of her wish to know and sympathize with 'the real India' has become distorted into a justifying fantasy in which Britain is raped by India."[3] There is little evidence to suggest that the mystery in the cave can be so easily resolved at an allegorical level. But even if we were to accept the English woman's accusation of rape as a fantasy generated by her guilt, the gender configuration of the allegory is askew. So long as Adela occupies the space of "woman" (and readings of her "hysteria" indicate that she does), she cannot figure the male-identified agency of a rape. As the gendering of the allegory starts to break down, one begins to suspect that the reading of a metaphoric rape is not derived from Forster's novel at all.[4]

The movement from the literal rape of an English woman to the figurative rape of India cannot be enacted through the simple reversal of assailant and victim that exists in *A Passage to India*. By its very definition, rape designates an unequal relationship of power and, as such, agent and object cannot be reversed. This may explain why the anti-imperialist message of Scott's fiction relies on the double-crossing of a chiasmus. *The Jewel in the Crown* is structured around a four-part figure of reversal that rotates the attributes of male and female, colonizer and colonized. Hari Kumar enters the feminized space of the rape victim when he is tortured, and Daphne Manners and Edwina Crane align themselves with the colonized in their refusal to testify. The rotation of attributes takes place on an allegorical level where "any person, any object, any relationship can mean absolutely anything else."[5] Hence, the novel produces its allegory of imperialism as rape through a sliding chain of signification from English woman to Indian man to India.

Salman Rushdie is perhaps not alone in noting that "if a rape must be used as the metaphor of the Indo-British connection, then surely, in the interests of accuracy, it should be the rape of an Indian woman by one or more Englishmen of whatever class—not even Forster dared to write about such a crime."[6] The question that needs to be asked, however, is not whether Forster could dare to represent an Indian woman being raped by an English man but whether that narrative possibility was historically available to him. I would say that it was not. *A Passage to India* does not provide even the slightest opening for considering the possibility that Rushdie suggests—an opening that is available in the denials of the Mutiny reports that British soldiers had raped Indian women. In Forster's novel, colonial violence against

Indian women is not disavowed so much as it is foreclosed. What is useful about the psychoanalytic concept of foreclosure is that it describes the disavowal of a reality, but one in which the object of disavowal is not recognized. A foreclosed event does not manifest itself as a symptom that "speaks" in its negation. Being barred or crossed out, it appears as a punctuation mark without a text.[7] In the absence of that text, we can only turn to the rape of English women to "act" in its place. What I am suggesting is that, given the overdeterminations of a discourse that presumes the agent of sexual violence to be an Indian male and the victim to be an English female, any other scene is so successfully effaced that there is no symptom in Anglo-Indian fiction for us to read. The violation of Indian women cannot be derived from a narrative in which its representation is foreclosed without writing it under the trope of Indian men raping English women. This is indeed what happens when we restore a literal meaning to Scott's anti-imperialist allegory.

It is perhaps no accident that *A Passage to India* has been read through Scott's fiction rather than the other way around, for the latter offers the interpretative system of an allegorical scheme. Unlike metaphor, which signifies a synchronic relationship between two signs, allegory (from *allos* and *agoreuein*, meaning "to speak otherwise") relies on complexes of codes for its meaning. It proceeds not only by metaphor (superimposed levels of meaning) but also by metonymy (a sequential relation of signs to anterior signs). Since each sign always refers to an anterior sign, allegory draws attention to the preexisting codes on which an interpretation relies. *The Jewel in the Crown* is a modern form of allegory in the sense that it does not simply rely on extrinsic conventions of reading but also supplies a system of codes that ensures a preferred meaning.[8] The reader is both reminded of conventional readings of the civilizing mission and provided with the codes for interpreting the colonizer/colonized relation as a rape. The interpretation of Forster's novel according to the narrative demands of Scott's shows the ability of an allegorical scheme to become detached from one text and lodged in other works. For this reason, I consider it important to unpack the discursive strategies of *The Jewel in the Crown*. My purpose is to interject the following cautionary note into any discussion of rape as a concept-metaphor for imperialism: that we are attentive to the geohistorical specificity of such figures and are keenly aware that they are received rather than invented.

Scott's understanding of allegory is given to us in the innocent voice of a child, who instructs the historian Guy Peron that "it means telling a story that's really two stories" (*ADS*, 505). From the moment we are first informed that "this is the story of a rape" (*JC*, 1), it is clear that the story is not of one violation but two. The narrator traces a chain of causality from the superimposed acts of love and violence in the Bibighar to a similar image of the British-Indian connection: "The affair that began on the evening of August 9th, 1942, in Mayapore, ended with the spectacle of two nations in violent opposition, not for the first time nor as yet for the last because they were then still locked in an imperial embrace of such long standing and subtlety it was no longer possible for them to know whether they hated or loved one another, or what it was that held them together and seemed to have confused the image of their separate destinies" (*JC*, 1). The opening sentence fuses the fate of individuals and nations into a single plot leading from a literal act of love and rape to the "imperial embrace" of Britain and India. This double narration is sustained throughout the novel. In this manner, the presence or absence of consent that is staged in Daphne's double sexual encounter with the native is extended to the novel's allegory of imperialism as rape. Hence, the British-Indian connection is expressed not only through metaphors of rape and sexual violence but also through marriage and romantic love. One of the objects of Scott's "story of a rape" is to provide the codes for reading imperialism according to the presence or absence of native consent, either as an illicit affair or as a violation.

The distinction the novel makes between love and rape suggests that imperialism is a violation only at the moment of an organized opposition to British rule—that is, when there is a viable national liberation movement. The Indian nationalist leadership, however, belonged to the same class that had historically provided colonialism with its ideological alibi. As a concept-metaphor, *rape* replaces, on the one hand, the presumed acquiescence of Indians with their resistance and, on the other hand, the benevolent use of colonial power with its abuse. The place of consent in Scott's anti-imperialist allegory thus conserves the idea of an imperial "love" at the origins, by focusing on "rape" as its corrupt and fallen form. But more than that, as I hope to demonstrate, it provides an interpretative system for reading the colonial male's exploitation of subaltern women as the expression of interracial love.

The Raj Nostalgia Mode

> I fell head over heels in love with India. If I'd gone there 100 years ago, I'd have left my bones there.
> —Enoch Powell, *The Times* (12 February 1968)

As a fiction whose narrative energy is generated around the barbaric attack of Indian peasants on white women, *The Jewel in the Crown* plays into the British racism of the 1970s and 1980s. First published in 1966, the novel appeared on the cusp of the British exit from India in 1947 and the arrival of "Asian" immigrants in Britain. The three subsequent novels of *The Raj Quartet* span the formation of what Rushdie calls "the new empire within Britain."[9] The new, imported empire is encapsulated in Enoch Powell's perception of Afro-Asian citizens as "detachments of communities in the West Indies, or India and Pakistan encamped in certain areas of England."[10] His words express an internal form of racism that addresses West Indians and Asians as "immigrants" (a phrase that is not associated with Commonwealth immigrants) in order to construct a nation that is white-identified. Stuart Hall describes the Powellism of the 1960s as a way of thinking that informed the official racism of Britain in the 1970s. Prior to Powellism, the nation suffered what he calls "a kind of historical amnesia, a decisive mental repression" about its imperial past.[11] The West Indian immigration that had been encouraged in the postwar era became a threat to the national character once black labor was no longer needed. Between 1968 and 1972, East African "Asians" were expelled from Kenya, Tanzania, and Uganda. Arriving in Britain as unwilling immigrants, they found themselves treated as second-class citizens. The internal racism constituted around the "immigration problem" perceives black Britain to be the legacy not of territorial conquest but rather of decolonization. In *Beyond the Pale*, Vron Ware alerts us to the feminization of Anglo-England in a Powellism that describes "the powerless and physical frailty of a white community threatened by the barbarism of the unwanted black 'immigrants' who neither understand nor have respect for the values of civilization."[12]

The representation of immigration as the triumph of *barbarism* over civilization might explain the popularity of documentary and fictional reenactments of the British exit from the Indian subcontinent, as it undergoes the violent splitting into India and Pakistan. Dramatizations of sectarian divisions "over there" confirm racist media images of Britain as an island race besieged by uncivilized "Asians" who are now the invaders.

The perceived threat of black immigration demanded a historical memory, and the entertainment industry manufactured one of epic proportions. The ongoing drama in films and television series like *Gandhi, A Passage to India, The Far Pavilions*, and *The Jewel in the Crown* transformed the raj into the spectacle of a Hollywood production. Thus forming a backdrop against which journalistic reports on bride-burning, ethnic strife, and political assassinations are to be read, the raj revival reanimates the great narrative of the civilizing mission. One sees in the everyday language of an advertisement for tea the empire that Britain never had but which it somehow seems to have lost. The newspaper advertisement, which shows sepoys in formation behind a lone British officer, invokes an almost Proustian moment in its suggestion of an imperial past springing from a mere cup of tea: "Assam tea brings back the strength of the good old days." Recollections of the raj do not appear as conscious re-creations; they are so immediate that the past itself seems to burst forth. Yet the raj revival does not revive a dead past so much as weave the living tapestry of a forgetting. As Michel de Certeau reminds us, "Forgetting is not something passive, a loss, but an action directed against the past."[13] The representation of decolonization as the moment of ruin (which is what we get in the raj revival) preserves a foundational moment of pomp and splendor as a monument to imperial greatness. If we instead look for the signs of ruin at the inception of the raj in 1858, then we begin to see the ignoble scenes of the charred remains of villages, the rubble of destroyed cities, and the shattered bodies of tens of thousands of Indians.

Ruins in the place of monuments, fragments where there should be continuity—this is what Benjamin suggests in the idea of history as allegory. In its simplest form, allegory is the representation of abstract ideas as concrete images, a language that "says one thing and means another."[14] Due to the incompatibility between tenor and vehicle, its exegesis relies on conventions of reading that codify the relationship between an allegorical sign and the idea it represents. Yet, for Benjamin, the demand for interpretation means that convention has the power to confer a meaning that it is unable to stabilize.[15] He thus defines allegory not simply in terms of preexisting codes of meaning but also in terms of the signification that exceeds what the codes can explain. The movement between the two poles of a fixed image (convention) and unfixing interpretation (expression) is what he calls the "antinomies of the allegorical."[16] Antinomies designate the contradictory impulse of allegory both to restore and destroy, to redeem and undermine. Scott's self-conscious project is to displace a monumental vision of empire with his anti-imperialist allegory of rape. Yet his epic account of the final years of the British in India is not allegorical in a Benjaminian sense. Rather, it belongs to what I call the raj nostalgia mode: a mourning for the loss of empire that masquerades as self-criticism, a resurrection of the civilizing mission from its ashes. The masquerade that is so central to the replaying of the last days of the raj might explain why *The Raj Quartet* has been described as both a self-conscious reflection on and "muted celebration" of Britain's imperial past.[17] Scott's semihistorical, semifictional plotting of rape exhibits the tension between these two positions.

The story of *The Jewel in the Crown* is presented as the efforts of one individual to reconstruct the events of 9 August 1942, which is the day after the Indian National Congress endorsed Gandhi's resolution for the British to quit India. The shadowy presence of this historian, known only to us as "the stranger," is evident to readers in his struggles to piece together the incidents that took place some twenty years or so earlier. His expressed desire is to map the unknown regions between an official version and the doubts that gossip and rumor have introduced. The Anglo-Indian community had believed the story circulated by Merrick—that Hari lured Daphne to a deserted spot, where he and five nationalist sympathizers were waiting to humiliate her. Among Indians, however, it was common knowledge that Merrick was determined to punish Hari for his friendship with Daphne and that he arrested the first five Indians he came across. To the police superintendent's good fortune, they turned out to be acquaintances of the prime suspect. Then the stranger has to contend with the rumors that unlawful methods were used to extract confessions and that the suspects had been held without trial. Determined to discover the truth, he carefully assembles a range of sources: the recollections of Lili Chatterjee,

Sister Ludmila, Mr. Poulson, and Mr. Srinivasan; a testimony by the ex-deputy commissioner, Robin White; the unpublished memoirs of Brigadier-General Reid; and the deposition of S. V. Vidyasagar, a nationalist imprisoned for printing pamphlets in protest of the arrests. The stranger also has access to Daphne Manners's journal, written "as an insurance against permanent silence" (*JC*, 349), and letters from her aunt, Lady Manners, reporting the circumstances of her death and Kumar's eventual release. Robin White's confirmation that "Miss Manners was obviously telling the truth" and "there seems small reason to doubt" Vidyasagar's deposition (*JC*, 312–14) lends credence to the two sources that are also the most explicitly detailed accounts of what happened. Daphne's journal reveals that five or six unknown assailants raped her in the Bibighar garden. Vidyasagar confirms that Hari and his fellow prisoners were indeed flogged, fed beef, and humiliated by Indian police, who were ordered to extract confessions from them.

Hari Kumar may be what Lady Manners calls "the left-over, the loose-end of our reign" (*JC*, 446), but the novel leaves no loose ends untied. Like a detective story, all is revealed at the end, and the reader is left with a vivid picture of the sequence of events. This is why the television serialization of *The Raj Quartet* could so easily reconstruct the rape story as a causal chain of events. Despite the fragmented narration of Scott's historical novel, there are no gaps or holes, no mystery in the cave or inquiry as to what constitutes the "real India." Rather, it gives the impression that what we are getting is history itself. "In 100 years' time when men are wondering what India in the 1940s was like," writes a reviewer for the *Daily Telegraph*, "they should read Mr Scott's quartet. It will not only describe events but, far more important, will give, by its shambling bulk, its hesitancies, its repetitions, headlong rushes and longeurs, a portrait of the real India in a way no formal history could."[18] What we have in the first book of *The Raj Quartet* is a carefully wrought narrative expressing the difficulty of explaining the "unrecorded moments of history" (*JC*, 334) placed over a powerful and singular masterplot. The effect of the masterplot is to bring together three historically distinct moments of unrest—1857, 1919, and 1942—into a single image of English women as the innocent victims of a native attack. As a result, the critical impulse to interrogate Britain's imperial past is neutralized by Scott's reliance upon the racial memory of the Mutiny as a normative text.

The novel's message is that British imperialism violated an entire race of people; however, the racial memory of the Mutiny serves as the model for that violation. Its plotting of racial antagonisms during the volatile years of decolonization works within (rather than against) a discourse that safeguards the moral value of colonialism. Upon exposing the British abuse of power in India, *The Jewel in the Crown* also consolidates a colonial discourse of rape.

Scott shows the idea of "an innocent white girl savaged and outraged by black barbarians" (*JC*, 150) to be a ruse for policing Indian nationalists. The information Merrick uncovers about the arrested men's acquaintance with a local nationalist confirms his suspicions regarding their unsavory character. Upon being forced to drop the rape charge when Daphne refuses to testify, he continues to hold his prisoners under the Defence of India Rules. The guilt or innocence of the six men is less important to Merrick than the message their arrests sends to Anglo-Indians and Indians alike. Reid confirms in his memoirs that "once the story got round that an English girl had been outraged there wasn't a white man or woman in the country who wouldn't rejoice that the suspects were already apprehended. The effect on the Indian population of knowing this kind of thing couldn't be got away with would also be exemplary" (*JC*, 289–90). From a military perspective, the meaning of the rape is inseparable from the threat that the national liberation movement poses. The attack on English women confirms the brigadier's belief that Gandhi's nonviolent, noncooperation movement is a plot to massacre all Europeans. From the Indian perspective, the arrest of Congress leaders was not a cause for the attack on English women; rather, the riots were a response to the injustices of arresting any Indian in the vicinity for the crime of rape.

The narrative function of Reid's memoirs is to demonstrate that the prominence of jingoistic generals like Dyer distorts the ambivalence that ran through the civil sector. Robin White undermines the military position when he claims that the brigadier's memoirs are filled with inaccuracies and that, if there had been no rebellion, he would have invented one. In his communications to the stranger, White attempts to map the unrecorded moments of history. However, because he cannot confront his own implication in the events that Reid describes, he does not proceed very far. Scott appears to share White's sense of guilt, especially concerning the massacre of unarmed Indian women and children in 1919—an incident for which the ex-deputy commissioner confesses he is "still deeply ashamed, after all these years" (*JC*, 323). The novel is so haunted by the specter of Amritsar that it both represents the events of the Punjab disturbances as occurring in 1942 *and* refers to 1919 as the historical referent for the fictional incidents it records. It is there, in the place where a literary imagination intersects with history, that Scott weaves the text of a forgetting.

The Jewel in the Crown is a semitransparent fiction through which the events at Amritsar are to be read. The locations of Daphne's rape and Hari's arrest, the Bibighar and Chillianwallah Bagh, allude to the historical sites that ring with the unjustified killing of unarmed women and children: the Bibighar at Cawnpore and the Jallianwalla Bagh at Amritsar. The nationalists who call for the release of "the six martyrs" and "innocent victims" of the Bibighar reverse the racial meaning of Cawnpore: The imperialists are now the violators, and the imprisoned men are their victims. Once again, as was the case in 1919, the colonizers are the object of their own emblem of barbarism. Yet the normative text for such violence remains the "native attack of English women." Behind the assult on the fictional character, Miss Crane, is the historical memory of Miss Sherwood, the missionary woman who was badly beaten on 9 April 1919, three days before the Amritsar massacre. In Scott's version, the assault on Miss Sherwood is both multiplied and sexualized in the attacks on Edwina Crane and Daphne Manners. There are other parallels between the historical and fictional incidents: The number of men charged with Daphne's rape corresponds to the number that General Dyer arrested for the attack on Miss Sherwood, and Reid, who represents the uncompromising position of the military sector, is a character modeled after the infamous general himself. According to Indian reports, "In those few days of Brigadier Reid, things had been almost as bad as in the days of General Dyer in Amritsar in 1919" (*JC*, 59). They are referring to the procedures Reid used to restore order after declaring martial law. In his memoirs, he claims to have faced a situation as grave as the civil strife in the Punjab, behind which lies the enormity of the Mutiny: "In 1919, as in 1942, the country was seething with unrest, and all the signs indicated open rebellion on a scale equal to that of the Mutiny in 1857" (*JC*, 278). The memoirs that exhibit what White calls "Reid's simple soldier attitude" (*JC*, 314) are countered by the Indian opinion that the rioting was triggered by the arrest and imprisonment of innocent men. Since one violent crime inevitably engenders another, each side claims a prior moment of victimization. The narrator appears to share the opinion of the magistrate, Mr. Poulson, that "at the time, there was no distinguishing cause from effect" (*JC*, 59). This position does not contend with the fact that the British alone have the power to enact martial law that sanctions the organized violence of the army and the police. The presupposed legitimacy of this power keeps the official version of what happened intact.

Upon comparing the sequence of events in the novel with those that occurred at Amritsar, one notices that the former establishes a chain of causality originating in the "attack of English women." The Punjab demonstrations in protest of O'Dwyer's arrest and deportation of two nationalist leaders were under control until the army fired into the crowd on two bridges on 10 April 1919.[19] At this point the demonstrators turned violent, burning and looting buildings and attacking five Europeans, including Miss Sherwood. An incident that resembles the bridge shootings occurs in *The Jewel in the Crown*, except that it takes place three days after Daphne's rape. Reid recounts how he ordered his men to fire on Indian demonstrators as they were crossing the Mandir Gate bridge. Unable to escape from the narrow bridge, many were trampled to death. Reid's action on the bridge is represented as a scaled-down version of Dyer's at the Jallianwalla Bagh, which occurred three days after the attack on Miss Sherwood. The bridge scene in the novel is thus represented as a *response* to the assault of Miss Crane and the rape of Daphne Manners. This chronology follows a colonial historiography that records military force as retribution for the violation of English womanhood. One might argue that Scott is simply shaping his fiction from an actual historical event. But by excluding the scene that marks the turning point in the series of events at Amritsar, *The Jewel in the Crown* repeats the narrative structure of a colonial historiography that posits the attack of English women as the primary cause for the British campaign of terror in 1857 as well as the massacre of 1919.

Given the care Scott takes in documenting his fiction as history, one has to confront his narrative as not only the reading but also the writing of a colonial discourse of rape. To begin with, Miss Sherwood was not sexually molested, although for all intents and purposes she could have been as far as the Anglo-Indian community was concerned. In addition, despite the demonstrations, riots, and growing force of the Quit India movement in 1942, the threat of rape did not emerge.[20] Scott endows the Anglo-Indian fear of rape with a concrete form in the graphic details he provides about the verbal and sexual abuse of two English women. By extending the racial memory of the 1857 revolt to what is referred to in the novel as the Congress "revolt" of 1942, he lends credence to the continuity of a colonial fear that was much more episodic.

To Speak Allegorically, to Speak of Rape Otherwise

My India made me talkative, Forster's stunned him into silence.
—Paul Scott, "India: A Post-Fosterian View" (5 December 1968)

Scott's self-conscious critique of imperialism appears in those aspects of the novel that destabilize the monumental vision of Empire represented in the "semi-historical, semi-allegorical" (*JC*, 17) painting entitled *The Jewel in Her Crown*. The title of the painting alludes to India as a prized possession: Being the largest and most valuable of its colonial territories, "she is spoken of, indeed, as 'the brightest jewel in the British crown.' "[21] The painting of Victoria seated on a canopied throne under the open sky is composed to demonstrate her temporal power. It depicts a single hierarchy from the angels poised over the golden throne of the queen-empress all the way down to the most humble of her Indian servants: "princes, landowners, merchants, moneylenders, sepoys, farmers, servants, children, mothers, and remarkably clean and tidy beggars" (*JC*, 18). Victoria is flanked by her soldiers and statesmen, including Prime Minister Disraeli holding up a map of India, while one of the princes is approaching her with a large and lustrous jewel on a velvet cushion. India is in Disraeli's hand, so to speak, even as "she" relinquishes her riches to England. The picture draws on Renaissance personifications of Asia as an exotic woman possessing the rare perfumes, precious stones, fine silks, and spices that Europe desired.[22] The allegorical emblem of India as a jewel in the British Crown subdues the subcontinent in the representation of her delivering her wealth to Europe. But there is also a historical referent for *The Jewel in Her Crown*, and it is Val C. Prinsep's well-known painting of the Delhi durbar at which Victoria was proclaimed empress of India.

In 1877, at the urging of Disraeli, an imperial assemblage was held to celebrate the addition of *Kaiser-i-Hind,* or "Empress of India," to Queen Victoria's titles. J. Talbot Wheeler, the man commissioned to write a commemorative book of the historic event, describes the Mogul ritual as "one of the oldest institutions in India."[23] The idea behind the title and ceremony was to represent the British rulers as the rightful heirs of the Mogul emperors. The monumental vision of the raj produced in the imperial assemblage thus constitutes a forgetting directed at the ignoble scenes out of which the Indian Empire emerged. "The tale of panic and revolt," continues Wheeler in allusion to the uprisings of 1857, "may well be forgotten in the story of the Imperial Assemblage at Delhi."[24]

The official story of the Imperial Assemblage of 1877 not only places the origins of empire in a distant past but also forgets the less-than-sacred character of the austere event. Native princes and dutiful subjects climbed the stairs to a central platform under an overdecorated, scarlet canopy to honor and pay tribute to their new empress. It was not the imposing gaze of Victoria that looked down on them but that of her framed image hanging on the tent wall. "Oh Horror! What have I to paint?" was the initial response of the artist commissioned to capture the Imperial Assemblage on canvas.[25] Facing Val C. Prinsep was the seemingly impossible task of transforming what he saw into a picture worth remembering:

> On the central erection they have heaped enormity on enormity—the Ossa of bad taste on the Pelion of shrieking colour. . . . Happily, I get out of painting it as it is, and find the Viceroy himself anxious that I should make rather a fancy picture of it. . . . Of necessity my picture must be a picture commemorative of the Assemblage rather than a faithful reproduction of the scene. . . . Pictorially, as I have already said, this thing cannot be rendered. I must try to put something into it which it had not—more dignity and distinction.[26]

Prinsep was entrusted with producing a sacred image of the ceremony for posterity. In other words, he was charged with covering over the excessiveness of piling one emblem of imperial power over the other that was itself the effort to conceal the horror of destruction. As if to make his task more difficult, elephants stampeded during the royal artillery salute and trampled Indian onlookers to death.[27] As the producer of a memory for future generations, the artist was assigned no lesser a task than that of imperial myth making. Perhaps out of a faithfulness to the picture he was to paint and the memory inscribed therein, Prinsep recorded the ceremony in his notebook as if Victoria were present.

Upon centering his fictional rendition of the Imperial Assemblage on the personage of the queen, Scott transforms Prinsep's painting into an allegory. As Edwina's friend Barbie Batchelor points out, the picture has to be read allegorically because "she [Victoria] never came to India" (*TS*, 64). In Scott's novel, the painting entitled *The Jewel in Her Crown* is intended to represent the imperial effort to stabilize the antinomies of the allegorical through a recovery of its redemptive side alone. The reader is initiated into interpreting the painting through the complexes of codes that are practically second nature to the Anglo-Indian characters. The missionary school teacher, Mr. Cleghorn, sees in the picture the abstract ideals of the civilizing mission: justice, goodwill, and benevolence. Private Clancy considers it to be a "nice old picture" (*JC*, 23) of a time when things were simpler. Edwina attempts to read in the figure of the queen the feminine qualities of self-sacrifice, devotion, and moral duty. She also knows, however, that "the India of the picture had never existed outside its gilt frame" (*JC*, 21). By drawing attention to the imperial myth making at work in the painting, Scott warns his readers against assuming the simple-soldier attitude of a Clancy or a Reid. Its depiction of loyal Indians standing quietly in their assigned places is at odds with the street scenes of demonstrators shouting for the British to quit India. The circumstances by which Edwina Crane acquired the picture also contribute to the novel's ironic comment on such gestures toward fixing the meaning of the imperial hierarchy in an image. She was awarded the painting in honor of defending the missionary schoolhouse and children from rioting Indians in 1914.

Whenever the missionary school teacher uses the picture to instruct Hindu and Muslim children in the English language, she has to inform them of its proper reading. The children think the title *The Jewel in Her Crown* refers to the precious stone the prince is carrying. Miss Crane tells them that the jewel is India, which was transferred to the British Crown in 1858. This is but one instance of the novel's insistence upon an oblique reading over a literal interpretation. There is a lesson to be learned from the children's (mis)reading, and it is this: The proper meaning of an allegory cannot be assumed. Yet there does exist an actual jewel that the British acquired as part of a settlement following the Anglo-Sikh War of 1848–49. Meaning "most precious or superb of its kind," the Koh-i-noor diamond was presented to Queen Victoria in 1850 to commemorate the two hundred and fiftieth anniversary of the East India Company. In 1937, the diamond was used as a centerpiece for the crown fashioned for Queen Elizabeth's coronation. Ten years later, India could no longer be called the brightest jewel in the British Crown; however, the Koh-i-noor glitters alongside the other crown jewels in the Tower of London, where they are secured for safekeeping. The gesture toward possessing "India" at the moment of its inevitable loss is a figure that underwrites the raj revival. In this regard, the children's direct reading reveals a sort of truth about Scott's fiction. The native rape of a white woman cannot figure the violence of imperialism except through the enforcement of an oblique reading. What this means is that the novel revives the racial memory of the Mutiny at the heart of its anti-imperialist critique.

Scott's semihistorical, semiallegorical fiction, *The Jewel in the Crown*, replaces the figure of the queen with the visual image of Daphne Manners fleeing from the scene of her rape. It presents an allegorical emblem that links Daphne's fate to the MacGregor and the Bibighar houses, which are also part of the picture. The novel opens with the narrator inviting the reader to visualize the emblem: "Imagine, then, a flat landscape, dark for the moment, but even so conveying to a girl running in the still deeper shadow cast by the wall of the Bibighar Gardens,an idea of immensity, of distance" (*JC*, 1). There is a detour into the story of Miss Crane (which is intimately connected to the iconography of rape) before we are presented with another piece to the picture: "Next, there is the image of a garden: not the Bibighar garden but the garden of the MacGregor House: intense sunlight, deep and complex shadows" (*JC*, 63). The allegorical emblem is completed by the written text that names the central figure: "Picture her then: Daphne Manners" (*JC*, 87). The image of Daphne sets in motion the antinomies of the allegorical that *The Jewel in Her Crown* attempts to stabilize. Her lovemaking with Hari undermines the racial hierarchy fixed in the monument to imperial greatness; her rape transforms the image of native subservience into one of racial antagonism.

Scott's allegorical scheme operates through a double reversal of racial attributes, one in which Daphne's crossing over between "the MacGregor and Bibighar [as] the place of the white and the place of the black" (*JC*, 136) is emblematic. The polarities of male/female and colonizer/colonized are reversed when Hari enters the feminized space of the rape victim and Daphne and Edwina "become" Indian. The two women are "disloyal to civilization," to invoke Adrienne Rich's well-known call for white women to refuse to participate in the enforcement of racial hierarchies.[28] Daphne and Edwina are not only Indian sympathizers, they also refuse to testify against their assailants. Daphne even goes so far as to suggest that, for all she knew, she could have been raped by English soldiers with blackened faces. The scandal of her remark, coupled with her refusal to identify the prisoners, turns the Anglo-Indian community against her. Sister Ludmila informs the stranger that for this action, Indians claimed her as one of their own: "That Daphne Manners had loved them. And had not betrayed them, even when it seemed that they had betrayed her. Few Indians doubted that she had indeed been raped by men of their own race. Only they did not believe that among the boys arrested there was even one of those responsible. And this, they felt, was a belief they held with her. A cross, if you like, that they shared with her" (*JC*, 152). Daphne may be a member of the colonizing race, but she allies herself with Indians by refusing to help the police in their investigations. The shared space of English women and the colonized is perhaps what gives the novel's anti-imperialist critique its appeal.

However, the colonial logic that frames the two women's actions reappropriates their acts of disloyalty in the interest of maintaining the superiority of Western civilization. Daphne refuses to identify the prisoners, not out of loyalty to the colonized but because she is afraid of implicating Hari in the rape. She does describe her assailants, over and over again, as "hooligans from some village" (*JC*, 413) in "peasant dress, dirty and smelly" (*JC*, 417), "men of that kind, labourers, hooligans, stinking to high heaven" (*JC*, 419) and "smelly peasants" (*JC*, 427). The same kind of men are also responsible for attacking Miss Crane on the road to Dibrapur. The betrayal that Edwina Crane first experienced when Gandhi called for the British to quit India is confirmed when nationalists beat her and kill Mr. Chaudhuri. She subsequently dons the white sari of a Hindu widow, locks herself in a garden shed, douses its walls with kerosene, and sets it on fire: "The story goes that for this act of becoming suttee ... she dressed for the first time in her life in a white saree, the saree for her adopted country, the whiteness for widowhood and mourning" (*JC*, 110). When Edwina dramatically assumes the role of a Hindu woman, it is as the "widow" of the country to which she was wedded. Yet, the image of sati is one that British colonialists have historically invoked to reconfirm both the oppressiveness of Indian culture and the racial memory of 1857.[29]

Scott's staging of the rape scene as a double encounter with the native splits the racial object of a colonial discourse of rape. The man who is saved from the label of rapist is one who possesses an English identity trapped inside an Indian body. Belonging to a class of Indian landowners and educated at an elite English school, Hari Kumar or Harry Coomer has a divided identity, as is evident in the double spelling of his name—one Indian and the other English. Daphne is not alone in noticing that "except for the colour of his skin he wasn't Indian at all" (*JC*, 357). Hari not only breaks the taboo of having a sexual relation with an English woman, but he is also the only Indian who is "man" enough to take her. The lovemaking between them is described as a forceful act in which Hari, having previously been emasculated because she is white and he only an inferior native, now asserts his manhood. When he remains silent under interrogation, he conducts himself with a chivalry, fortitude, and manly restraint that are signs to the reader of his Englishness. As the deputy commissioner's wife confesses to Daphne: "You know if Hari Kumar had been an Englishman I could have understood his silence better, although even then it would have had to be a silence imposed on him by a woman" (*JC*, 439). As readers, we know that Daphne's last words to Hari before they parted in the Bibighar was that he should say nothing. The masculine ethos of imperialism is thus reaffirmed through the same Indian man that is the inappropriate object of colonial racism.

The return of a Western value system in the shape of a colonial Other is characteristic of neocolonial forms of knowledge. The novel's anti-imperialist allegory works through a figure of reversal in which the colonizer and colonized exchange discursive places. Since Hari is in essence English, however, and Daphne and Edwina are Indian only inasmuch as they are the objects of an Indian national (rather than British colonial) violence, the attributes of colonizer and colonized cross back over again, and the racial memory of the Mutiny is kept in place.

With regard to the agents of the racial and sexual violence, there is no similar crossing of attributes but a splitting that scape-goats a group or individual—the peasants on the Indian side and Ronald Merrick on the British. Merrick, like the wretchedly poor and uneducated peasants, is characterized by Daphne as a "spoiler." Since he lacks the class privilege of his fellow imperialists, he is threatened by Hari's Englishness and public-school education, which he himself was denied. But more than that, Merrick sexually desires the handsome young Indian, and his repressed homosexuality feeds his racism.[30] By making the agent of Hari's metaphoric rape a sadistic homosexual, Scott identifies the decline of the moral ideals of imperialism as the corruption of Victorian manliness. Thus isolating homosexuality as an inferior form of masculinity for which the pretensions of racial superiority compensate, the novel safeguards Victorian manliness and the homosocial relations of colonialism.[31] In this manner, Scott frames and contains the exorbitant signification of Forster's novel. The subaltern-as-untouchable in *A Passage to India* shows the existence of hierarchies that cannot be explained simply in terms of the courtroom drama centering on the trial of an educated colonial. In *The Jewel in the Crown*, on the other hand, the subaltern-as-peasant is represented as having committed the crime for which the English-educated Indian stands accused. Whereas the homosexual elements of Forster's novel express the desire to overcome race, class, and caste hierarchies, in Scott's novel homosexual desire is isolated as a psychological condition that gives white superiority its oppressive form.

The story of a doomed love between a white woman and brown-skinned man, a story that Anglo-Indians can read only according to the sexual violence of rape, is one that reinforces a Victorian ideal of manliness. This may explain why, when deployed as a concept-metaphor for imperialism, "rape" does not designate the penetration and control of a female colonial body; rather, it designates the emasculation of a male one. "The whole bloody affair of us in India ... was based on a violation," Daphne writes in her journal. "What happens when you unsex a nation, treat it like a nation of eunuchs? Because that's what we've done, isn't it?" (*JC*, 400). She is alluding not only to colonial constructions of Indian masculinity as effeminate but also to the memsahib's attitude of racial superiority that emasculates the Indian male.[32] Further on in her journal, she metaphorically extends the signification of her own rape to an Indian woman, but it is only to negate the possibility of a similar violation:

There is that old, disreputable saying, isn't there? "When rape is inevitable, lie back and enjoy it." *Well, there has been more than one rape.* I can't say, Auntie, that I lay back and enjoyed mine. But Lili was trying to lie back and enjoy what we've done to her country. I don't mean done in malice. Perhaps there was love. Oh, somewhere in the past, and now, and in the future, love as there was between me and Hari. But the spoilers are always there, aren't they? (*JC*, 434)

This passage sums up the sentiment of Scott's anti-imperialist allegory—namely, imperialism is a violation only when the class of Indians that has historically benefited from British rule demands independence. Daphne's reading is confirmed by the imposing Rajput woman, Lili Chatterjee, who gives us a slightly different version of the sexual analogy: "I have a feeling that when it was written into our constitution that we should be a secular state we finally put the lid on our Indianness, and admitted the *legality* of our long years of living in sin with the English. Our so-called independence *was* rather like a shot-gun wedding. The only Indians who don't realise that we are now really westerners are our peasants" (*JC*, 68). Both Daphne's and Lili's testimonies reproduce the primary ideological effect of the civilizing mission, which is to substitute metonymically the Western educated colonial for the native as such.

The presence or absence of consent that the love/rape in the Bibighar stages is at the heart of how we read the British-Indian connection: either as an illicit affair or as a rape. This sexual analogy presents a double bind for the feminist critic. To acknowledge the complicity of the comprador class means reading rape according to a masculinist desire that asserts female consent. To overturn this logic—that is, to deny the consent of the violated party—is to ignore the overdeterminations of colonial relations, whereby the British ruled with the approval of an intermediary class of natives. Because it is a reductive model that works in the interests of conserving the binarism of colonizer and colonized, the concept-metaphor of rape cannot address the fractured scene of colonialism.

Throughout this book, I have been arguing that the persistence of colonial structures of knowledge points to a greater continuity between past and present than the rupture of postcolonialism might suggest. What *The Jewel in the Crown* shows is how those age-old stories can be revived so long as they are told by a native informant. In the aftermath of decolonization, when imperialism has fallen into disrepute, Western representation seeks its authority in the authenticating signature of a racial Other. Yet, the countersignatures offer no guarantee that we have the story right. As an Indian woman who is also a narrator, Lili Chatterjee perhaps speaks for all native women in the novel. Her sexual analogy, however, represents an old colonial understanding of the master/concubine relationship as "living in sin." As an interpretative code for reading the nineteenth-century stories woven into the novel's anti-imperialist allegory, her words do no less than reconfirm what the colonizers have known all along.

A Return to the "House of the Ladies"

Have you yet seen Bibighar? ... The Europeans seldom went, except to look and sneer and be reminded of that other Bibighar in Cawnpore.
— Sister Ludmila in *The Jewel in the Crown*

Behind the allegorical picture of Daphne running from the Bibighar to MacGregor House are anterior signs and the historical layering of prior stories. We are told that the place known as MacGregor House was originally built in the late eighteenth century by a native prince for the woman he loved. She was a classical singer whose voice so enchanted him that he asked nothing of her except to hear her sing. After her death, the house fell into ruin. As a comment on his father's reticence, the prince's corrupt son built a second house, the Bibighar, where he kept his courtesans. Accused of poisoning an Englishman visiting his court, the son was later deposed, and Mayapore was annexed by the British. From this point on, there are several versions of the story. According to the European version, a God-fearing Scotsman named MacGregor took over the two houses shortly after annexation. He rebuilt the singer's house and burned the Bibighar for being an "abomination." Sister Ludmila, however, provides evidence that contradicts the depiction of MacGregor as a morally upright European. He was no company officer but a private merchant, a latter-day nabob who came to Mayapore in 1853, some thirty years after annexation and four years before the Mutiny. Practically a local ruler, he managed to amass a small fortune through bribery and corruption. According to the Indian version of the story, he burned the Bibighar, not because it was a house of sin, but "because he fell in love with an Indian girl and lost her to a boy whose skin was the same colour as her own" (*JC*, 135). At this point even the Indian version diverges. One account claims that MacGregor destroyed the Bibighar because it was the place where his mistress held secret meetings with her Indian lover, and another claims that she ran away with the lover after MacGregor decided to marry an English woman and move her out of his own home into the Bibighar. The romance plot is thus presented as the rivalry between a Scotsman and an anonymous Indian man, and/or the sexual competition between his English wife and Indian mistress.

The so-called Indian versions of the MacGregor story belong to the myth of the destructive female, which posits an intimacy between English men and Indian women prior to the arrival of the memsahib. Their narrative function is to show the interracial love that Daphne imagines must have existed in the past. Or maybe they tell the story that confirms her remark that "although a white man could make love to a black girl, the black man and white girl association was still taboo" (*JC*, 355). Although the gender roles are reversed, MacGregor shares with Daphne the love for a native that tragically ends in death. In 1857, the Scotsman, his wife, Janet, and baby are all killed by mutinous sepoys. "History was left the impression," Sister Ludmila informs the stranger, "that nothing could have saved MacGregor because the sepoys knew he had burned the Bibighar and it was rumoured that his Indian mistress and her lover died in the fire" (*JC*, 136).

It is no accident that the house in whose ruins Daphne's rape takes place is called "Bibighar." The name is an anglicization of *bibi khana*, the "house of women" (or "ladies" as they were known), which was where high-ranking colonialists kept their Indian mistresses. As a proper name, it refers to the infamous house at Cawnpore where English women and children were held as Nana Sahib's prisoners. According to colonial historiography, the Bibighar at Cawnpore was a small Oriental-style house that had originally been built by a British officer for his Indian mistress but that had since become the residence of a Eurasian clerk.[33] After 1857, the "house of the ladies" takes on a new meaning: Once a place of concubinage, it now designates the murder of English women; a prior sexual violence is thus covered over. *The Jewel in the Crown* does not efface the history that precedes Daphne's rape. Rather, a return to the Mutiny scene rewrites the prehistory of a colonial discourse of rape as the tragic story of interracial love.

Historically, the relationship between a British colonialist and his Indian mistress, or *bibi*, was no romantic love. Rather, she performed in the capacity of a servant who tended to her master's needs, including his sexual ones. The bibi was often (though not always) a village woman sold into prostitution as repayment for family debts. This aspect of the Indian sex trade was but an extension of the debt-bondage system. As was the case with the export of coolie labor to remote corners of the Empire, the British did not destroy indigenous forms of the sex trade so much as incorporate them into modern colonialism. Since enlisted British soldiers could not afford to bring their wives out to India (as did their officers), the government regulated prostitution through the Indian Contagious Diseases Act of 1868, "lock" hospitals, and *lal bazaars* (regimental brothels), licensed for European clients alone.[34] Although the maintenance of concubines was discouraged after the Mutiny, the practice continued until the 1920s.[35] The British men who purchased bonded women differed little from their Indian counterparts, although Anglo-Indian fiction depicts them as kinder and more enlightened masters. Yet one need only turn to Kenneth Ballhatchet's description of the English civil surgeon who beat his bibi daily for yet another image of the "gentle" colonial master.[36] In Steel's Mutiny novel, *On the Face of the Waters*, Jim Douglas's purchase of a Persian girl from a house of prostitution is represented as a noble act of liberation and romantic gesture on his part, even though the reader is informed that her confinement to their rooftop home brings about her early death.

How does one begin to read the relationship of an Indian woman who "lives in sin" with a white man? In *The Jewel in the Crown*, the elopement of the bibi with her Indian lover suggests that she is with MacGregor of her own free will and that she leaves because she does not want to be displaced by the English woman who is her rival. If this is the case, then the telling of an interracial love story at the beginning as opposed to the end of Empire hinges on the Indian woman's desire. Yet there is no interpretative text for establishing the desire of the sexed subaltern—we do not even know her name. Rather, the codes for understanding the relation between MacGregor and his mistress are derived from the sex/rape opposition that is staged in the Bibighar garden and the consent/refusal opposition belonging to an allegorical reading of imperialism as rape.[37] To transform the meaning of the MacGregor story from interracial "love" to "rape" by demonstrating force where there was previously consent does not break with the interpretative system of the novel. Rather, it restores a literal meaning to the concept-metaphor of rape. Upon performing such a restoration, the critic is forced into reading the place of the sexed subaltern as identical to that of an English woman who is the victim of an interracial rape. In addition, that, by extending the status of victim and violated object—a status that allows no place for woman's desire for agency—to the everyday life of the Indian mistress, this reading reproduces a colonial construction of the native woman as an object to be saved.[38] Instead of extending the Mutiny signification of *Bibighar* to a prior moment of racial and sexual violence, we need to maintain the two scenes as discontinuous.

As a gesture in this direction, I conclude my own narration with a different kind of frame for the painting *The Jewel in Her Crown* than Scott's image of interracial rape. While on a fact-finding mission to investigate government-licensed prostitution in India, the social reformer Alfred Dyer was horrified at the sight that assaulted his eyes: "Conspicuously displayed in one of the shops of this licensed market of sin, I noticed a large framed portrait of 'Victoria, Queen of Great Britian and Empress of India.'"[39] Here sits the queen-empress, not under a sacred canopy for Indian princes to pay their respect, but in a regimental brothel for British foot soldiers to visit. The scandal for a moral reformer like Dyer is that the immorality of the colonial sex trade should touch the royal personage of the queen. But, for us, there is another reading to be derived from the picture of Victoria in an Indian house of prostitution. When placed alongside the allegorical emblem of Daphne fleeing from the Bibighar, it shifts the meaning of the "House of the Ladies" from the native rape of a white woman to the colonial exploitation of Indian women, also a scene of racial and sexual violence. But more than that, it allows us to recognize the figure of the female rebel in the novels and colonial documents I have been reading. She is the harlot who stirs up sepoys to mutiny and the bazaar whore from whose lips come the word of revolt. But she is also

MacGregor's bibi who, like so many other Indian servants, heard the news that British rule had ended—and ran away. I leave my readers with the image of an Indian woman who escapes not only from the master's house but also from the frame of a modern-day allegory of Empire.

Appendix

I. Unpublished Sources

(1) India Office Library (London)

Jackson, Madeline. A Personal Narrative of the Indian Mutiny 1857 (written c. 1880). Photo EUR 41.

Mill, Maria. Memoir by Wife of Major John Mill Describing Her Escape from Fyzabad to Gorakhpur (1857). EUR Mss B 414.

Sneyd, Elizabeth. Reminiscences of the Dreadful Mutiny in India in 1857. Volume 1: Narrative Referring to the Years 1853–57. Photo EUR 44.

Vansittart, Mary Amelia. Diary. EUR Mss B 167.

(2) British Museum Library (London)

Horne, Amelia. "Miss Amy Haine's Narrative." Mss 41488, ff. 53–95.

II. Published Sources

Bartrum, Katherine Mary. *A Widow's Reminiscences of the Siege of Lucknow.* London: James Nisbet, 1858.

Becher, Augusta. *Personal Reminiscences in India and Europe, 1830–1888.* Edited by H. G. Rawlinson. London: Constable, 1930.

Case, Adelaide. *Day by Day at Lucknow: A Journal of the Siege of Lucknow by Mrs. Adelaide Case, Widow of Colonel Case.* London: Richard Bentley, 1858.

Coopland, R. M. *A Lady's Escape from Gwalior and Life in the Fort of Agra during the Mutinies of 1857.* London: Smith, Elder, 1859.

Duberly, Mrs. Henry. *Campaigning Experiences in Rajpootana and Central India during the Suppression of the Mutiny, 1857–1858.* London: Smith, Elder, 1859.

Forbes, Mrs. Hamilton. *Some Recollections of the Siege of Lucknow.* Exminister: Edwin Snell, 1905.

Germon, Maria. *Journals of the Siege of Lucknow: An Episode of the Indian Mutiny.* Edited by Michael Edwardes. London: Constable, 1958.

Haldane, Julia. *Story of Our Escape from Delhi in 1857.* Agra: S. Brown, 1888.

Harris, Katherine. *A Lady's Diary of the Siege of Lucknow.* London: John Murray, 1858.

Inglis, Julia Selina. *Letters Containing Extracts from a Journal Kept by Mrs. Julia Inglis during the Siege of Lucknow.* London, privately printed, 1858.

———. *The Siege of Lucknow, a Diary.* London: James R. Osgood, McIlvaine, 1892.

Muter, Mrs. Dunbar Douglas. *My Recollections of the Sepoy Revolt (1857–1858).* London: John Long, 1909.

———. *Travels and Adventures of an Officer's Wife in India, China, and New Zealand.* 2 volumes. London: Hurst & Blackett, 1864.

Ouvry, Matilda H. *A Lady's Diary before and during the Indian Mutiny.* Lymington: Chas. T. King, 1892.

Paget, Mrs. Leopold. *Camp and Cantonment: A Journal of Life in India in 1857–1859.* London: Longman, Green, Longman, Roberts & Green, 1865.

Peile, Mrs. Fanny. *History of the Delhi Massacre, Its Supposed Origin, and the Means Being Adopted to Avenge the Murder of the British Subjects.* Liverpool: C. Tinling, 1858.

Soppitt, Mrs. *Diary of an Officer's Wife.* Rptd. in W. H. Fitchett, *Tale of the Great Mutiny.* London: Smith, Elder, 1939, 453–70.

Tytler, Harriet. *An Englishwoman in India: The Memoirs of Harriet Tytler, 1828–1858.* Edited by Anthony Sattin. Oxford: Oxford University Press, 1986.

Wagentreiber, Miss. *The Story of Our Escape from Delhi in May, 1857.* Delhi: Imperial Medical Hall Press, 1894.

Notes

1. Introduction: Neocolonial Conditions of Reading

1. I use *colonial* to refer to relations in the colonies and *imperial* to denote the remote seat of government for overseas territories—although the distinction between colonialism and imperialism is also a historical one having to do with the consolidation of Empire in the latter half of the nineteenth century. The term *imperialism* gained currency in the 1870s, following the scramble of European nations for global territorial control. See Raymond Williams, *Keywords: A Vocabulary of Culture and Society* (London: Flamingo, 1983), 159, and Richard Koebner and Helmut Dan Schmidt, *Imperialism: The Story and Significance of a Political Word, 1840–1960* (Cambridge: Cambridge University Press, 1964).

2. Indian soldiers in the British army were called sepoys. The 1857 rebellion was more than a mutiny, although the British recorded it as such.

3. The British used *Hindoo, Indian*, and *native* as interchangeable terms for the heterogeneous peoples of the Indian subcontinent. My own use of *native* is intended to retain the historical traces of the homogenization of indigenous populations within colonial discourse.

4. I use the term *Anglo-Indian* in its historical sense, that is, to designate the British residents of India. Anglo-Indians did not comprise a white settler colony so much as a community in exile.

5. David Maughan-Brown, *Land, Freedom and Fiction: History and Ideology in Kenya* (London: Zed Books, 1985), 55, 124.

6. Patrick Brantlinger, *Rule of Darkness: British Literature and Imperialism, 1830–1914* (Ithaca, N.Y.: Cornell University Press, 1988), 210.

7. O. Mannoni, *Prospero and Caliban: The Psychology of Colonization*, trans. Pamela Powesland (Ann Arbor: University of Michigan Press, 1990), 110–11.

8. Ibid., 110. In his foreword to *Prospero and Caliban*, Maurice Bloch describes how Mannoni's psychology of colonialism relies on the same set of assumptions as the official explanation for the rebellion (v–xx). For other critiques of Mannoni, see Frantz Fanon, *Black Skin, White Masks*, trans. Charles Lam Markmann (New York: Grove Press, 1967), ch. 4, and Aimé Césaire, *Discourse on Colonialism*, trans. Joan Pinkham (New York: Monthly Review Press, 1972), 40–43.

9. "Colonialism cannot be understood without the possibility of torturing, of violating, or of massacring" (Frantz Fanon, "Algeria Face to Face with the French Torturers," in *Toward the African Revolution*, trans. Haakon Chevalier [New York:

Grove Press, 1967], 66). "Order, as an idiom of state violence . . . in colonial India . . . was allowed to intrude again and again into many such areas of the life of the people as would be firmly kept out of bounds in metropolitan Britain" (Ranajit Guha, "Dominance without Hegemony and Its Historiography," in *Subaltern Studies VI: Writings on South Asian History and Society*, ed. Ranajit Guha [Delhi: Oxford University Press, 1989], 237).

10. I locate the beginnings of modern colonialism in what L. S. Stavrianos designates as the second phase of colonialism (*Global Rift: The Third World Comes of Age* [New York: William Morrow, 1981]). Stavrianos divides colonialism into four phases: 1400 to 1770, which is dominated by mercantile capitalism and an exploitation of the Americas; 1770 to 1870, which involved the rise of industrial capitalism and a search for overseas markets; 1870 to 1914, the moment of monopoly capitalism and global conquest; and from 1914 to the present, which is characterized by the shift from defensive monopoly capitalism and decolonization to a system of multinational corporations and neocolonialism (41–43).

11. Stuart Hall, "Race, Articulation and Societies Structured in Dominance," in *UNESCO, Sociological Theories: Race and Colonialism* (Paris: UNESCO Press, 1980), 338.

12. Peter Fryer, *Staying Power: The History of Black People in Britain* (London: Pluto, 1984), 133–90; Michael Omi and Howard Winant, *Racial Formation in the United States: From the 1960s to the 1980s* (New York: Routledge & Kegan Paul, 1986), 57–69. In *The Black Image in the White Mind: The Debate on Afro-American Character and Destiny, 1817–1914* (New York: Harper & Row, 1972), 43–58, George M. Fredrickson traces a coherent argument for Negro inferiority to the period following the Nat Turner uprising of 1831 and the abolitionist offensive against slaveholders. In *White over Black: American Attitudes toward the Negro, 1550–1812* (Baltimore: Penguin, 1969), 304–11, Winthrop D. Jordan locates the beginnings of the racial argument in the earlier Revolutionary period of the 1770s. A similar pattern of racism as proslavery defensiveness can be identified in the British West Indies during the years between the early abolitionist attack in the 1770s and the successful San Domingo rebellion of 1804 that led to the free black nation of Haiti.

13. As a category that arranges different families of people into a fixed hierarchy, race belongs to the epistemic formation of man as a subject who knows and an object of knowledge. Foucault's description of this epistemic formation in *The Order of Things: An Archaeology of the Human Sciences* (New York: Vintage, 1973) is noticeably race-blind. He does not mention the theories of racial degeneracy and comparative anatomy of the French biologist Georges Cuvier, the Orientalism of Bopp and his fellow philologists, and the non-Western peoples that are the object of ethnology, even though he devotes a section to each of these scientific discourses.

14. Nancy Stepan, *The Idea of Race in Science: Great Britain 1800–1960* (London: Macmillan Press, 1982), 1.

15. I take the notion of the instrumentality of woman from Gayatri Chakravorty Spivak, "The Rani of Sirmur," in *Europe and Its Others*, 2 vols., ed. Francis Barker et al. (Colchester: University of Essex, 1985), 1: 128–51, and *In Other Worlds* (New York: Methuen, 1987), 215–19. All further references to *In Other Worlds*, abbreviated *IOW*, will be included in the text.

16. Thomas Babington Macaulay, "Government of India: A Speech Delivered in the House of Commons on the 10th of July, 1833," in *Macaulay: Prose and Poetry*, ed. G. M. Young (London: Rupert Hart-Davis, 1952), 717. In this memorable statement, Macaulay not only anticipates the civilizing mission but also prefigures neocolonialism, a system of political independence and economic dependency.

17. David Brion Davis, "Slavery and 'Progress,'" in *Anti-Slavery, Religion, and Reform*, ed. Christine Bolt and Seymour Drescher (Hamden, Conn.: Archon, 1980),

353. In *British Colonial Theories* (Toronto: University of Toronto Press, 1944), Klaus Knorr explains that the idea of the moral obligation to spread Western civilization was first introduced at the end of the eighteenth century in response to attacks on the economic feasibility of Britain maintaining its overseas colonies (247).

18. The historical incident that prompted Kipling to write "The White Man's Burden" (1899) was the Filipino attack on the Americans who had "saved" them from Spanish rule.

19. Edward W. Said, *The World, the Text, and the Critic* (Cambridge, Mass.: Harvard University Press, 1983), 221.

20. Michel Foucault, *Discipline and Punish: The Birth of the Prison*, trans. Alan Sheridan (New York: Vintage, 1979), 29, 194; Michel Foucault, "Two Lectures" and "Truth and Power," in *Power/Knowledge: Selected Interviews and Other Writings 1972–1977*, trans. Colin Gordon et al. (New York: Pantheon, 1980), 78–133.

21. Louis Althusser, "Ideology and Ideological State Apparatuses (Notes towards an Investigation)," *Lenin and Philosophy and Other Essays*, trans. Ben Brewster (New York: Monthly Review Press, 1971), 127–86.

22. Louis Althusser, *For Marx*, trans. Ben Brewster (London: Verso, 1979), 233–34.

23. Stuart Hall, "Encoding/Decoding," in Centre for Contemporary Cultural Studies, *Culture, Media, Language: Working Papers in Cultural Studies, 1972–79* (London: Hutchinson, 1980), 128–38. My understanding of ideology is indebted to Hall's extensive writings on the subject. Two essays I have found particularly useful are "The Problem of Ideology—Marxism Without Guarantees," in *Marx: A Hundred Years On*, ed. Betty Matthews (London: Lawrence & Wishart, 1983), 57–85, and "Culture, the Media and the 'Ideological Effect,'" in *Mass Communication and Society*, ed. James Curran et al. (Beverly Hills, Calif.: Sage, 1979), 315–48.

24. Hall, "Encoding/Decoding," 137.

25. Hall, "Culture, the Media and the 'Ideological Effect,'" 327.

26. I use *English* and *England* in their historical sense, that is, to designate a national culture that brings the "Celtic fringe" of Scotland, Wales, and Cornwall under its hegemony. An excellent introduction to Englishness as a discourse of nation and ethnicity at home and of empire and race in the colonies can be found in Robert Miles, "Recent Marxist Theories of Nationalism and the Issue of Racism," *British Journal of Sociology* 38, no. 1 (March 1987): 24–43. Also see Philip Corrigan and Derek Sayer, *The Great Arch: English State Formation as Cultural Revolution* (London: Basil Blackwell, 1985), and Robert Colls and Phillip Dodd, eds., *Englishness: Politics and Culture 1880–1920* (London: Croom Helm, 1987).

27. Walter Benjamin, *Illuminations*, ed. Hannah Arendt, trans. Harry Zohn (New York: Schocken, 1969), 257.

28. Walter Benjamin, *The Origin of German Tragic Drama*, trans. John Osborne (London: Verso, 1987).

29. Ibid., 178.

30. Ibid.

31. Edward W. Said, *Orientalism* (New York: Vintage, 1978), 12.

32. Robert Young, *White Mythologies: Writing History and the West* (London: Routledge, 1990), 140.

33. Walter Benjamin, "Eduard Fuchs, Collector and Historian," in *One-Way Street and Other Writings*, trans. Edmund Jephcott and Kingsley Shorter (London: Verso, 1985), 352.

34. Benita Parry, "Problems in Current Theories of Colonial Discourse," *Oxford Literary Review* 9, nos. 1–2 (1987): 35.

35. Mieke Bal, "The Rhetoric of Subjectivity," *Poetics Today* 5, no. 2 (1984): 337–76.

36. Antonio Gramsci, *Selections from the Prison Notebooks*, ed. and trans. Quintin Hoare and Geoffrey Nowell Smith (New York: International Publishers, 1985), 323–77.

37. Ibid., 330.

38. Ranajit Guha, ed., *Subaltern Studies: Writings on South Asian History and Society*, vols. 1–6 (New Delhi: Oxford University Press, 1982–89).

39. Ranajit Guha, "On Some Aspects of the Historiography of Colonial India," in *Selected Subaltern Studies*, ed. Ranajit Guha and Gayatri Chakravorty Spivak (New York: Oxford University Press, 1988), 1–12.

40. Commenting on the way her notion of "strategic essentialism" has been taken up, Spivak notes that "just as 'the personal is political' because, finally, in our personalist ideology, 'Only the personal is political,' in the same way, the strategic use of essentialism became a kind of carte blanche for being an essentialist when one wanted to be" ("Gayatri Spivak on the Politics of the Subaltern," interview by Howard Winant, *Socialist Review* 20, no. 3 [July–September 1990]: 93).

41. Gayatri Chakravorty Spivak, "Can the Subaltern Speak?" in *Marxism and the Interpretation of Culture*, ed. Cary Nelson and Lawrence Grossberg (Urbana: University of Illinois Press, 1988), 271–313.

42. This problem is also present in Gramsci's definition of popular philosophies as the expression of collective political action (*Selections from the Prison Notebooks*, 326–27).

43. "Naming Gayatri Spivak," interview by Maria Koundoura, *Stanford Humanities Review* 1, no. 1 (Spring 1989): 88–91.

44. Ibid., 89.

45. Geoffrey Moorhouse, *India Britannica* (London: Paladin Books, 1983), 144.

46. James Clifford and George Marcus, eds., *Writing Culture: The Poetics and Politics of Ethnography* (Berkeley: University of California Press, 1986); George Marcus and Michael Fischer, *Anthropology as Cultural Critique* (Chicago: University of Chicago Press, 1986); James Clifford, *The Predicament of Culture: Twentieth-Century Ethnography, Literature, and Art* (Cambridge, Mass.: Harvard University Press, 1988).

47. Thomas Babington Macaulay, "Indian Education: Minute of the 2nd. of February 1835," in *Macaulay: Prose and Poetry*, 722.

48. Gauri Viswanathan, *Masks of Conquest: Literary Study and British Rule in India* (New York: Columbia University Press, 1989).

49. Gramsci uses the term *common sense* for philosophical thinking that has since passed into popular use as the taken-for-granted assumptions of everyday or common language: "Every philosophical current leaves behind a sedimentation of 'common sense': this is the document of its historical effectiveness. Common sense is not something rigid and immobile, but is continually transforming itself, enriching itself with scientific ideas and with philosophical opinions which have entered ordinary life" (*Selections from the Prison Notebooks*, 326n).

50. Pierre Macherey, *The Theory of Literary Production*, trans. Geoffrey Wall (London: Routledge & Kegan Paul, 1978).

51. Said, *Orientalism*, 16.

52. My understanding of allegories of reading is from Paul de Man, *Allegories of Reading: Figural Language in Rousseau, Nietzsche, Rilke, and Proust* (New Haven, Conn.: Yale University Press, 1979), 76–77, 205, 247.

2. The Rise of Women in an Age of Progress: *Jane Eyre*

1. After the Emancipation Act went into effect on 1 August 1834, slavery was replaced by a four-year transitory system of apprenticeship that did not noticeably im-

prove the condition of the slaves. The emancipation date is thus more accurately represented as 1838.

2. Anthropos, *The Rights of Man (Not Paines) But the Rights of Man, in the West Indies* (London: Knight & Lacey, 1824), 40.

3. Ibid., 35.

4. *Patterns of Racism* (London: Institute of Race Relations, 1982), 26–27.

5. Charlotte Brontë, *Jane Eyre* (New York: Norton, 1971). All further references to this work, abbreviated *JE*, will be included in the text.

6. Kathleen Tillotson, *Novels of the Eighteen-Forties* (Oxford: Clarendon Press, 1954), 287.

7. Walter Benjamin, "Eduard Fuchs, Collector and Historian," in *One-Way Street and Other Writings*, trans. Edmund Jephcott and Kingsley Shorter (London: Verso, 1985), 351.

8. Gayatri Chakravorty Spivak, "Three Women's Texts and a Critique of Imperialism," in *"Race," Writing, and Difference*, ed. Henry Louis Gates, Jr. (Chicago: University of Chicago Press, 1986), 262–80.

9. May Ellis Gibson, "The Seraglio or Suttee: Brontë's *Jane Eyre*," *Postscript* 4 (1987): 1–8; Laura E. Donaldson, "The Miranda Complex: Colonialism and the Question of Feminist Reading," *Diacritics* 18, no. 3 (Fall 1988): 65–77; Susan L. Meyer, "Colonialism and the Figurative Strategy of *Jane Eyre*," *Victorian Studies* 3, no. 2 (Winter 1990): 247–68.

10. Spivak, "Three Women's Texts," 264. Spivak uses the term *individualist* to distinguish the epistemology of individualism from an ontology of the *individual* as an essential category of being.

11. Gibson, "The Seraglio or Suttee," 5.

12. Donaldson, "The Miranda Complex," 75.

13. Jacques Derrida, "White Mythology: Metaphor in the Text of Philosophy," in *Margins of Philosophy*, trans. Alan Bass (Chicago: University of Chicago Press, 1982), 207–71.

14. Meyer is more attentive to the tropological turns in the novel's colonial references. She sees a radical potential in Brontë's suggestion that white women share a common oppression with black slaves and Asian women. But she also unpacks a discursive strategy in which the novel displaces racial and sexual oppression onto dark-skinned races. Despite her care in distinguishing gender from racial hierarchies, however, Meyer presumes a unified field of otherness in which the color black represents all members of the colonies. Hence, she effaces the place of the white Jamaican as one who is neither English nor black, and she treats the West Indian and Asian woman as interchangeable figures of enslavement and/or resistance.

15. Paul de Man, *Allegories of Reading: Figural Language in Rousseau, Nietzsche, Rilke, and Proust* (New Haven, Conn.: Yale University Press, 1979), 163.

16. Patricia Meyer Spacks, *The Female Imagination* (New York: Alfred A. Knopf, 1975), 35.

17. Elaine Showalter, *A Literature of Their Own: British Women Novelists from Brontë to Lessing* (Princeton, N.J.: Princeton University Press, 1977), 112. Also see Patricia Beer, *Reader, I Married Him: A Study of the Women Characters of Jane Austen, Charlotte Brontë, Elizabeth Gaskell and George Eliot* (London: Macmillan, 1974); Spacks, *Female Imagination*; Ellen Moers, *Literary Women: The Great Writers* (Garden City, N.Y.: Doubleday, 1976); Sandra M. Gilbert and Susan Gubar, *The Madwoman in the Attic: The Woman Writer and the Nineteenth-Century Literary Imagination* (New Haven, Conn.: Yale University Press, 1980).

18. Sidonie Smith, *A Poetics of Women's Autobiography: Marginality and the Fictions of Self-Representation* (Bloomington: Indiana University Press, 1987).

19. For a poststructural critique of the autobiographical subject, see Michael Sprinker, "Fictions of the Self: The End of Autobiography," in *Autobiography: Essays Theoretical and Critical*, ed. James Olney (Princeton, N.J.: Princeton University Press, 1980), 321–42. Since Sprinker does not address the question of gender, a good supplement to his essay is Barbara Johnson, "My Monster/My Self," *Diacritics* 12, no. 2 (Summer 1982): 2–10. The following is a select list of recent studies of women's autobiography: Estelle C. Jelinek, ed., *The Tradition of Women's Autobiography: From Antiquity to the Present* (Boston: Twayne, 1986); Domna C. Stanton, ed., *The Female Autograph: Theory and Practice of Autobiography from the Tenth to the Twentieth Century* (Chicago: University of Chicago Press, 1987); Smith, *A Poetics of Women's Autobiography*; Bella Brodzki and Celeste Schenck, eds., *Life/Lines: Theorizing Women's Autobiography* (Ithaca, N.Y.: Cornell University Press, 1988); Shari Benstock, ed., *The Private Self: Theory and Practice of Women's Autobiographical Writings* (Bloomington: Indiana University Press, 1988); Carolyn G. Heilbrun, *Writing a Woman's Life* (New York: Norton, 1988); Felicity A. Nussbaum, *The Autobiographical Subject: Gender and Ideology in Eighteenth-Century England* (Baltimore: Johns Hopkins University Press, 1989); Holly Laird, ed., special issue entitled "Women Writing Autobiography," *Tulsa Studies in Women's Literature* 9, no. 1 (Spring 1990); Shari Benstock, "The Female Self Engendered: Autobiographical Writing and Theories of Selfhood," *Women's Studies* 20, no. 1 (1991): 5–14.

20. Brodzki and Schenck, *Life/Lines*, 1–2.

21. Paul de Man, "Autobiography as De-Facement," in *The Rhetoric of Romanticism* (New York: Columbia University Press, 1984), 70.

22. Nussbaum, *The Autobiographical Subject*, xii–xiii.

23. Ibid., 39.

24. Michel Foucault, *The History of Sexuality, Volume I: An Introduction*, trans. Robert Hurley (New York: Vintage Books, 1980), 62.

25. Jacques Derrida, *The Ear of the Other: Otobiography, Transference, Translation*, trans. Avital Ronell (New York: Schocken, 1985), 1–38, 49–53.

26. The term *gynocritics*, which designates a criticism centered on women's writing, was introduced by Elaine Showalter in "Toward a Feminist Poetics." The essay has been reprinted in *The New Feminist Criticism: Essays on Women, Literature, and Theory*, ed. Elaine Showalter (New York: Pantheon Books, 1985), 125–43. For a critique of the racial assumptions of gynocritics, see Susie Tharu and K. Lalita, eds., *Women Writing in India*, vol 1: *600 B.C. to the Early Twentieth Century* (New York: Feminist Press, 1991), 12–33.

27. Showalter, *A Literature of Their Own*, 106.

28. Peggy Kamuf, "Writing Like a Woman," in *Women and Language in Literature and Society*, ed. Sally McConnell-Ginet, Ruth Borker, and Nelly Furman (New York: Praeger, 1980), 284–99.

29. Ibid., 285–86.

30. Peggy Kamuf, *Signature Pieces: On the Institution of Authorship* (Ithaca, N.Y.: Cornell University Press, 1988), 13.

31. Nancy K. Miller, *Subject to Change: Reading Feminist Writing* (Ithaca, N.Y.: Cornell University Press, 1988), 67–76. This essay first appeared as "The Text's Heroine: A Feminist Critic and Her Fictions," *Diacritics* 12, no. 2 (Summer 1982): 48–53.

32. Ibid., 72.

33. Ibid., 106.

34. Nancy Armstrong, *Desire and Domestic Fiction: A Political History of the Novel* (Oxford: Oxford University Press, 1987), 28–58.

35. Ibid., 41.

36. Ibid., 42–43.

37. Mary Poovey, *Uneven Developments: The Ideological Work of Gender in Mid-Victorian England* (Chicago: University of Chicago Press, 1988), 125.

38. Thomas James Ewise, ed., *The Brontës: Their Lives, Friendships and Correspondence* (1933; reprint, Philadelphia: Porcupine Press), 1 November 1849, III: 31.

39. An unsigned review, *Era* 9 (14 November 1847), in *The Brontës: The Critical Heritage*, ed. Miriam Allott (London: Routledge & Kegan Paul, 1974), 79.

40. [G. H. Lewes], *Fraser's Magazine* 36 (December 1847): 686–95, in *The Brontës: The Critical Heritage*, 84, 85.

41. [Edwin Percy Whipple], "Novels of the Season," *North American Review* cxli (October 1848): 354–69; [James Lorimer], from an unsigned review, *North British Review* 11 (August 1849): 455–93, in *The Brontës: The Critical Heritage*, 98, 116.

42. The "edited by" was deleted in subsequent editions.

43. Armstrong, *Desire and Domestic Fiction*, 53.

44. Terry Eagleton, *Myths of Power: A Marxist Study of the Brontës* (London: Macmillan, 1975), 15–32; Helene Moglen, *Charlotte Brontë: The Self Conceived* (New York: Norton, 1976), 115–27; Gilbert and Gubar, *The Madwoman in the Attic*, 336–71.

45. In *Moral Imperium: Afro-Caribbeans and the Transformation of British Rule, 1776–1838* (Westport, Conn.: Greenwood Press, 1987), Ronald Kent Richardson explains abolitionism as a selective humanitarianism that emerged in response to slave rebellions, because they threatened Christianity and a Western system of values. The standard histories of West Indian slave rebellions are Eugene D. Genovese, *From Rebellion to Revolution: Afro-American Slave Revolts in the Making of the New World* (New York: Vintage, 1981), and Michael Craton, *Testing the Chains: Resistance to Slavery in the British West Indies* (Ithaca, N.Y.: Cornell University Press, 1982). For slave women's resistance, see Barbara Bush, *Slave Women in Caribbean Society, 1650–1838* (London: James Curry, 1990), 51–82, and Stella Dadzie, "Searching for the Invisible Woman: Slavery and Resistance in Jamaica," *Race and Class* 32, no. 2 (October–December 1990): 21–38. I have not had a chance to look at Moira Ferguson's *Subject to Others: British Women Writers and Colonial Slavery, 1670–1834* (New York: Routledge, 1992), which was published after I completed this manuscript.

46. For the popularity of the antislavery position in England, see Seymour Drescher, "Public Opinion and the Destruction of British Colonial Slavery," in *Slavery and British Society: 1776–1846*, ed. James Walvin (Baton Rouge: Louisiana State University Press, 1982), 22–48, and James Walvin, "The Public Campaign in England against Slavery, 1787–1834," in *The Abolition of the Atlantic Slave Trade: Origins and Effects in Europe, Africa, and the Americas*, ed. David Eltis and James Walvin (Madison: University of Wisconsin Press, 1981), 63–79. The antislavery issue was still current in the 1840s, as emancipation had not yet been achieved in the United States.

47. William Thompson, *Appeal of One-Half the Human Race, Women, against the Pretensions of the Other Half, Men, to Retain Them in Political and Thence in Civil and Domestic Slavery; in Reply to a Paragraph of Mr Mill's Celebrated "Article on Government"* (1825), 86, cited by Barbara Taylor, *Eve and the New Jerusalem: Socialism and Feminism in the Nineteenth Century* (New York: Pantheon, 1983), 35.

48. For a discussion of working-class hostility to abolitionism, see Patricia Hollis, "Anti-Slavery and British Working-Class Radicalism in the Years of Reform," in *Anti-Slavery, Religion, and Reform*, ed. Christine Bolt and Seymour Drescher (Hamden, Conn.: Archon, 1980), 294–315. By focusing on the post- rather than the pre-Emancipation period, Betty Fladeland makes the counterargument that the working class forged alliances with abolitionists. See " 'Our Cause being One and the

Same': Abolitionists and Chartism," in *Slavery and British Society, 1776–1846*, ed. Walvin, 69–99. For a reading of the worker/slave metaphor in the English industrial novel, see Catherine Gallagher, *The Industrial Reformation of English Fiction: Social Discourse and Narrative Form, 1832–1867* (Chicago: University of Chicago Press, 1985), ch. 1.

49. Anthropos, *The Rights of Man (Not Paines) But the Rights of Man, in the West Indies*, 14, 16.

50. Thomas Cooper, *Facts Illustrative of the Condition of the Negro Slaves in Jamaica* (London, 1824), 13, 14.

51. Franco Moretti, *The Way of the World: The Bildungsroman in European Culture* (London: Verso, 1987).

52. Gilbert and Gubar, *The Madwoman in the Attic*, 370.

53. For a discussion of women's negotiations within the doctrine of "woman's mission," see Barbara Taylor, *Eve and the New Jerusalem*, 123–30, and Leonore Davidoff and Catherine Hall, *Family Fortunes: Men and Women of the English Middle Class, 1780–1850* (Chicago: University of Chicago Press, 1987), 114–18, 180–88.

54. Sarah Lewis, *Woman's Mission* (New York: Wiley & Putnam, 1839), 14.

55. Ibid., 47.

56. Ibid., 49. Sarah Ellis makes a similar argument in *The Women of England, Their Social Duties, and Domestic Habits* (London: Fisher, 1838), 52–81.

57. The following list is by no means exhaustive: Showalter, *A Literature of Their Own*, 118–22; Maurianne Adams, *"Jane Eyre: Woman's Estate,"* in *The Authority of Experience: Essays in Feminist Criticism*, ed. Arlyn Diamond and Lee Edwards (Amherst: University of Massachusetts Press, 1977), 146; Barbara Hill Rigney, *Madness and Sexual Politics in the Feminist Novel: Studies in Brontë, Woolf, Lessing, and Atwood* (Madison: University of Wisconsin Press, 1978), 20–29; Marxist-Feminist Literary Collective, "Women's Writing: *Jane Eyre, Shirley, Villette, Aurora Leigh*," *Ideology and Consciousness*, 3 (Spring 1978): 34–35; Cora Kaplan, *Sea Changes: Culture and Feminism* (London: Verso, 1986), 171–74; Pat Macpherson, *Reflecting on Jane Eyre* (London: Routledge, 1989), 10–58.

58. Gilbert and Gubar, *The Madwoman in the Attic*, 359–60.

59. Meyer, "Colonialism and the Figurative Strategy," 252–59. With the exception of this important difference, my reading of West Indian slavery overlaps with that of Meyer. An earlier version of my conclusions, which I arrived at independently of her essay, appears in "Scenes of an Encounter: A Double Discourse of Colonialism and Nationalism" (Ph.D. diss., University of Texas at Austin, 1987), 94–127.

60. C. Duncan Rice, "Literary Sources and British Attitudes to Slavery," in *Anti-Slavery, Religion, and Reform*, ed. Bolt and Drescher, 328–29. Wylie Sypher quotes extensively from I. B. Moreton's *Manners and Customs in the West India Islands* (1790) for outlining the characteristic qualities of the creole "type": "The men, he says, are 'of a sickly, pale, yellowish complexion, meager, weak, and emaciated as to appearance'; yet they are 'open-hearted, generous, kind and hospitable to excess; proud, vain, high-spirited and flighty to an extreme; lazy, dull, and indolent . . . ; and volatile as air where drinking, whoring, gaming, or any kind of dissipation invites; so that their hearts and fortunes seldom agree.' Moreton declares that the creole gentleman keeps wenches until 'a day or two before . . . marriage,' and that one may see his 'white, mestee, quadroon, and mulatto children, all brothers and sisters, playing together.' He also disapproves of the creole girl; though many are 'prudent, chaste, and fine women,' they are generally lascivious and overdressed" ("The West-Indian as a 'Character' in the Eighteenth Century," *Studies in Philology* 36, no. 3 [July 1939]: 503–20). As a member of the Jamaican plantocracy, Edward Long describes "the native white men, or Creoles, of Jamaica" in decidedly more noble terms, as "lovers of

freedom, fond of social enjoyments, tender fathers, humane and indulgent masters" (*The History of Jamaica* , 3 vols. [London, 1774], 2: 261). For an etymology of *creole* in Jamaica, see Edward Brathwaite, *The Development of Creole Society in Jamaica, 1770–1820* (Oxford: Clarendon Press, 1971), xiv–xvi, and in the Americas, José Juan Arrom, *Certidumbre de America* (Madrid: Gredos, 1971), 11–26. Sir Walter Scott's characterization of George Staunton in *The Heart of Midlothian* (1818) ([London: Collins Classics, 1963], 313–14), is a good example of the Creole stereotype in nineteenth-century British literature: "The father of George Staunton had been bred a soldier, and, during service in the West Indies, had married the heiress of a wealthy planter. By this lady he had an only child, George Staunton, the unhappy young man who has been so often mentioned in this narrative. He passed the first part of his early youth under the charge of a doting mother, and in the society of negro slaves, whose study it was to gratify his every caprice.... When he was about ten years old, and when his mind had received all the seeds of those evil weeds which afterwards grew apace, his mother died, and his father, half-heart-broken, returned to England.... He took his son to reside with him at the rectory; but he soon found that his disorders rendered him an intolerable inmate. And as the young men of his own rank would not endure the purse-proud insolence of the Creole, he fell into that taste for low society, which is worse than 'pressing to death, whipping, or hanging.' " When read alongside Brontë's representation of the creole woman as the source of Bertha's madness, Scott's characterization of Staunton's mother as indulgent shows the emergent duty of English mothers to raise a superior race for nation and Empire.

61. Long, *The History of Jamaica*, 2: 321.

62. Denise Riley, *"Am I That Name?" Feminism and the Category of "Women" in History* (Minneapolis: University of Minnesota Press, 1988), 41. I. B. Schneewind describes how the ethical agency of the individual is contingent upon social and political structures; see "The Use of Autonomy in Ethical Theory," in *Reconstructing Individualism: Autonomy, Individuality, and the Self in Western Thought*, ed. Thomas Heller et al. (Stanford, Calif.: Stanford University Press, 1986), 64–75.

63. A public address given in the 1860s.

64. Elizabeth Missing Sewell, *Principles of Education, Drawn from Nature and Revelation, and Applied to Female Education in the Upper Classes* (London, 1865), II: 240, cited by M. Jeanne Peterson, "The Victorian Governess: Status, Incongruence in Family and Society," in *Suffer and Be Still: Women in the Victorian Age*, ed. Martha Vicinus (Bloomington: Indiana University Press, 1972), 9–10.

65. Poovey, *Uneven Developments*, 126–63.

66. William Wilson Hunter, "England's Work in India," in *The India of the Queen and Other Essays* (London: Longmans, Green, 1903), 127.

67. The following discussion of sati is based on Lata Mani's important essay, "The Production of an Official Discourse on Sati," in *Europe and Its Others*, 2 vols., ed. Francis Barker et al. (Colchester: University of Essex Press, 1985), 1: 107–27.

68. As Mani points out, an attention to agency is imperative for displacing a colonial construction of the widow as an object to be saved. She also issues the warning, however, that we treat First World and Third World feminist discourses as discontinuous. An insistence on the widow's agency could have detrimental effects in India, where "current legislation of sati, by making women attempting sati liable to punishment, implicitly conceives of them as 'free agents' " ("Multiple Mediations: Feminist Scholarship in the Age of Multinational Reception," *Feminist Review* 35 [July 1990]: 37–38).

69. Lata Mani, "Cultural Theory, Colonial Texts: Reading Eyewitness Accounts of Widow Burning," in *Cultural Studies*, ed. Lawrence Grossberg, Cary Nelson, and Paula Treichler (New York: Routledge, 1992), 397.

70. Parliamentary Papers on Hindu Widows (1825, xxiv, 243), cited by Mani, "The Production of an Official Discourse," 122.

71. Davidoff and Hall, *Family Fortunes*, 111–12.

72. C. Duncan Rice explains the emblematic value of Christian martrydom to the overseas missions: "Much of the tension created by commitment [to the missions] could be resolved by exposure to violence and suffering.... To risk martyrdom, real or imagined, was a fruitful means of releasing such tensions.... Livingstone's demise came to provide one of the most celebrated scenes in the Victorian iconography of death" ("The Missionary Context of the British Anti-Slavery Movement," in *Slavery and British Society*, 158).

73. Interestingly enough, a collector's wife, Fanny Parks, describes sati as the "grilling" of widows in her travel journal, *Wanderings of a Pilgrim in Search of the Picturesque*, 2 vols., reprint edition (1836; Karachi: Oxford University Press, 1975), 1: 162.

74. Carol Ohmann, "Historical Reality and 'Divine Appointment' in Charlotte Brontë's Fiction," *Signs* 2, no. 4 (1977): 757.

75. Spivak, "Three Women's Texts," 264.

3. The Civilizing Mission Disfigured

1. Virginia Woolf, *Mrs. Dalloway* (New York: Harcourt Brace Jovanovich, 1953), 271.

2. With the expansion and consolidation of British territories in the first half of the nineteenth century, the company governed under the fiction that it was the "protector" of the Mogul emperor at Delhi. As John Kaye explains, the sovereignty of the king of Delhi was a "political paradox" by which "he was to be a King, yet no King,—a something and yet a nothing—a reality and a sham at the same time" (John W. Kaye, *Kaye's and Malleson's History of the Indian Mutiny of 1857–8*, 6 vols., 2d ed. [London: Longmans, Green, 1898], 2: 4). The king maintained his sovereignty, if only in name, until the 1857 uprisings, when Bahadur Shah II attempted to restore the Mogul Empire. Following the defeat of the rebellion, he was charged with "not regarding his allegiance" as a British subject, and the royal family was subsequently exiled to Rangoon.

3. *Times*, 15 June 1857.

4. Editorial, *Times*, 23 June 1857. It is perhaps worth noting that the Irish supported the sepoys and criticized the British army for its attacks on the Indian peasantry. The *Times* makes a point of expressing its disapproval of the "foolish fanatics in Ireland who write Sepoy sentences, and paste Sepoy placards on walls and gateposts, calling upon Ireland to awake, and rise up, and 'give 3 cheers for old Ireland, and 3 more for the Sepoys'" (8 November 1857).

5. S. N. Mukherjee, "Class, Caste and Politics in Calcutta, 1815–38," in *Elites in South Asia*, ed. Edmund Leach and S. N. Mukherjee (Cambridge: Cambridge University Press, 1970), 33–78.

6. Alexander Duff, *The Indian Rebellion: Its Causes and Results* (London: James Nisbet, 1858), 54–55.

7. S. B. Chaudhuri vividly describes the participants in the 1857–58 rebellion in the opening to his *Theories of the Indian Mutiny (1857–59)* (Calcutta: World Press, 1965): "The villagers impeded the march of the British avenging army by withholding supplies and information which they freely gave to the rebel forces; wage earners vented their rage on the system of foreign exploitation by a wholesale destruction of the British-owned factories; the social destitutes to whom borrowing was the only

means of livelihood turned against the bankers, *mahajans* (capitalists) and usurers, the class protected by the British courts; the priests and prophets preached jehad against the *feringhis;* and other elements of society, not always amenable to law and order, broke out into uncontrollable fury, attacked police and revenue establishments, destroyed government records and court-buildings and telegraph poles, in fact everything which could remind them of the English" (1). Although he acknowledges the heterogeneity of the uprising, Chaudhuri discusses the rebellions in terms of the leadership of the landed class. Gautam Bhadra, writing against an elite Indian historiography, reconstructs the undocumented leadership of a small landlord, a peasant cultivator, a tribal youth, and a Maulvi (Muslim religious scholar). See his "Four Rebels of Eighteen-Fifty-Seven," in *Selected Subaltern Studies*, ed. Ranajit Guha and Gayatri Chakravorty Spivak (New York: Oxford University Press, 1988), 129–75.

8. Ranajit Guha, *Elementary Aspects of Peasant Insurgency in Colonial India* (Delhi: Oxford University Press, 1983), 259. My account of the 1857 uprisings relies heavily on this work.

9. Ibid., 255–60.

10. "Eating the Company's salt" was a figure of speech that expressed the contractual relationship of the sepoy's loyal service in exchange for fair treatment from the British.

11. The threat of an alliance is evident in the following letter from Governor-General Canning to the president of the Board of Control, dated 21 November 1857: "If we destroy or desecrate Mussalman Mosques or Brahmin temples we do exactly what is wanting to band the two antagonist *races* against ourselves. . . . As we must rule 150 million people by a handful (more or less small) of Englishmen, let us do it in the manner best calculated to leave them divided (as in religion and national feeling they already are) and to inspire them with the greatest possible awe of our power and with the least possible suspicion of our motives." Cited by Peter Hardy, *The Muslims of British India* (London: Cambridge University Press, 1972), 72.

12. For the significance of religious discourse to peasant mobilization, see Ranajit Guha, "The Prose of Counter-Insurgency," in *Subaltern Studies II: Writings on South Asian History and Society*, ed. Ranajit Guha (Delhi: Oxford University Press, 1983), 34–38.

13. Christopher Hibbert, *The Great Mutiny, India 1857* (London: Penguin, 1980), 79, 82, 85.

14. Pat Barr, *The Memsahibs: The Women of Victorian India* (London: Secker & Warburg, 1976), 143.

15. Sir George Campbell, *Memoirs of My Indian Career*, vol. 1, ed. Sir Charles E. Bernard (London: Macmillan, 1893), 400.

16. *News of the World*, 19 July 1857.

17. See the Appendix for a listing of the English women's Mutiny writings on which I base my discussion.

18. Honoria Lawrence reports that thirty was a modest number of servants in *The Journals of Honoria Lawrence: India Observed 1837–1854*, ed. John Lawrence and Audrey Woodiwiss (London: Hodder & Stoughton, 1980), 42.

19. R. M. Coopland, *A Lady's Escape from Gwalior and Life in the Fort of Agra during the Mutinies of 1857* (London: Smith, Elder, 1859), 110.

20. Thomas Babington Macaulay, "Government of India: A Speech Delivered in the House of Commons on the 10th of July, 1833," in *Macaulay: Prose and Poetry*, ed. G. M. Young (London: Rupert Hart-Davis, 1952), 699.

21. A. R. Desai, *Peasant Struggles in India* (Bombay: Oxford University Press, 1979); Guha, *Elementary Aspects*.

22. Coopland, *A Lady's Escape from Gwalior*, 107–8.

23. Barr, *The Memsahibs*, 113.

24. Kaye, *Kaye's and Malleson's History of the Indian Mutiny of 1857–8*, 2: 299. The famous war correspondent William Howard Russell records in his diary: "I have been very anxious to find out all particulars about the Cawnpore massacre; but as yet all is obscure.... One fact is clearly established; that the writing behind the door, on the walls of the slaughterhouse, on which so much stress was laid in Calcutta, did not exist when Havelock entered the place, and therefore was not the work of any of the poor victims. It has excited many men to fury—the cry has gone all over India" (*My Diary in India*, vol. 1 [London, 1860], 191).

25. John W. Kaye, *A History of the Sepoy War in India 1857–58*, vol. 2, rev. ed. (London: W. H. Allen, 1876), 354.

26. Versions of the following excerpt from a letter that was originally published in the *Times* reappeared in speeches and popular histories: "After we stormed and entered Delhi, we saw a poor woman crucified naked, and nailed up in the same manner as our Lord and Saviour is represented" (April 1858). Cited by Edward Leckey, *Fictions Connected with the Outbreak of 1857 Exposed* (Bombay: Chesson & Woodhall, 1858), 115.

27. *News of the World*, 30 June 1857.

28. Monique Plaza, "Our Damages and Their Compensation, Rape: The Will Not to Know of Michel Foucault," *Feminist Issues* 1 (Summer 1981): 27.

29. *Times*, 25 August 1857.

30. Karl Marx, *On Colonialism and Modernization*, ed. Shlomo Avineri (Garden City, N.Y.: Anchor, 1969), 226.

31. Leckey, *Fictions Connected with the Outbreak of 1857 Exposed*, xvi.

32. Plaza, "Our Damages and Their Compensation, Rape," 29.

33. Elizabeth Cowie, "Woman as Sign," *m/f* 1 (1978): 49–63.

34. Colin Campbell, *Narrative of the Indian Revolt from Its Outbreak to the Capture of Lucknow* (London: George Victers, 1858), 20.

35. Miss Wagentreiber, *The Story of Our Escape from Delhi in May, 1857* (Delhi: Imperial Medical Hall Press, 1894), 12–13.

36. Helen Mackenzie, *Life in the Mission, the Camp and the Zenana; or, Six Years in India*, vol. 1 (London: Richard Bentley, 1853), 353.

37. *The History of the Indian Revolt and of the Expeditions to Persia, China, and Japan 1856–7–8* (London: Chambers, 1859), 139–40. The statements of the British spy, Myoor Tewaree, and the ayah, Marian, who both claimed to have witnessed the events, are included in N. A. Chick, *Annals of the Indian Rebellion 1857–58*, ed. David Hutchinson (Calcutta, 1859–60; reprint, London: Charles Knight, 1974), 178–84.

38. G. O. Trevelyan, *Cawnpore* (London: Macmillan, 1865), 254–55. It was also reported that Miss Wheeler was seen riding with the mutineers on an English sidesaddle obtained for her by the sowar who had abducted her. See Montgomery R. Martin, *The Indian Empire*, vol. 2 (London, 1858–61), 263, and Leckey, *Fictions Connected with the Outbreak of 1857 Exposed*, 113.

39. Hibbert, *The Great Mutiny*, 195.

40. Chick, *Annals of the Indian Rebellion*, 189.

41. Amelia Horne, "Miss Amy Haine's Narrative," MSS 41488, ff. 53–95. (British Museum Library, London).

42. Trevelyan, *Cawnpore*, 255.

43. The following disclaimer in *The History of the Indian Revolt and of the Expeditions to Persia, China, and Japan 1856–7–8*, 311, is paradigmatic of this type of denial: "One thing, however, the British soldiers did *not* do; they did not murder

women and children. This humanity, heroism, justice, or whatever it may best be called, was more than the natives generally expected: the leaders in the revolt had sedulously disseminated a rumour that the British would abuse all the women, and murder them and their children" (emphasis in original).

44. *News of the World*, 22 November 1857.

45. See, for instance, Catharine A. MacKinnon, "Feminism, Marxism, Method, and the State: Toward Feminist Jurisprudence," *Signs* 8, no. 4 (Summer 1983): 635–58. MacKinnon sums up her position in the following statement: "To be rap*able*, a position which is social, not biological, defines what a woman *is*" (651).

46. For a study of the Rani as a heroic figure in Indian literature, see Joyce Lebra-Chapman, *The Rani of Jhansi: A Study in Female Heroism in India* (Honolulu: University of Hawaii Press, 1986).

47. *Times*, 16 October 1885, cited by An Indian Student, *India, Before and After the Mutiny* (Edinburgh: Livingstone, 1886), 40.

48. *Bombay Times*, 31 March 1858, cited by Leckey, *Fictions Connected with the Outbreak of 1857 Exposed*, 171–72.

49. Hibbert, *The Great Mutiny*, 209–10.

50. Campbell, *Memoirs of My Indian Career*, 231.

51. In *English Historical Writings on the Indian Mutiny, 1857–1859* (Calcutta: World Press, 1979), S. B. Chaudhuri documents how colonial historiography records British acts of violence as the retribution for massacres that chronologically occurred later (106–7).

52. Cited by Francis Cornwallis Maude, *Memories of the Mutiny, with Which Is Incorporated the Personal Narration of John Walter Sherer*, 2 vols. (London: Remington, 1894), 1: 71.

53. Cited by Hibbert, *The Great Mutiny*, 210.

54. Maude, *Memories of the Mutiny, 1: 70*.

55. *Board's Collection* 2714 (195690): To the Court of Directors from the Government of Bengal; Fort Williams, 19 October 1857 (India Office Library, London).

56. Chick, *Annals of the Indian Rebellion*, 173.

57. Michel Foucault, *Discipline and Punish: The Birth of the Prison*, trans. Alan Sheridan (New York: Vintage, 1979), 14. With the disappearance of public execution, the power to punish is hidden and anonymous, whereas it was once manifest in the person of the king, dispersed throughout society rather than attached to the crime. The body is an instrument of correction, whereas it was once a ledger of pain, and the crime now faceless instead of being displayed upon the tortured body of the criminal. In short, the technologies of modern surveillance and self-control (which find their ideal form in Bentham's Panopticon) constitute a code of normalization that produces docile bodies for a disciplinary society.

58. Ibid., 16.

59. For a brief discussion of the Panopticon prison in India, see Eric Stokes, *The English Utilitarians and India* (Oxford: Clarendon Press, 1959), 149–50; 325.

60. Foucault, *Discipline and Punish*, 50.

61. See the pamphlet *By Authority! A Full Exposure of All the Horrible Tortures Inflicted on the Natives of India, by Officers of the East India Company* (London: C. Elliot, n.d.), which was published in response to the "Investigation of Alleged Cases of Torture," 16 April 1855. In January 1856, the Madras Native Association expressed its dissatisfaction with the offical report on torture in Madras. "The origin of this coercion," write the petitioners, "is not with the physical perpetrators of it, but descends to them from the officials immediately their superiors, which latter again are answerable for the estimated amount of the collection to their European superiors, these are also

being responsible on the same head to the highest authority of the Government." Cited by Marx, *On Colonialism and Modernization*, 230.

62. Ranajit Guha, "Dominance without Hegemony and Its Historiography," in *Subaltern Studies VI: Writings on South Asian History and Society*, ed. Ranajit Guha (Delhi: Oxford University Press, 1989), 238.

63. Ibid., 234–37.

64. The Permanent Settlement was a politically motivated reform to ensure the allegiance of a wealthy class of Hindus by making them the proprietors (*zamindars*) of rural land for which there was no precedent of entitlement.

65. Rhoda Reddock, "Freedom Denied: Indian Women and Indentureship in Trinidad and Tobago, 1845–1917," *Economic and Political Weekly* 20, no. 43 (26 October 1985): WS 79–87; Narendra K. Sinha, *The Economic History of Bengal, 1793–1848*, vol. 3 (Calcutta: Firma K. L. Mukhopadhyay, 1970), 31.

66. Bernard S. Cohn, "Representing Authority in Victoria India," in *The Invention of Tradition*, ed. Eric Hobsbawm and Terence Ranger (Cambridge: Cambridge University Press, 1984), 165–209.

67. *Board's Collection* 2714 (195701): Petition of the British Inhabitants of Calcutta to the Lords and Commons of Great Britain and Ireland in Parliament Assembled, 3 August 1857 (India Office Library, London).

4. The Rise of Memsahibs in an Age of Empire: *On the Face of the Waters*

1. Inscription on the well at Cawnpore, cited by Vincent Smith, *The Oxford History of India*, 2d ed. (Oxford: Clarendon Press, 1923), 719. The plaque was removed along with other colonial historical markers after Indian independence.

2. "The Indian Mutiny in Fiction," *Blackwood's Edinburgh Magazine* 161 (February 1897): 218.

3. For an annotated biobliography of Mutiny writings in English, see Janice M. Ladendorf, *The Revolt in India, 1857–58* (Zug: Inter Documentation, 1966); and for one on Mutiny fiction, see Brijen K. Gupta, *India in English Fiction, 1800–1970: An Annotated Bibliography* (Metuchen, N.J.: Scarecrow, 1973). Shailendra Dhari Singh reviews fifty Mutiny novels in his *Novels on the Indian Mutiny* (Delhi: Arnold-Heinemann, 1980).

4. James Grant, *First Love and Last Love: A Tale of the Indian Mutiny* (1868; London: Routledge, 1887), 165.

5. *Maurice Dering; or, The Quadrilateral*, by the author of "Guy Livingstone" (New York: Harper, 1864), 108.

6. Louis Tracy, *The Red Year, a Story of the Indian Mutiny* (London: White, 1908), and Charles E. Pearce, *Red Revenge: A Romance of Cawnpore* (London: Stanley Paul, 1909).

7. Fredric Jameson, "Criticism in History," *The Ideologies of Theory*, vol. 1 (Minneapolis: University of Minnesota Press, 1988), 125.

8. Flora Annie Steel, *The Garden of Fidelity* (London: Macmillan, 1929), 15.

9. Flora Annie Steel, *On the Face of the Waters: A Tale of the Mutiny* (New York: Macmillan, 1911). All further references to this work, abbreviated *OFW*, will be included in the text.

10. Steel, *The Garden of Fidelity*, 226–29; Daya Patwardhan, *A Star of India: Flora Annie Steel, Her Works and Times* (Poona: Lokasangraha Press, 1963); Violet Powell, *Flora Annie Steel: Novelist of India* (London: Heinemann, 1981), 77–81.

11. Steel, *The Garden of Fidelity*, 203–12.

12. Ibid., 228.

13. "The Indian Mutiny in Fiction," 229.

14. Mrinalini Sinha, " 'Chathams, Pitts and Gladstones in Petticoats': The Politics of Gender and Race in the Ilbert Bill Controversy, 1883–84," in *Western Women and Imperialism: Complicity and Resistance*, ed. Nupur Chaudhuri and Margaret Strobel (Bloomington: Indiana University Press, 1992).

15. Ronald Hyam, *Britain's Imperial Century, 1815–1914: A Study of Empire and Expansion* (London: B. T. Batsford, 1976), 233.

16. Margaret MacMillan, *Women of the Raj* (London: Thames & Hudson, 1988), 221–22.

17. *Pioneer*, 3 March 1883.

18. These letters are cited in Edwin Hirschmann, *"White Mutiny": The Ilbert Bill Crisis in India and Genesis of the Indian National Congress* (New Delhi: Heritage Publishers, 1980), 142–43.

19. Annette Ackroyd Beveridge, "A Lady's View of Mr. Ilbert's Bill," *Englishman*, 6 March 1883.

20. For a discussion of Annette Ackroyd Beveridge's involvement in the Bengali social reform movement, see Meredith Borthwick, *The Changing Role of Women in Bengal 1849–1905* (Princeton, N.J.: Princeton University Press, 1984), 88–92; Barbara N. Ramusack, "Cultural Missionaries, Maternal Imperialists, Feminist Allies: British Women Activists in India, 1865–1945," *Women's Studies International Forum* 13, no. 4 (Winter 1990): 309–21; and Vron Ware, *Beyond the Pale* (London: Verso, 1992), ch. 3.

21. Annette Ackroyd Beveridge, cited in Lord Beveridge, *India Called Them* (London: George Allen & Unwin, 1947), 90.

22. Hilary Callan and Shirley Ardener, eds., *The Incorporated Wife* (London: Croom Helm, 1984).

23. In the army, the term *memsahib* was used for officers' wives alone, with soldiers' wives being referred to as *women*.

24. Wilfred Scawen Blunt, *Ideas about India* (London: Kegan Paul, Trench, 1885), 47.

25. Margaret Strobel, *European Women and the Second British Empire* (Bloomington: Indiana University Press, 1991), 1–15. An earlier version of her argument appears in "Gender and Race in the Nineteenth- and Twentieth-Century British Empire," *Becoming Visible: Women in European History*, 2d ed., ed. Renate Bridenthal et al. (Boston: Houghton Mifflin, 1987), 375–96.

26. The following excerpt from an official document shows how an increasingly large Eurasian population presented a problem for the racial division on which the company's hiring policy was based: "The next object of consideration is the offspring of a connection between a European and a half caste. . . . The Candidates for admission to the Company's service who have been of this class of persons, have since 1791 been subjected to the examination of one of the Committees of the Direction; and if they have exhibited signs of Native origin in their colour or otherwise, have been accepted or rejected by the Committee according to the degree in which their hue appeared objectionable or unobjectionable. These rejections . . . have produced some anomalies. One Brother has been accepted, another rejected. Europeans whose parents were both European, have been on the brink of Rejection for their dark complexion." Cited by Gayatri Chakravorty Spivak, "Imperialism and Sexual Difference," *Oxford Literary Review* 8, nos. 1–2 (1986): 236.

27. For a particularly insightful discussion of the part domesticity played in "imperial designs," see Mary Poovey's chapter on the social construction of Florence Nightingale in *Uneven Developments: The Ideological Work of Gender in Mid-Victorian England* (Chicago: University of Chicago Press, 1988), 164–98.

28. Flora Annie Steel and Grace Gardiner, *The Complete Indian Housekeeper and Cook* (1888; rev. ed. London: Heinemann, 1898), 9.

29. Beverley Gartrell, "Colonial Wives: Villians or Victims?" in Callan and Ardener, *The Incorporated Wife*, 165–85; Janice Brownfoot, "Memsahibs in Colonial Malaya: A Study of European Wives in a British Colony and Protectorate, 1900–1940" in Callan and Ardener, *The Incorporated Wife*, 186–210; and Claudia Knapman, *White Women in Fiji, 1835–1930: The Ruin of Empire?* (Sydney: Allen & Unwin, 1986).

30. Helen Callaway, *Gender, Culture and Empire: European Women in Colonial Nigeria* (Urbana: University of Illinois Press, 1987); Mary Ann Lind, *The Compassionate Memsahibs: Welfare Activities of British Women in India, 1900–1947* (New York: Greenwood Press, 1988); Nupur Chaudhuri, "Memsahibs and Motherhood in Nineteenth-Century Colonial India," *Victorian Studies* 31, no. 4 (Summer 1988): 517–35; Ramusack, "Cultural Missionaries, Maternal Imperialists, Feminist Allies"; Chilla Bulbeck, "New Histories of the Memsahib and Missus: The Case of Papua New Guinea," *Journal of Women's History* 3, no. 2 (Fall 1991): 82–105.

31. Callaway, *Gender, Culture and Empire*, 243–44.

32. Jane Haggis, "Gendering Colonialism or Colonising Gender? Recent Women's Studies Approaches to White Women and the History of British Colonialism," *Women's Studies International Forum* 13, nos. 1/2 (1990): 113. Haggis primarily reviews Knapman and Callaway.

33. Antoinette M. Burton, "The White Woman's Burden: British Feminists and the Indian Woman, 1865–1915," *Women's Studies International Forum* 13, no. 4 (Winter 1990): 295. Also see her essay "The Feminist Quest for Identity: British Imperial Suffragism and 'Global Sisterhood,' 1900–1915," *Journal of Women's History* 3, no. 2 (Fall 1991): 46–81, and Ware, *Beyond the Pale*.

34. Geraldine H. Forbes, "In Search of the 'Pure Heathen': Missionary Women in Nineteenth-Century India," *Economic and Political Weekly* 21, no. 17 (26 April 1986): WS 2–8, and Janaki Nair, "Uncovering the Zenana: Visions of Indian Womanhood in Englishwomen's Writings, 1813–1940," *Journal of Women's History* 2, no. 1 (Spring 1990), 8–34.

35. Forbes, "In Search of the 'Pure Heathen.'"

36. J. E. Dawson, "Woman in India: Her Influence and Position" and "The Englishwoman in India: Her Influence and Responsibilities," *Calcutta Review* 83, no. 167 (October 1886): 347–70. All further references to this work, abbreviated *WI*, will be included in the text. Although the author's gender cannot be established with any certainty, the women's issues raised in this and other essays published under the same name have led me to conclude that Dawson is a woman.

37. Pat Barr, *The Memsahibs: The Women of Victorian India* (London: Secker & Warburg, 1976), 197.

38. G. A. Henty, *Rujub the Juggler* (London: Chatto & Windus, 1893), 300.

39. "The Indian Mutiny in Fiction," 226.

40. Bithia Mary Croker, *Mr. Jervis: A Romance of the Indian Hills* (Philadelphia: Lippincott, 1895), 230.

41. The famous general that Steel admires in her work was known for his obsessive desire to pass a bill that would rank the punishment of rebels according to the severity of each crime. See Christopher Hibbert, *The Great Mutiny, India 1857* (London: Penguin, 1980), 293–94.

42. Lieutenant Hodson, who headed the Department of Intelligence during the Mutiny, has been described both as "a free lance of the Middle Ages" and as "the most notorious looter in the whole army." See George B. Malleson, *Kaye's and Malleson's History of the Indian Mutiny of 1857–8*, 6 vols., 2d ed. (London: Longmans, Green, 1898), 5: 52. The reference in Steel's novel is to the report made by Hodson's second-

in-command, Lieutenant MacDowell. According to MacDowell, Hodson ordered the princes to strip naked and shot them after they had laid down their arms and surrendered. A complete description of the incident appears in Hibbert, *The Great Mutiny*, 315–17.

43. For a discussion of the orthodox Hindu position on sati, see Gayatri Chakravorty Spivak, "Can the Subaltern Speak?" in *Marxism and the Interpretation of Culture*, ed. Cary Nelson and Lawrence Grossberg (Urbana: University of Illinois Press, 1988), 294–308, and Lata Mani, "Contentious Traditions: The Debate on *Sati* in Colonial India," in *Recasting Women: Essays in Colonial History*, ed. Kumkum Sangari and Sudesh Vaid (Delhi: Kali for Women, 1989), 106–9.

44. Spivak, "Can the Subaltern Speak?" 303.

45. Jean Rhys, whose own mother was a creole, writes: "When I read *Jane Eyre* as a child, I thought, why should she think Creole women are lunatics and all that? What a shame to make Rochester's first wife, Bertha, the awful madwoman, and I immediately thought I'd write the story as it might really have been. She seemed such a poor ghost. I thought I'd try to write her a life" (Elizabeth Vreeland, "Jean Rhys: The Art of Fiction LXIV," Interview, *Paris Review* 76 [1979]: 235). Rhys's response was her novel *Wide Sargasso Sea* (1966), which tells the story of Bertha Mason prior to her arrival in England. The ending of Rhys's novel shatters the spectacle of death in *Jane Eyre* by fracturing it with fragments of a West Indian past. Cutting back and forth between Bertha's dream of the death scene from *Jane Eyre* and her memories of Jamaica, Rhys ends the story with Bertha's beginning her ascent to the roof—at which point she is brought into Brontë's novel. By giving the creole woman a West Indian history, Rhys explains her suicide as something other than an unconscious act of madness or conscious taking of her life. I am interested in seeing if there is a similar explanation for Tara Devi's death to be derived from Steel's fiction?

46. For a description of *sat*, see K. Sangari and S. Vaid, "Sati in Modern India: A Report," *Economic and Political Weekly* 16, no. 3 (1 August 1981): 1286.

47. Rajeswari Sunder Rajan, "The Subject of Sati: Pain and Death in the Contemporary Discourse on Sati," *Yale Journal of Criticism* 3, no. 2 (Spring 1990): 15.

48. Uma Chakravarti, "Whatever Happened to the Vedic *Dasi*? Orientalism, Nationalism and a Script for the Past," in *Recasting Women: Essays in Colonial History*, ed. Sangari and Vaid, 71.

49. Patwardhan, *A Star of India*, 34.

50. *Saturday Review* (28 November 1896): 569.

51. Rajan, "The Subject of Sati," 17.

5. The Unspeakable Limits of Civility: *A Passage to India*

1. For a documentation of the battle over the meaning of 1857, see Ainslie Embree, ed., *1857 in India: Mutiny or War of Independence?* (Boston: Heath, 1963).

2. Vinayak D. Savarkar, *The Indian War of Independence: 1857* (Bombay: Phoenix, 1947).

3. Allen J. Greenberger, *The British Image of India: A Study in the Literature of Imperialism 1880–1960* (London: Oxford University Press, 1969).

4. Cited by Correlli Barnett, *The Collapse of British Power* (London: Eyre Methuen, 1972), 76.

5. *Report of the Committee Appointed by the Government of India to Investigate the Disturbances in the Punjab, etc.* (London, 1920), 112.

6. Derek Sayer, "British Reaction to the Amritsar Massacre, 1919–1920," *Past and Present* 131 (May 1991): 132.

7. Michael O'Dwyer, *India As I Knew It, 1885–1925* (London: Constable, 1925), 263–317.

8. For descriptions of these and other forms of punishment that were administered under martial law, see the *Report of the Committee*, 83–86.

9. *Times*, 15 December 1919.

10. "Amritsar, by an Englishwoman," *Blackwood's Magazine* 207 (April 1920): 446.

11. Sayer, "British Reaction to the Amritsar Massacre, 1919–1920," 158; Margaret MacMillan, *Women of the Raj* (London: Thames & Hudson, 1988), 226.

12. Edward Thompson, *The Other Side of the Medal* (London: Hogarth Press, 1925), 95. All further references to this work, abbreviated *OS*, will be included in the text. Thompson, whose writings include novels and histories on India, served as an educational missionary in Bengal. He resigned from the ministry upon his return to England in 1923 and for the next ten years taught Bengali at Oxford. His son is the well-known cultural Marxist and pacifist E. P. Thompson.

13. Vincent Smith, *The Oxford History of India*, 2d ed. (Oxford: Clarendon Press, 1923), 723.

14. *Report of the Committee*, 53; O'Dwyer, *India As I Knew It, 1885–1925*, 291–92. Also see MacMillan, *Women of the Raj*, 225.

15. "Notes on the English Character" (1920), in *Abinger Harvest* (London: Edward Arnold, 1936), 13.

16. Forster's outline for the 1912–13 manuscript reads as follows:

> Aziz & Janet [Adela's name in the early manuscript] drift into one another's arms —then apart, \Marriage impossible./ She—theoretically—immoral: he practically, but believes it impossible with an Englishwoman. \She is ugly./ Discovers she loves him—less offensive\than Englishmen/ . . .
>
> A's Horror of falling in love with Englishwomen—not due to natural reverence but since they could be only obtained on terms of marriage which is impossible & since of purity of blood.

Oliver Stallybrass, *The Manuscripts of* A Passage to India (New York: Holmes & Meier, 1978), 580.

17. E. M. Forster, *The Hill of Devi* (New York: Harcourt, Brace, 1953), 238. For readings of *A Passage to India* as a commentary on the political instability of the 1920s, see Jeffrey Meyers, *Fiction and the Colonial Experience* (Totowa, N.J.: Rowman & Littlefield, 1973), 29–53; Molly Mahood, *The Colonial Encounter: A Reading of Six Novels* (London: Rex Collings, 1977), 65–91; Hunt Hawkins, "Forster's Critique of Imperialism in *A Passage to India*," *South Atlantic Review* 48, no. 1 (1983): 54–65; Frances B. Singh, "*A Passage to India*, the National Movement, and Independence," *Twentieth Century Literature* 35, nos. 2/3 (Summer/Fall 1985): 265–78.

18. G. K. Das maps the fictional events onto historical ones in *E. M. Forster's India* (London: Methuen, 1977), 46–54.

19. E. M. Forster, *A Passage to India* (New York: Harcourt Brace Jovanovich, 1952). All further references to this work, abbreviated *PI*, will be included in the text.

20. The following select list gives some indication of the pervasiveness of the explanation that the accusation of rape is the product of a sexually repressed woman's imagination: Louise Dauner, "What Happened in the Cave? Reflections on *A Passage to India*," in *Perspectives on E. M. Forster's A Passage to India*, ed. V. A. Shahane (New York: Barnes, 1968), 51–64; Benita Parry, *Delusions and Discoveries: Studies on India in the British Imagination* (London: Allen Lane, 1972), 294–95; Barbara Rosencrance, *Forster's Narrative Vision* (Ithaca, N.Y.: Cornell University Press, 1982), 207; Abdul R.

JanMohamed, "The Economy of Manichean Allegory: The Function of Racial Difference in Colonialist Literature," in *"Race," Writing and Difference*, ed. Henry Louis Gates, Jr. (Chicago: University of Chicago Press, 1986), 94–95; David Rubin, *After the Raj: British Novels of India Since 1947* (Hanover: University Press of New England, 1986), 66; Sara Suleri, "The Geography of *A Passage to India*," in E. M. Forster's *A Passage to India*, ed. Harold Bloom (New York: Chelsea House, 1987), 109–10.

21. Elaine Showalter, *"A Passage to India* as 'Marriage Fiction': Forster's Sexual Politics," *Women & Literature* 5, no. 2 (1977): 3–16.

22. Brenda Silver, "Periphrasis, Power, and Rape in *A Passage to India*," *Novel* 22 (Fall 1988): 100. A shorter version of this essay appears in *Rape and Representation*, ed. Lynn A. Higgins and Brenda R. Silver (New York: Columbia University Press, 1991), 115–37.

23. Showalter, *"A Passage to India* as 'Marriage Fiction,' " 6.

24. Paul de Man, "Crisis and Criticism," *Blindness and Insight: Essays in the Rhetoric of Contemporary Criticism*, 2d ed. (Minneapolis: University of Minnesota Press, 1983), 8.

25. *The Manuscripts of* A Passage to India, 242–43.

26. Silver, "Periphrasis, Power, and Rape," 86; Frances Restuccia, " 'A Cave of My Own': The Sexual Politics of Indeterminacy," *Raritan* 9, no.2 (Fall 1989): 117.

27. Silver, "Periphrasis, Power, and Rape," 97–98.

28. Stuart Hall, "Race, Articulation and Societies Structured in Dominance," *UNESCO, Sociological Theories: Race and Colonialism* (Paris: UNESCO Press, 1980), 336.

29. Eugene Genovese, *Roll, Jordan, Roll: The World the Slaves Made* (New York: Vintage, 1976), 462.

30. Ida B. Wells-Barnett, *On Lynchings: Southern Horrors, A Red Record, Mob Rule in New Orleans* (reprint Salem, N.H.: Ayer, 1987).

31. Angela Davis, *Women, Race and Class* (New York: Random House, 1981), ch. 11; Jacqueline Dowd Hall, *Revolt against Chivalry: Jessie Daniel Ames and the Women's Campaign against Lynching* (New York: Columbia University Press, 1979), ch. 5, and Hall, " 'The Mind That Burns in Each Body': Women, Race, and Racial Violence," in *Powers of Desire: The Politics of Sexuality*, ed. Ann Snitow, Christine Stansell, and Sharon Thompson (New York: Monthly Review, 1983), 328–49; Hazel V. Carby, " 'On the Threshold of Woman's Era': Lynching, Empire, and Sexuality in Black Feminist Theory," in Gates, *"Race," Writing and Difference*, 301–16.

32. Silver, "Periphrasis, Power, and Rape," 97; Restuccia, " 'A Cave of My Own,' " 114, also suggests that Aziz is "raped" by British imperialism.

33. Silver, "Periphrasis, Power, and Rape," 88.

34. Ibid., 104–5.

35. Geraldine Forbes, "Caged Tigers: 'First Wave' Feminists in India," *Women's Studies International Forum* 5, no. 6 (1982): 525–36; Joanna Liddle and Rama Joshi, "Gender and Imperialism in British India," *South Asia Research* 5, no. 2 (November 1985): 147–65, and Liddle and Joshi, *Daughters of Independence: Gender, Caste and Class in India* (New Brunswick, N.J.: Rutgers University Press, 1986); Romila Thapar, "The History of Female Emancipation in Southern Asia," in *Women in the New Asia: The Changing Social Roles of Men and Women in South and South-East Asia*, ed. Barbara E. Ward (Paris: UNESCO, 1968), 473–99.

36. Meyers, *Fiction and the Colonial Experience*, 35, for example, commends Forster for "expertly portray[ing] the Indians speaking to each other in the vernacular and to the British in colloquial Indianized English."

37. Barbara Joshi, ed., *Untouchable! Voices of the Dalit Liberation Movement* (London: Zed Books, 1986), 1–14. The contradictions in Gandhi's political thought are

best understood in terms of Partha Chatterjee's distinction between Gandhi the man, who held moral beliefs that were fundamentally at odds with nationalism, and Gandhism the movement, which involved "the political appropriation of the subaltern classes by a bourgeoisie aspiring for hegemony in the new nation-state" (*Nationalist Thought and the Colonial World: A Derivative Discourse* [London: Zed Books, 1986], 100). Today, militant untouchables call themselves *dalits*, a name that includes "members of Scheduled Castes and Tribes, neo-Buddhists, the working people, the landless and poor peasants, women and all those who are being exploited politically, economically and in the name of religion" ("Dalit Panthers Manifesto" [Bombay, 1973], in Joshi, ed., *Untouchable! Voices of the Dalit Liberation Movement*, 145).

38. Jacques Derrida, *Of Grammatology*, trans. Gayatri Chakravorty Spivak (Baltimore: Johns Hopkins University Press, 1978), 157–64.

39. Steve Neale, "Masculinity as Spectacle: Reflections on Men and Mainstream Cinema," *Screen* 24, no. 6 (November–December 1983): 2–16.

40. For a discussion of Forster's homosexual relationships with Egyptian and Indian men, see Rustom Bharucha, "Forster's Friends," *Raritan* 5, no. 4 (Spring 1986): 105–22.

41. Derrida, *Of Grammatology*, 163 (my modification).

6. The Ruins of Time: *The Jewel in the Crown*

1. Paul Scott, *The Raj Quartet* (New York: William Morrow, 1976). The four novels that make up *The Raj Quartet*— *The Jewel in the Crown* (1966), *The Day of the Scorpion* (1968), *The Towers of Silence* (1971), and *A Division of the Spoils* (1975)— were published in one volume in 1976 by William Heinemann in London and William Morrow in New York. All further references, which are to the William Morrow edition, will be included in the text and abbreviated as *JC, DS, TS*, and *ADS*.

2. By *concept-metaphor*, I mean the metaphoric extension of sexual violence to imperialism and not the general, nongendered usage of *rape*, meaning "to take by force."

3. David Rubin, *After the Raj: British Novels of India since 1947* (Hanover, N.H.: University Press of New England, 1986), 66.

4. Brenda Silver, for instance, supports her reading of Aziz's metaphoric rape with evidence from *The Raj Quartet* ("Periphrasis, Power, and Rape in *A Passage to India*," *Novel* 22 [Fall 1988]: 94).

5. Walter Benjamin, *The Origin of German Tragic Drama*, trans. John Osborne (London: Verso, 1987), 175.

6. Salman Rushdie, "Outside the Whale," in *Imaginary Homelands: Essays and Criticism 1981–1991* (London: Granta Books, 1991), 89.

7. Jacques Lacan, "Réponse au commentaire de Jean Hyppolite sur la 'Verneinung' de Freud," *Écrits* (Paris: Seuil, 1966), 388.

8. Gayatri Chakravorty Spivak divides allegory into three broad historical periods, each of which identifies the relationship of an allegorical iconography to extrinsic conventions of reading. Medieval and Renaissance allegory relies on the double structure of an external typology and its correspondence to systematized signs in the text. In the late seventeenth and eighteenth centuries, the correspondences are mechanical. With the discrediting of allegory in the nineteenth century, the shared referential system between allegorist and audience is no longer presumed. Modern allegories thus replace the uniformity of a metasemantic system with systematized codes in the text that the reader can construct into a typology ("Thoughts on the Principle of Allegory," *Genre* 5, no. 4 [December 1972]: 327–52).

9. Rushdie, "The New Empire within Britain," in *Imaginary Homelands*, 129–38.

10. Enoch Powell, *Freedom and Reality* (London: Paperfront, 1969), 311.

11. Stuart Hall, "Racism and Reaction," *Five Views of Multi-Racial Britain: Talks on Race Relations Broadcast by BBC TV* (London: Commission for Racial Equality, 1978), 25. For a description of Powellism, see Tom Nairn, "English Nationalism: The Case of Enoch Powell," in *The Break-Up of Britain: Crisis and Neo-Nationalism*, 2d expanded ed. (London: Verso, 1981), 256–90. For a history of the official racism of Britain, see A. Sivanandan, *A Different Hunger: Writings on Black Resistance* (London: Pluto Press, 1982), 1–54, 99–140.

12. Vron Ware, *Beyond the Pale: White Women, Racism and History* (New York: Verso, 1992), 5–6.

13. Michel de Certeau, *Heterologies: Discourse on the Other*, trans. Brian Massumi (Minneapolis: University of Minnesota Press, 1986), 3.

14. Angus Fletcher, *Allegory: The Theory of a Symbolic Mode* (Ithaca, N.Y.: Cornell University Press, 1964), 2.

15. Benjamin's use of allegory belongs to what Maureen Quilligan calls *allogoresis*, an exegesis that emphasizes discontinuity over coherence ("Allegory, Allegoresis, and the Deallegorization of Language," in *Allegory, Myth, and Symbol*, ed. Morton W. Bloomfield [Cambridge, Mass.: Harvard University Press, 1981], 184).

16. Benjamin, *The Origin of German Tragic Drama*, 174–75.

17. Benita Parry, "Paul Scott's Raj," *South Asian Review* 8, no. 4 (July/October 1975): 359–69; Max Beloff, "The End of the Raj: Paul Scott's Novels as History," *Encounter* 272 (May 1976): 65–70; Allen Boyer, "Love, Sex, and History in *The Raj Quartet*," *Modern Language Quarterly* 46 (March 1985): 64–80; Margaret Scanlan, "The Disappearance of History: Paul Scott's *Raj Quartet*," *Clio* 15, no. 2 (Winter 1986): 153–69.

18. David Holloway, "Requiem for India," *Daily Telegraph* (London), 8 May 1977, 12.

19. Derek Sayer, "British Reaction to the Amritsar Massacre, 1919–1920," *Past and Present* 131 (May 1991): 137.

20. Margaret MacMillan, *Women of the Raj* (London: Thames & Hudson, 1988), 230.

21. Marianne Postans, *Western India in 1838*, 2 vols. (London: Sunder & Otley, 1839), 2: 283.

22. In allegorical personifications of the four continents as women, Asia was characteristically more richly dressed than Europe. See Clare le Corbeiller, "Miss America and Her Sisters: Personifications of the Four Parts of the World," *Metropolitan Museum of Art Bulletin* 19, no. 8 (April 1961): 209–22.

23. J. Talbot Wheeler, *The History of the Imperial Assemblage at Delhi* (London, 1877; reprint ed. Delhi: R. K. Publishing House, 1982), 42.

24. Ibid.

25. Val C. Prinsep, *Imperial India: An Artist's Journal*, 2d ed. (London: Chapman & Hall, 1879), 20.

26. Ibid., 34–36.

27. Marian Fowler, *Below the Peacock Fan: First Ladies of the Raj* (London: Viking, 1987), 200.

28. Adrienne Rich, "Disloyal to Civilization: Feminism, Racism, Gynephobia," in *On Lies, Secrets and Silence: Selected Prose 1966–1978* (New York: Norton, 1979), 275–310.

29. In this regard, the image of Edwina as a sati plays into a Powellism that feminizes Anglo-England—as, for instance, those newspaper stories that dramatized the threat of Asian immigration through headlines such as "Britain is not Asia's fiancée."

30. That Merrick's cruel racism is the expression of his class inferiority and repressed homosexuality is explicitly spelled out at the end of the quartet, when Count Bronowsky explains the circumstances of his mysterious death following a sado-masochistic relation with an Indian boy: "I think it likely that what he did with, and to, Aziz revealed something to him about himself that utterly appalled him ... I don't mean the revelation of his latent homosexuality and his sado-masochism. These must have been apparent to him for many many years and every now and again given some form of expression. What I mean by a revelation is revelation of the connexion between the homosexuality, the sado-masochism, the sense of social inferiority and the grinding defensive belief in his racial superiority" (*ADS*, 571).

31. The term *homosocial* is a neologism coined by Eve Kosofsky Sedgwick in *Between Men: English Literature and Male Homosocial Desire* (New York: Columbia University Press, 1985). Sedgwick uses homosocial to designate a desire between men that passes through women as exchange objects. Since it works in the interest of male bonding and enforced heterosexuality, homosocial relations are generally accompanied by a fear or denial of homosexuality.

32. In her study of masculinity and imperialism, Mrinalini Sinha notes that Bengali "effeminacy" is not the opposite of Victorian manliness but, like homosexuality, is constructed as its "bastardized or incomplete form" ("Gender and Imperialism: Colonial Policy and the Ideology of Moral Imperialism in Late Nineteenth-Century Bengal," in *Changing Men: New Directions in Research on Men and Masculinity*, ed. Michael S. Kimmel [London: Sage, 1987], 230).

33. John William Kaye, *A History of the Sepoy War in India 1857–58*, vol. 2, rev. ed. (London: W. H. Allen, 1876), 352.

34. Kenneth Ballhatchet, *Race, Sex and Class under the Raj: Imperial Attitudes and Policies and Their Critics, 1793–1905* (New York: St. Martin's Press, 1980).

35. Ann L. Stoler, "Making Empire Respectable: The Politics of Race and Sexual Morality in 20th-Century Colonial Cultures," *American Ethnologist* 16, no. 4 (1989): 653n.

36. Ballhatchet, *Race, Sex and Class under the Raj*, 144–45.

37. This understanding is not restricted to Scott's fiction, as the following remark from a history of imperialism and the sex trade demonstrates: "Sexual relationships soldered together the invisible bonds of empire. In the erotic field, as in administration and commerce, some degree of 'collaboration' from the indigenous communities was essential to the maintenance of imperial systems.... Sexual preoccupation may well be even more pervasive than we can document, but its expression is likely to have been generally less exploitative than the records suggest; at any rate, I cannot accept the feminist contention that it was fundamentally undesirable." Ronald Hyam, "Empire and Sexual Opportunity," *Journal of Imperial and Commonwealth History* 14, no. 2 (January 1986): 75.

38. For a discussion of the ways in which a feminist discourse of rape negates female subjectivity, see Ellen Rooney, " 'A Little More than Persuading': Tess and the Subject of Sexual Violence," in *Rape and Representation*, ed. Lynn A. Higgins and Brenda R. Silver (New York: Columbia University Press, 1991), 87–114.

39. *Sentinel*, January 1888, cited by Ballhatchet, *Race, Sex and Class under the Raj*, 125.

Index

Jenny Sharpe received her Ph.D. in comparative literature at the University of Texas at Austin and is now an assistant professor of English at the University of California at Los Angeles. She has contributed articles to *Modern Fiction Studies, Genders, differences,* and *boundary 2.*